WINDOWS VISTA™
QuickSteps

MARTY MATTHEWS

New York Chicago San Francisco
Lisbon London Madrid Mexico City
Milan New Delhi San Juan
Seoul Singapore Sydney Toronto

The McGraw·Hill Companies

McGraw-Hill books are available at special quantity discounts to use as premiums and sales promotions or for use in corporate training programs. For more information, please write to the Director of Special Sales, Professional Publishing, McGraw-Hill, Two Penn Plaza, New York, NY 10121-2298. Or contact your local bookstore.

WINDOWS VISTA™ QUICKSTEPS

234567890 CCI CCI 01987

ISBN-13: 978-0-07-226382-4
ISBN-10:   0-07-226382-2

SPONSORING EDITOR / Roger Stewart

EDITORIAL SUPERVISOR / Jody McKenzie

PROJECT MANAGER / Samik Roy Chowdhury

SERIES CREATORS AND EDITORS / Marty and Carole Matthews

ACQUISITIONS COORDINATOR / Carly Stapleton

TECHNICAL EDITOR / John Cronan

COPY EDITOR / Lisa McCoy

PROOFREADER / Joette Lynch

INDEXER / Valerie Perry

PRODUCTION SUPERVISOR / Jim Kussow

COMPOSITION / International Typesetting and Composition

ILLUSTRATION / International Typesetting and Composition

SERIES DESIGN / Bailey Cunningham

ART DIRECTOR, COVER / Jeff Weeks

COVER DESIGN / Pattie Lee

Contents at a Glance

Chapter 1 **Stepping into Windows Vista** 1
Start and log on to Windows Vista; use the mouse, screen, window, and Start menu; exit Windows Vista; get help; have fun

Chapter 2 **Customizing Windows Vista** 19
Personalize Windows; change the desktop, icons, Start menu, date/ time, sounds, and regional settings; use Quick Launch toolbar

Chapter 3 **Storing Information** 45
Display files and folders; change Explorer views; create folders; copy, move, rename, delete, and zip files and folders

Chapter 4 **Using the Internet** 69
Connect to the Internet, set up communications, search the Internet, control security, use e-mail, participate in newsgroups.

Chapter 5 **Managing Windows Vista** 99
Start, stop, switch, and schedule programs; use Task Manger and Run; update and restore Windows; add/remove software

Chapter 6 Working with Documents and Pictures 129
Create and print documents and pictures; use cameras and scanners; handle fonts; set up, send, and receive a fax

Chapter 7 Working with Multimedia 159
Play CDs, listen to a radio station, locate music, copy and burn CDs, play DVDs, make a movie, explore Media Center

Chapter 8 Controlling Security 189
Set up users and passwords, switch users, set parental controls, share files, encrypt files, set up an Internet firewall

Chapter 9 **Setting Up Networking** 213
Select a network, set up and enable a wired and a wireless network, configure and test networking, review security

Chapter 10 **Using Networking** 233
Explore a network, use network addressing, find and copy network files, use Remote Desktop, use a wireless network

Index 253

1
2
3
4
5
6
7
8
9
10

Carole Boggs Matthews...

Writing partner, parenting partner, life partner, and spouse for almost
35 years—a most exceptional person. I am truly lucky to be able to spend my life
with you. I treasure your constant support and encouragement and
for being there at all times. I love you, Carole!

—Marty

Acknowledgments

This book is a team effort of truly talented people. Among
them are:

John Cronan, technical editor, corrected many errors, added
many tips and notes, and greatly improved the book. John is
also a good friend and an author in his own right. Thanks, John!

Lisa McCoy, copy editor, added to the readability and
understandability of the book while always being a joy to
work with. Thanks, Lisa!

Valerie Perry, indexer, who adds so much to the usability of the
book, and does so quickly and without notice. Thanks, Valerie!

Jody McKenzie, editorial supervisor, and **Samik Roy
Chowdhury**, project manager, who greased the wheels and
straightened the track to make a smooth production process.
Thanks, Jody and Sam!

Roger Stewart, sponsoring editor, believed in us enough
to sell the series and continues to stand behind us as we go
through the second edition. Thanks, Roger!

Kim and **Lee Bandy**, friends and island neighbors, who are not
only good friends, but also do what they can to support our
writing efforts. Thanks, Kim and Lee!

About the Author

Marty Matthews has used computers for over 40 years, from
some of the early mainframe computers to recent personal
computers. He has done this as a programmer, systems analyst,
manager, vice president, and president of a software firm. As a
result, he has firsthand knowledge of not only how to program
and use a computer, but also how to make the best use of all that
can be done with a computer.

Over 27 years ago, Marty wrote his first computer book on how
to buy mini-computers. Over 23 years ago, Marty and his wife
Carole began writing books as a major part of their occupation. In
the intervening years, they have written over 70 books, including
ones on desktop publishing, Web publishing, Microsoft Office,
and Microsoft operating systems—from MS-DOS through
Windows Vista. Recent books published by **McGraw-Hill** include
Windows XP QuickSteps, *Windows XP Professional: A Beginner's
Guide*, *Windows Server 2003: A Beginner's Guide*, and *Microsoft
Office Word 2003 QuickSteps*.

Marty and Carole live on an island in Puget Sound, where, on
the rare moments when they can look up from their computers,
they look west across seven miles of water and the main shipping
channel to the snow-capped Olympic Mountains.

Contents

Acknowledgments iv

Introduction X

Chapter 1 **Stepping into Windows Vista** 1
    Start Windows 2
        Log On to Windows...3
        Using the Mouse..4
        Use the Mouse 4
        Use the Screen 4
        Using the Notification Area 5
        Open the Start Menu 6
        Use the Start Menu 6
        Starting a Program 8
        Use a Window 9
        Changing Window Layout...11
        Use a Menu 11
        Use a Dialog Box 11
        End Your Windows Session..13
        Get Help 15
        Play FreeCell...15
        Having Fun with Windows...16

Chapter 2 **Customizing Windows Vista** 19
    Change the Look of Windows Vista.....................................19
        Use the Personalization Window 19
        Add Windows Program Icons...26
        Change Desktop Icons 26
        Adding Other Program Icons to the Desktop 27
        Change the Start Menu 28
        Changing Taskbar Properties...31
        Change the Taskbar 31
        Changing the Notification Area 33
        Use the Quick Launch Toolbar...33
        Rearranging the Quick Launch Toolbar 35
    Change How Windows Vista Operates 36
        Set and Use the Date and Time..36
        Change Ease of Access Settings 37
        Using the Control Panel...39
        Customize the Mouse...39
        Customize the Keyboard 41
        Change Sounds 42
        Change Regional Settings..43
        Manage the Windows Sidebar 43

3 Chapter 3 **Storing Information** 45

Use the Windows File System 46
 Open Windows Explorer 46
 Changing Windows Explorer Layout 48
 Customize Windows Explorer 48
 Use Windows Explorer Menus 50
Locate and Use Files and Folders 51
 Identify Storage Devices 51
 Select and Open Drives and Folders 52
 Navigate Through Folders and Disks 53
 Renaming and Deleting Files and Folders 55
 Create New Folders 55
 Select Multiple Files and Folders 55
 Use the Recycle Bin 56
 Create Shortcuts 58
 Search for Files and Folders 58
 Copying and Moving Files and Folders 59
 Create Files 60
 Encrypt Files and Folders 61
 Change Other File and Folder Attributes 62
 Zipping Files and Folders 63
 Back Up Files and Folders 63
 Write Files and Folders to a CD or DVD 65
Managing Disks 67
 Clean Up a Disk 67
 Check for Errors 67
 Defragment a Disk 68

4 Chapter 4 **Using the Internet** 69

Connect to the Internet 70
 Set Up Communications 70
 Configure an Internet Connection 74
 Browsing the Internet 75
Use the World Wide Web 75
 Search the Internet 75
 Keep a Favorite Site 78
 Use Tabs 78
 Organizing favorite sites 81
 Change Your Home Page 81
 Access Web History 82
 Controlling Internet Security 84
 Copy Internet Information 85
 Play Internet Audio and Video Files 87
Use Internet E-Mail 88
 Establish an E-Mail Account 88
 Create and Send E-Mail 89
 Receive E-Mail 90
 Using the Contacts List 91
 Respond to E-Mail 91

Use Stationery 92
Apply Formatting 92
🔍 Using Web Mail...94
Attach Files to E-Mail 95
Participate in Newsgroups 96

Chapter 5 **Managing Windows Vista**.. 99

Start and Stop Programs...99
Automatically Start Programs 100
Start Programs Minimized 101
Schedule Programs 102
🔍 Switching Programs 104
Control with the Task Manager 104
🔍 Stopping Programs...106
Start a Program in Run 106
Start Older Programs...107
Control Automatic Programs 108
Control Windows Indexing...108
🔍 Running Accessory Programs...110
Maintain Windows Vista..111
Update Windows Vista 111
Restore Windows Vista 112
Get System Information 116
Set Power Options 118
Add and Remove Software 119
Add Hardware 121
Use Remote Assistance 122

Chapter 6 **Working with Documents and Pictures** 129

Create Documents and Pictures...129
🔍 Acquiring a Document..130
Create a Picture 130
Install Cameras and Scanners 131
Scan Pictures..133
Import Camera Images 134
Work with Photo Gallery Pictures...136
🔍 Viewing Other Pictures...138
Print Documents and Pictures...138
Install a Printer 138
🔍 Printing 142
Print Pictures 143
Print to a File..143
Print Web Pages 145
Configure a Printer 145
Control Printing 148
🔍 Handling Fonts 152
Fax Documents and Pictures..153
Set Up Faxing 153
Send and Receive Faxes 153
Create a Fax Cover Page 156

7   Chapter 7   **Working with Multimedia** 159

     Work with Audio 160
         Play CDs...160
         Control the Volume...162
         Listen to Radio Stations 163
         Locate Music on the Internet..164
         Copy (Rip) CDs to Your Computer 165
         Organize Music 167
         Make (Burn) a Music CD 167
       Changing the Visualizations in Windows Media Player.......................169
         Copy to (Sync with) Music Players 169
     Work with Video 171
         Play DVDs...171
       Preparing to Make a Movie..172
         Import Video from a Camcorder 172
         Make a Movie 173
         Select Video Clips...176
         Edit Video Clips 177
         Import Other Files 180
         Add Titles to a Movie..181
       Employing Effects and Transitions 183
         Add Sound to a Movie..184
         Publish a Movie..186
       Exploring Windows Media Center 187

8   Chapter 8   **Controlling Security** 189

     Control Who Is a User...189
         Set Up Users 190
       Understanding User Account Control 191
       Setting Passwords...193
         Reset a Password 193
         Replace Passwords 195
         Customize a User Account 196
         Switch Among Users 197
         Control What a User Does 197
         Set Parental Controls 198
     Control What Parts of Windows Can Be Used....................................200
         Set File and Folder Sharing 200
       Testing an Internet Firewall 202
         Use and Add Groups...207
       Understanding Permissions..208
     Protect Stored Data..209
         Protect Files and Folders..209
       Locking a Computer 211
         Use Encrypted Files and Folders...212

Chapter 9   **Setting Up Networking** 213

Plan a Network..214
Select a Type of Network 214
🌐Selecting Wired Ethernet Hardware 216
Select a Network Standard 216
🌐Selecting Wireless Hardware 219
Set Up a Network...220
Set Up Network Interface Cards...220
Enable Vista's Networking Functions..222
Configure a Networking Protocol 224
🌐Getting a Block of IP Addresses 226
Test a Network Setup and Connection 228
Review Network Security...229

Chapter 10   **Using Networking** 233

Access Network Resources 234
Explore a Network..234
Permanently Connect to a Network Resource 236
Connect Outside Your Workgroup or Domain..........................237
🌐Using Network Addresses 238
Copy Network Files and Information...238
🌐Finding or Adding a Network Printer.......................................239
Print on Network Printers 239
Access a Network Internet Connection 239
Let Others Access Your Resources..239
Share Your Files..240
Share Folders 241
Work Remotely..242
Set Up a Remote Desktop Connection..243
Connect to a Remote Desktop over a LAN.................................245
Use a Remote Desktop Connection...246
Set Up and Use a Wireless Network 248
Set Up a Wireless Connection 248
Manage Wireless Network Sharing..250
🌐Implementing Windows Defender 251
Use a Wireless Network...251

Index 253

9

10

Introduction

QuickSteps books are recipe books for computer users. They answer the question "how do I…" by providing a quick set of steps to accomplish the most common tasks with a particular operating system or application.

The sets of steps are the central focus of the book. QuickSteps sidebars show how to quickly perform many small functions or tasks that support the primary functions. Notes, Tips, and Cautions augment the steps, and are presented in a separate column so as not to interrupt the flow of the steps. The introductions are minimal, and other narrative is kept brief. Numerous full-color illustrations and figures, many with callouts, support the steps.

QuickSteps books are organized by function and the tasks needed to perform that function. Each function is a chapter. Each task, or "How To," contains the steps needed for accomplishing the function, along with the relevant Notes, Tips, Cautions, and screenshots. You can easily find the tasks you want to perform through:

- The table of contents, which lists the functional areas (chapters) and tasks in the order they are presented

- A How To list of tasks on the opening page of each chapter

- The index, which provides an alphabetical list of the terms that are used to describe the functions and tasks

- Color-coded tabs for each chapter or functional area, with an index to the tabs in the Contents at a Glance (just before the Table of Contents)

Conventions Used in This Book

Windows Vista QuickSteps uses several conventions designed to make the book easier for you to follow. Among these are:

- A 🔍 or a 🔍 in the table of contents or the How To list in each chapter references a QuickSteps or QuickFacts sidebar in a chapter.

- **Bold type** is used for words on the screen that you are to do something with, like "…click the **File** menu, and click **Save As**."

- *Italic type* is used for a word or phrase that is being defined or otherwise deserves special emphasis.

- <u>Underlined type</u> is used for text that you are to type from the keyboard.

- SMALL CAPITAL LETTERS are used for keys on the keyboard, such as ENTER and SHIFT.

- When you are expected to enter a command, you are told to press the key(s). If you are to enter text or numbers, you are told to type them.

How to...

- Log On to Windows
- Using the Mouse
- Use the Mouse
- Use the Screen
- Using the Notification Area
- Open the Start Menu
- Use the Start Menu
- Starting a Program
- Use a Window
- Changing Window Layout
- Use a Menu
- Use a Dialog Box
- End Your Windows Session
- Get Help
- Having Fun with Windows
- Play FreeCell

Chapter 1

Stepping into Windows Vista

Windows Vista is an *operating system.* Operating systems perform *the* central role in managing what a computer does and how it is done. An operating system provides the interface between you and the computer hardware: it lets you store a file, print a document, connect to the Internet, or transfer information over a local area network (LAN) without knowing anything about how the hardware works.

This chapter explains how to start and/or log on to Windows Vista; how to use its screens, windows, menus, and dialog boxes; and how to shut it down. You will also learn how to get help and discover some ways to have fun with Windows.

NOTE

The desktop on your screen may be different from the one shown in Figure 1-1. Each manufacturer has its own default desktop, and if you upgrade to Windows Vista, you will see still a different one.

Start Windows

To start Windows, you need to turn on the computer. Sometimes, that is all you need to do. If, when you turn on the computer you see a screen similar to Figure 1-1, then you have started Windows. In many cases, in addition to turning on the computer, you also need to log on.

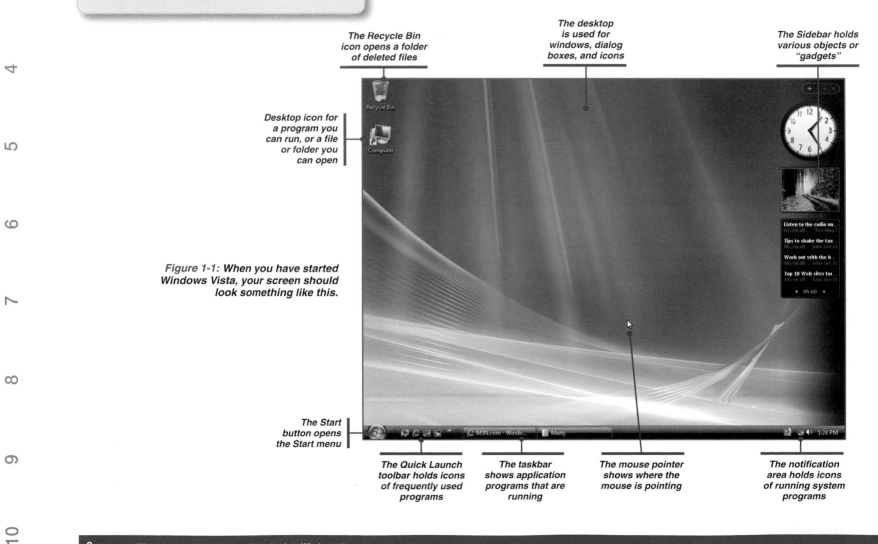

The Recycle Bin icon opens a folder of deleted files

The desktop is used for windows, dialog boxes, and icons

The Sidebar holds various objects or "gadgets"

Desktop icon for a program you can run, or a file or folder you can open

Figure 1-1: When you have started Windows Vista, your screen should look something like this.

The Start button opens the Start menu

The Quick Launch toolbar holds icons of frequently used programs

The taskbar shows application programs that are running

The mouse pointer shows where the mouse is pointing

The notification area holds icons of running system programs

NOTE

If you are logging on to a domain (see Chapter 9), you will be asked to press **CTRL+ALT+DEL** all together. Do so, then enter your user name and password, and press **ENTER** or click **OK**.

Log On to Windows

If, when you start Windows, you see the Log On screen shown in Figure 1-2, click your name or that of the default user and, if requested, enter your password. Windows will log you on to the system. If someone else, such as a system administrator installed Windows Vista on your computer, he or she should have given you a user name and password, if one is needed. If you purchased a computer with Vista installed on it or upgraded to Vista, then a default user is shown on the logon page. As you will see in Chapter 8, you can change and add users if you wish.

Figure 1-2: If you see this logon screen, select a user and enter a password if you need to.

2

3

4

5

6

7

8

9

10

USING THE MOUSE

HIGHLIGHT AN OBJECT ON THE SCREEN

Highlight an *object* (a button, an icon, a border, etc.) on the screen by pointing to it. *Point* at an object on the screen by moving the mouse until the tip of the pointer is on top of the object.

Recycle Bin

SELECT AN OBJECT ON THE SCREEN

Select an object on the screen by clicking it. *Click* means to point at an object you want to select and quickly press and release the left mouse button.

OPEN AN OBJECT OR START A PROGRAM

Open an object or start a program by double-clicking it. *Double-click* means to point at an object you want to select and press and release the mouse button twice in rapid succession.

OPEN A CONTEXT MENU FOR AN OBJECT

Open a context menu, which allows you to do things specific to an object, by right-clicking it. *Right-click* means to point at an object you want to select and quickly press and release the right mouse button.

Recycle Bin

| Open |
| Explore |
| Empty Recycle Bin |
| Create Shortcut |
| Delete |
| Rename |
| Properties |

MOVE AN OBJECT ON THE SCREEN

Move an object on the screen by dragging it. *Drag* means to point at an object you want to move, then press and hold the mouse button while moving the mouse. You will drag the object as you move the mouse. When the object is where you want it, release the mouse button.

Use the Mouse

A *mouse* is any pointing device—including trackballs, pointing sticks, and graphic tablets—with two or more buttons. This book assumes you are using a two-button mouse. Moving the mouse moves the pointer on the screen. You *select* an object on the screen by moving the pointer so that it is on top of the object and then pressing the left button on the mouse.

You can control the mouse with either your left or right hand; therefore, the buttons may be switched. (See Chapter 2 to switch the buttons.) This book assumes you are using your right hand to control the mouse and that the left mouse button is "the mouse button." The right button is always called the "right mouse button." If you switch the buttons, you must change your interpretation of these phrases.

Use the Screen

The Windows Vista screen can hold windows and other objects. In its simplest form, shown in Figure 1-1, you see a background scene, a bar at the bottom with a button on the left and the time on the right, some objects on the right side of the screen, and some icons on the left.

The parts of a screen are:

- The **desktop**, which takes up most of the screen.
- The **Start button** in the lower-left, which open the Start menu.
- The **taskbar** across the bottom, which identifies programs that are running.
- The **notification area** in the lower-right, which holds icons of running system programs.
- **Desktop icons**, which can be in any number and anywhere on the desktop, are in the upper-left of Figure 1-1. Desktop icons are used to start programs or open files or folders.
- The **mouse pointer**, which can be anywhere on the screen.
- The **Sidebar**, which is on the right, holds various objects or "gadgets."

QUICKSTEPS

USING THE NOTIFICATION AREA

The *notification area* on the right of the taskbar contains the icons of special programs as well as the time of day.

OPEN A PROGRAM

Click the program icon.

SEE THE DAY AND DATE

Point to the time.

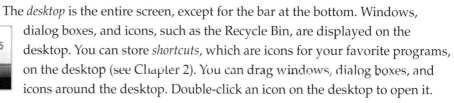

Sunday, September 17, 2006

7:22 PM

SET THE TIME AND DATE

Double-click the time.

NOTE

The icons you have in the notification area will depend on the programs and processes you have running. Others that you may have include the Safely Remove Hardware ⬛, Change Volume 🔊, Network Connection 🖥, and Windows Security Alerts icons 🛡.

- The **Quick Launch** toolbar to the left of the taskbar (and to the right of the Start button) is used to hold the icons of programs you frequently use.

USE THE DESKTOP

The *desktop* is the entire screen, except for the bar at the bottom. Windows, dialog boxes, and icons, such as the Recycle Bin, are displayed on the desktop. You can store *shortcuts*, which are icons for your favorite programs, on the desktop (see Chapter 2). You can drag windows, dialog boxes, and icons around the desktop. Double-click an icon on the desktop to open it.

USE THE START BUTTON

The *Start button*, on the left of the taskbar, opens the Start menu when clicked. This provides you with primary access to the programs, utilities, and settings that are available in Windows.

USE THE TASKBAR

The *taskbar* at the bottom of the screen contains the active *tasks*, which are icons and titles of the programs that are running on the computer or folders that are open. The taskbar also holds the Start button on the left and the notification area on the right. Click a program on the taskbar to open it.

Start button — Quick Launch toolbar — Active programs or open folders — Notification area

Windows Media Ce... — Computer — 10:13 PM

NOTE

Your taskbar may have more or fewer objects than those shown in the illustration. The Quick Launch toolbar may not appear on your computer; and you may have more or fewer icons and active programs across all of your taskbar. The Quick Launch toolbar is described in Chapter 2.

USE A DESKTOP ICON

A *desktop icon* represents a program or folder that can be started or opened and moved about the screen. The Recycle Bin is a desktop icon for a folder that contains all of the files that have been deleted since the Recycle Bin was last emptied. Double-click a desktop icon to open or start what it refers to.

1

NOTE

The two steps describing how to open the Start menu can be replaced with the two words "click **Start**." You can also open the Start menu by pressing the Windows flag key [⊞] on your keyboard, if you have that key, or by pressing both the **CTRL** and **ESC** keys together (**CTRL+ESC**). In the rest of this book, you will see the phrase "click **Start**." This means open the Start menu using any technique you wish.

USE THE MOUSE POINTER

The *mouse pointer*, or simply the *pointer*, shows where the mouse is pointing. Move the mouse to move the pointer.

Open the Start Menu

To open the Start menu:

1. Point at the **Start** button by moving the pointer so that it is over the Start button. You will see that the button changes color. When this happens, the button is said to be selected or *highlighted*.

2. Press and release the left mouse button (given that your mouse buttons have not been switched) while the pointer is on the Start button. The Start menu will open, as you can see in Figure 1-3.

Use the Start Menu

The Start menu contains icons for programs and folders, as well as access to control functions and other menus, as shown in Figure 1-3. The most important menu item is All Programs, which opens a menu within the Start menu of all your programs. The buttons in the lower-right —Sleep, Lock, and session-ending choices—are important control functions discussed later in this chapter. The text box in the lower-left allows you to enter criteria and search the files and folders on the computer or the Internet for those that contain a match. All other options on the menu open folders or start programs, or both. The eight lower icons on the left change to reflect the programs you have used most recently (which are probably different from those shown here). In most cases, these are the programs that Windows Vista initially displays.

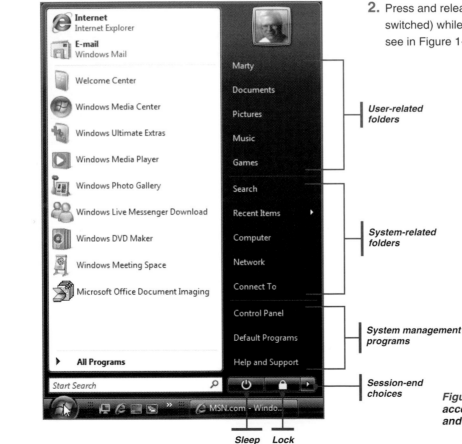

Figure 1-3: The Start menu provides access to the programs, utilities, and settings in Windows.

The remaining icons in the Start menu fall into three categories: Internet programs, user- or system-related folders and programs, and system management options.

START INTERNET-RELATED PROGRAMS

The two icons in the upper-left of the Start menu start programs that use the Internet. Internet Explorer lets you browse the World Wide Web, while Windows Mail (formerly Outlook Express) opens an e-mail program to send and receive messages. These programs are described in Chapter 4.

> **Internet**
> Internet Explorer
>
> **E-mail**
> Windows Mail

OPEN USER-RELATED FOLDERS

The top five options on the right in Figure 1-3 (including the user's name at the top) are used to access folders related to the user who is logged on. These options start the Windows Explorer program and display the folder identified. Clicking the user's name opens a folder containing the four folders beneath the name, plus others. Windows Explorer will be discussed later in this chapter and again in Chapter 3.

OPEN SYSTEM-RELATED FOLDERS

The five options in the middle on the right in Figure 1-3 are used to access folders other than those belonging to the logged-on user. The Computer and Network options start the Windows Explorer program and display disks on the computer or on the network the computer is connected to. The Search, Recent Items, and Connect To options open specific objects for those functions, all of which are discussed either later in this chapter or in the following chapters.

OPEN SYSTEM MANAGEMENT PROGRAMS

The remaining three icons in the bottom-right of the Start menu help you manage your computer and its resources or get help. The function of each is as follows:

- **Control Panel** provides access to many of the settings that govern how Windows and the computer operate. This allows you to customize much of Windows and to locate and solve problems. Control Panel is discussed primarily in Chapter 2.

QUICKSTEPS

STARTING A PROGRAM

The method for starting a program depends on where the program icon is located. Here are the alternatives:

ON THE DESKTOP

Double-click the program icon, or "shortcut," on the desktop.

ON THE START MENU

Click the program icon on the Start menu.

IN THE NOTIFICATION AREA

Click the program icon in the notification area.

ON THE ALL PROGRAMS MENU

1. Click **Start**.

2. Click **All Programs**.

3. Click the relevant folder or folders.

4. Click the program icon, as shown in Figure 1-4.

USING THE RUN COMMAND

1. Click **Start** and click **All Programs**.

2. Click **Accessories** and then click **Run**.

3. Type the path and program name, and press **ENTER** or click **OK**.

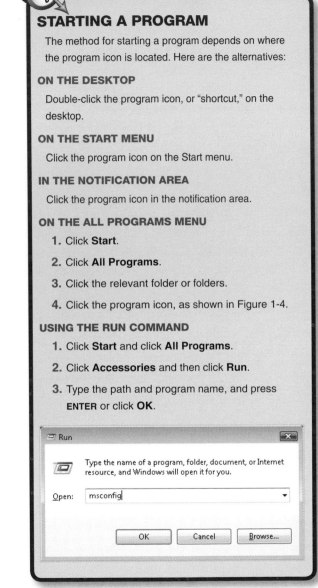

Figure 1-4: All Programs on the Start menu may lead you through several folders before you find the program you want.

- **Default Programs** allows you to associate a program with a file type and automatically start that program when you double-click that type of file.

- **Help And Support** opens a window from which you can search for information on how to use Windows Vista. It includes a tutorial and a troubleshooting guide. Help is discussed in more detail later in this chapter.

Your computer's manufacturer may have added an icon that connects you to the manufacturer's Internet Help center.

Use a Window

When you start a program or open a folder, the program or folder appears in a "window" on your screen, as shown with the Windows Explorer window in Figure 1-5.

Figure 1-5: The Windows Explorer window has a number of different features that allow you to perform many tasks.

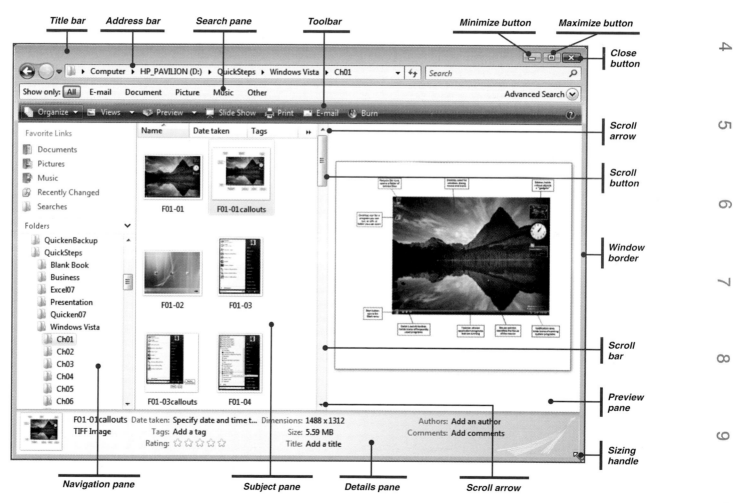

Title bar   Address bar   Search pane   Toolbar   Minimize button   Maximize button

Close button

Scroll arrow

Scroll button

Window border

Scroll bar

Preview pane

Sizing handle

Navigation pane   Subject pane   Details pane   Scroll arrow

The window in Figure 1-5 has a number of features that are referred to in the remainder of this book. Not all windows have all of the features shown in the figure, and some windows have features unique to them.

- The **title bar** is used to drag the window around the screen, and may contain the name of the program or folder in the window (the Windows Explorer window in Windows Vista does not contain a name in the title bar).

- The **address bar** displays the complete address of what is being displayed in the subject pane. In Figure 1-5, this is the Ch01 folder, in the Windows Vista folder, in the QuickSteps folder, on drive D: of the local computer.

- The **search pane** provides a set of tools you can use to search for files and folders. By default, the search pane is turned off.

- The **toolbar** contains tools related to the contents of the window. Click a tool to use it. The toolbar is always displayed.

- The **Minimize button** decreases the size of the window so that you see it only as a task on the taskbar.

- The **Maximize button** increases the size of the window so that it fills the screen. When the screen is maximized, the button becomes the **Restore button**, which, when clicked, returns the screen to its previous size.

- The **Close button** shuts down and closes the program, folder, or file in the window.

- **Scroll arrows** move the window contents in small increments in the direction of the arrow.

- The **scroll button** can be dragged in either direction to move the contents accordingly.

- The **scroll bar** allows you to move the contents of the pane within the window so that you can see information that wasn't displayed. Clicking the scroll bar itself moves the contents in larger increments.

- The **window border** separates the window from the desktop, and can be used to size the window horizontally or vertically by dragging a horizontal or vertical border, respectively.

- The **sizing handle** in each corner of the window allows it to be sized diagonally, increasing or decreasing the window's height and width when you drag a handle.

- The **preview pane** displays the object selected in the subject pane. For example, in Figure 1-5, the navigation pane points to a particular folder whose files of screenshots

TIP

Double-clicking a window's title bar toggles between maximizing and restoring a window to its previous size. This is much easier than clicking the **Maximize** and **Restore** buttons.

NOTE

All windows have a title bar with the Minimize, Maximize, and Close buttons. The title bars of program windows also have a control menu icon on the left of the title bar and the program name in the middle of the title bar. All windows also have a border and sizing handle, both of which can be used to change the size of the window. *Almost* all windows have a menu bar. Other features are optional.

are shown in the subject pane, where one particular file is selected and displayed in the preview pane. By default, the preview pane is turned off.

- The **details pane** displays detailed information about the object that is selected in the subject pane. The details pane is turned on by default.

- The **subject pane** displays the principal subject of the window, such as files, folders, programs, documents, or images. The subject pane is always on.

- The **navigation pane** provides links to the most commonly used folders related to the user who is logged on, as well as an optional hierarchical list of disks and folders on the computer. The folders list is not displayed by default, and can be seen by dragging it up from the bottom of the window. The navigation pane is turned on by default.

Use a Menu

A *menu* provides a way of selecting an action, such as Create Shortcut, on an object, such as a folder, as shown in Figure 1-6. To use a menu in an open window:

1. Click the menu name on the menu bar.
2. Move the pointer to the option you want.
3. Click the option you want.

Use a Dialog Box

Dialog boxes gather information. A *dialog box* uses a common set of features called *controls* to accomplish its purpose. Figures 1-7 and 1-8 show two frequently used dialog boxes with many of the controls often seen.

Figure 1-6: By default, menus are turned off in Windows Explorer, but you can turn them on if you wish.

QUICKSTEPS

CHANGING WINDOW LAYOUT

The window shown in Figure 1-5 has all of its panes turned on. By default, the preview and search panes are not visible. You can turn these panes on and turn other panes off.

TURN ON PANES

Click **Organize** on the toolbar, click **Layout**, and click **Preview Pane.** The search pane appears when you do a search.

TURN OFF PANES

Click **Organize** on the toolbar, click **Layout**, and click **Details Pane** or **Navigation Pane**.

TURN ON CLASSIC MENUS

If you miss the menus that were in Windows Explorer in earlier versions of Windows, you can turn them on.

Click **Organize** on the toolbar, click **Layout**, and click **Classic Menus**.

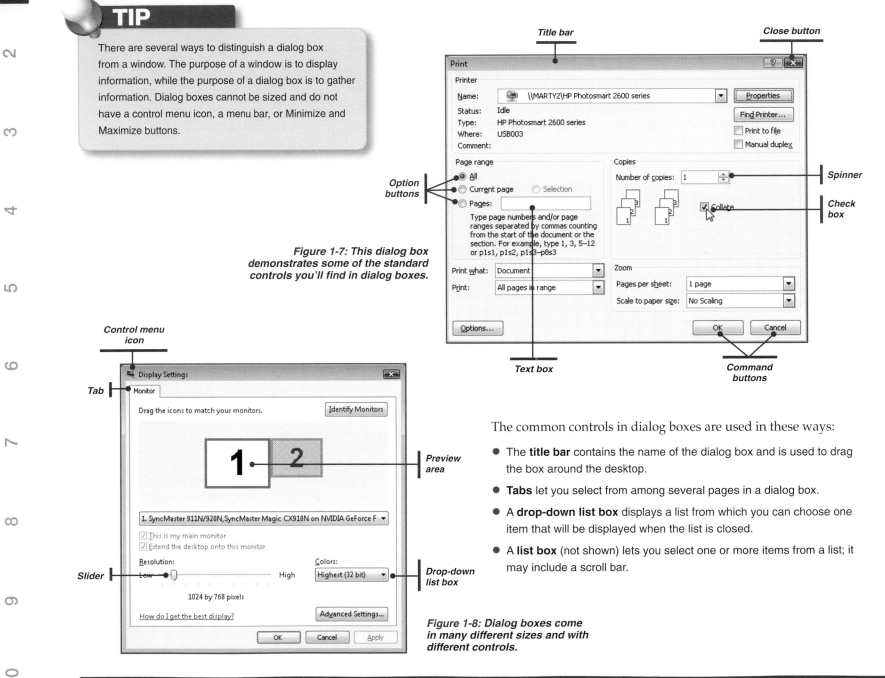

TIP

There are several ways to distinguish a dialog box from a window. The purpose of a window is to display information, while the purpose of a dialog box is to gather information. Dialog boxes cannot be sized and do not have a control menu icon, a menu bar, or Minimize and Maximize buttons.

Title bar

Close button

Figure 1-7: This dialog box demonstrates some of the standard controls you'll find in dialog boxes.

Option buttons

Spinner

Check box

Text box

Command buttons

Control menu icon

Tab

Preview area

Slider

Drop-down list box

Figure 1-8: Dialog boxes come in many different sizes and with different controls.

The common controls in dialog boxes are used in these ways:

- The **title bar** contains the name of the dialog box and is used to drag the box around the desktop.

- **Tabs** let you select from among several pages in a dialog box.

- A **drop-down list box** displays a list from which you can choose one item that will be displayed when the list is closed.

- A **list box** (not shown) lets you select one or more items from a list; it may include a scroll bar.

- **Option buttons**, also called radio buttons, let you select one among mutually exclusive options.
- **Check boxes** let you turn features on or off.
- A **preview area** shows you the effect of the changes you make.
- A **text box** lets you enter and edit text.
- **Command buttons** perform functions such as closing the dialog box and accepting any changes (the OK button), or closing the dialog box and ignoring the changes (the Cancel button).
- A **spinner** lets you select from a sequential series of numbers.
- A **slider** lets you select from several values.

You will have a great many opportunities to use dialog boxes. For the most part, you can try dialog boxes and see what happens; if you don't like the outcome, you can come back and reverse the setting.

TIP

If you are not sure what a dialog box control does, try it. In almost every circumstance, you can come back to the dialog box and reverse what ever you did, and in many dialog boxes you can preview the effects without leaving the dialog box.

End Your Windows Session

You have seven ways you can end your Windows session, depending on what you want to do. All of these can be found on the Start menu:

Click **Start**, click the session-end choices right-arrow, and click the option you want.

Connect To	Switch User
	Log Off
Control Panel	Lock
Default Programs	Restart
	Sleep
Help and Support	Hibernate
	Shut Down

Your options are:

- **Switch User** leaves all active programs, network connections, and your user account active but hidden while you let another person use the computer.

NOTE

Sleep and Lock have their own buttons at the bottom-right of the Start menu. The Sleep button can be changed to shut down the computer or put it into hibernation when the button is clicked (see Chapter 5).

TIP

It is recommended that you use Sleep when you leave a computer for any time up to a couple of days and not shut it down, because it actually uses less power than the power consumed during shut down and start up of the computer. Your computer's power light will either stay on or blink.

- **Log Off** closes all active programs, network connections, and your user account but leaves Windows Vista and the computer running so another person can log on.

- **Lock** leaves all active programs, network connections, and your user account active but displays the Welcome screen, where you must click your user icon and potentially enter a password, if you have established one, to resume using the computer.

- **Restart** closes all active programs, network connections, and logs off all users so that no information is lost. Windows is then shut down and restarted. This is usually done when there is a problem that restarting Windows will fix or to complete setting up some programs.

- **Sleep** leaves all active programs, network connections, and your user account active and in memory, but also saves the state of everything on disk. Your computer is then put into a low power state that allows you to quickly resume working exactly where you were when you left. In a desktop computer, it is left running in this low power state for as long as you wish. In a mobile computer (laptops, notebooks, and tablet PCs), after three hours or if the battery is low, your session is again saved to disk and the computer is turned off.

- **Hibernate**, which is by default only on mobile computers, saves the current state of the computer, including the open programs and files and the active network connections to your hard disk, and then turns off the computer. When you start up the computer, you can resume working with exactly the same programs, files, and network connections that you had open when you went into hibernation.

- **Shut Down** closes all active programs and network connections and logs off all users so that no information is lost, and then turns off the computer (if it is done automatically) or tells you when it is safe for you to turn it off. When you start up the computer, you must reload your programs and data and reestablish your network connection to get back to where you were when you shut down.

RESUME FROM SLEEP

There are several ways to resume operation after a computer has been put into Sleep mode, which depend on your type of computer, how it was put to sleep, and how long it has been sleeping. A computer can be put into Sleep mode either by your action on the Start menu or as the result of the computer not being used for a period of time, which is controlled in the Power Options (see Chapter 5). The ways to resume include:

- Press any key on your keyboard. This works with most desktop computers and mobile computers that have only been asleep a short time.

- Quickly press the power button on your computer. This works with most recent computers of all types. Holding down the computer's power button will, in most cases, either fully turn off the computer or cause it to restart (shut fully down and then restart).

- Open the top. This works with most mobile computers.

RESTART FROM HIBERNATE

Hibernate is like shutting down, except that your entire session is saved on disk and then restored when you restart the computer. Therefore, from hibernate, you need to press the power button on your computer as you normally would.

Get Help

Windows Vista Help provides both built-in documentation and online assistance that you can use to learn how to work with Windows Vista. For example, to use Help to start a program:

1. Click **Start** and click **Help And Support**. The Help And Support Center window, like the one shown in Figure 1-9, opens.

2. Under Find An Answer, click **Windows Basics**, scroll down, click **Using Programs**, and then click **Starting A Program** in the right-hand column. Steps and notes related to starting a program will be displayed.

3. Click the **Close** button to close the Help And Support Center.

Play FreeCell

There are a number of games you can play in Windows Vista. Probably the most addictive of them all is FreeCell, which is a solitaire-like card game. To start playing:

1. Click **Start**, click **All Programs**, click **Games**, and click **FreeCell**. The game board will be displayed.

Windows Help and Support

ⓘ Do you want to get the latest online content when you search Help?

If you choose No, when you search Help you will get only the content that came with your version of Windows.

[Yes] [No]

Microsoft cares about your privacy. Read the privacy statement online

QUICKSTEPS

HAVING FUN WITH WINDOWS

Windows Vista has a number of games besides FreeCell. Here is how to play three more:

PLAY HEARTS

Hearts is a card game that can be played by as many as four people on the network.

1. Click **Start**, click **All Programs**, click **Games**, and click **Hearts**. The game board will appear. By default, you will have three simulated opponents.

2. Click three cards you want to give away, and click the arrow to give your cards to the person in the direction of the arrow.

The objective is to have the lowest score by *not* taking tricks with hearts or the queen of spades in them *unless* you can take all such tricks. You take a trick by playing the highest card in the suit led for that trick. You begin the game by passing three cards from your hand to another player. You want to pass your highest hearts and spades. The person with the two of clubs leads. You must follow suit if you can. If you can't, you may throw away your high hearts or spades or any other card. Whoever takes a trick plays the first card for the next trick. Play continues until all cards have been played. At the end of a game, one point is assessed for each heart in the tricks you took plus 13 points for the queen of spades. If you get all the hearts plus the queen of spades, you get zero points and all other players get 26 points.

PLAY MINESWEEPER

Minesweeper is a game of chance in which you try to accumulate points by not encountering mines.

Continued...

Figure 1-9: *The Windows Vista Help And Support Center window provides you with several ways of getting Help on many different topics.*

2. Click **Game** and then click **New Game**. A deck of cards will be spread out. The objective is to get the complete set of cards in each of the four suits in order from ace to king in the home cells in the upper-right. You can temporarily place up to four cards in the free cells in the upper-left. You can also temporarily place a card on the next highest card of the opposite color in the stacks at the bottom.

QUICKSTEPS

HAVING FUN WITH WINDOWS *(Continued)*

1. Click **Start**, click **All Programs**, click **Games**, and click **Mine-sweeper**. The first time you play, you are asked to click the level of difficulty you want to use. The game board will then appear.

   The object is to find the mines hidden in the squares without clicking one. Click a square. You will see a number or a mine. The number tells you how many mines are contained in the eight surrounding squares. Mark the suspected mines with the right mouse button. Clicking a mine ends the game.

2. To restart the game, click **Play Again** or click **Exit**.

PLAY SOLITAIRE

Solitaire is a game of chance and strategy. The object of the game is to end up with the deck of cards arranged sequentially in suits from ace to king.

1. Click **Start**, click **All Programs**, click **Games**, and click **Solitaire**. The game board is displayed.

   You will see a row of seven stacks of cards; all are face-down except the top card. In the upper-left of the board is another turned-down stack of cards, which you can click. In the upper-right are four empty cells, where you will place the suits, beginning with the aces.

2. Start a new game by clicking **Game** and clicking **Deal**.

3. To move a card, click it and then click where you want it to go. If it is not a legal move, you will be told that. If you get an empty column at the bottom, you can build your own sequence in it.

   The secret is to think several moves in the future and never fill up the free cells without having a way to empty them. The game is lost if you have no moves left and haven't moved all the cards to the home cells. Figure 1-10 shows a game that was played for a few minutes and is all but won. The king of hearts is the only card left to move. When all your cards are in order, they will be moved to the home cells automatically and you will be told you won.

4. When you are done playing, click **Close** and then click **Yes** to "resign" from the game if you did not finish it.

TIP

Windows Vista has added two neat features to FreeCell. You can now undo your moves (Game menu Undo, or press **CTRL+Z**) and get a hint (Game menu Hint, or press **CTRL+H**).

Figure 1-10: *A great many people spend a lot of time playing FreeCell.*

How to...

- *Use the Personalization Window*
- *Add Windows Program Icons*
- *Change Desktop Icons*
- *Adding Other Program Icons to the Desktop*
- *Change the Start Menu*
- *Changing Taskbar Properties*
- *Change the Taskbar*
- *Changing the Notification Area*
- *Use the Quick Launch Toolbar*
- *Rearranging the Quick Launch Toolbar*
- *Set and Use the Date and Time*
- *Change Ease of Access Settings*
- *Using the Control Panel*
- *Customize the Mouse*
- *Customize the Keyboard*
- *Change Sounds*
- *Change Regional Settings*
- *Manage the Windows Sidebar*

Chapter 2

Customizing Windows Vista

Windows Vista has many features that can be customized. You can keep the default Windows Vista setup; or you can change the display, Start menu, taskbar, Windows Sidebar, and sounds. You can also rearrange the desktop and enable accessibility options.

Change the Look of Windows Vista

An important aspect of Windows that leads to your enjoyment and efficient use of it is how it looks. Windows Vista provides significant flexibly in this area. You can change how the screen looks, including the desktop, the Start menu, and the taskbar.

Use the Personalization Window

Much of what you see on the Windows Vista screen is controlled by the Display Properties dialog box. Open it to make many of the changes in this chapter.

In Windows Vista, when you first attempt to change various aspects of the program, you'll see a User Account Control (UAC) dialog box appear and tell you that Windows needs your permission to continue. This prevents a hacker from changing your system over the Internet or malicious software from harming your computer. When you see these dialog boxes and if you are an administrator and, in fact, want to continue, click **Continue**. If you are not logged on as an administrator, you will need to enter a password. If you don't want to do whatever is being requested, click **Cancel**. To simplify the instructions in this book, I have left out the UAC dialog box and its associated steps. If you see one while following the instructions here, just process it as you want and continue with the instructions. UAC is discussed in depth in Chapter 8.

Figure 2-1: The Personalization window lets you change the appearance of Windows Vista.

(Several of the features controlled in the Personalization window, such as sounds and the mouse pointer, are discussed on their own later in this chapter.)

1. With Windows Vista running and displayed on your computer, right-click a blank area of the desktop. The desktop *context menu* is displayed.

2. Click **Personalize**. The Personalization window opens, as shown in Figure 2-1.

CHANGE THE RESOLUTION AND COLOR

Depending on your computer and monitor, you can display Windows Vista with various resolutions and

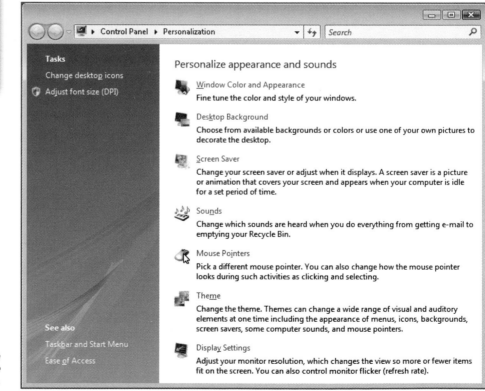

NOTE

The Advanced button at the bottom of the Display Settings dialog box will provide access to settings that are specific to your display hardware.

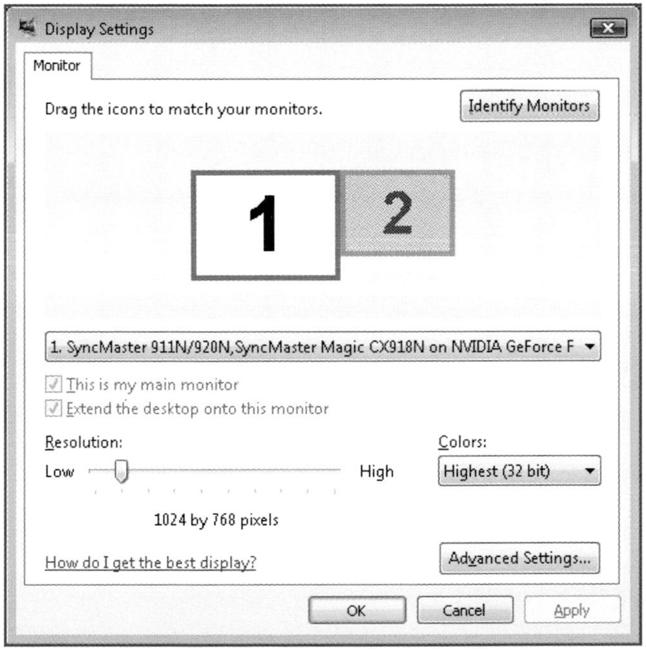

color quality. You can select the resolution and color in the Display Settings dialog box. From the Personalization window:

1. Click **Display Settings**. The Display Settings dialog box will appear, as shown in Figure 2-2.

2. Drag the **Resolution** slider to the right for a higher resolution or to the left for a lower resolution. (You can try this, and if you don't like it, come back and change it.)

3. Click the **Colors** drop-down list, and choose the color quality you want.

4. Click **OK** to close the Display Settings dialog box.

ALTER THE APPEARANCE OF OBJECTS

You can alter the appearance of windows, icons, and dialog boxes, changing their shapes and colors, as well as the font used in those objects. From the Personalization window:

1. Click **Windows Color And Appearance**. The Appearance Settings dialog box will appear, as shown in Figure 2-3.

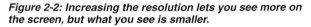

Figure 2-2: Increasing the resolution lets you see more on the screen, but what you see is smaller.

Figure 2-3: Look at possible changes in the Appearance Settings dialog box without affecting the actual screen.

2. Click:

- **Windows Aero** for the fanciest look (if your computer doesn't support this, this option won't be displayed)
- **Windows Vista Basic** for a modern look
- **Windows Standard** for a Windows 2000 look
- **Windows Classic** for the look of Windows 98
- One of the **High Contrast** choices for visual assistance

3. Click **Effects** to open the Effects dialog box, select the options that are correct for you, and click **OK** to close the Effects dialog box.

4. Click **Advanced** to open the Advanced Appearance dialog box. Select an object whose color and/or font you want to change, make those changes, and click **OK**. Some changes work with all color schemes, while others only work with Windows Classic.

5. When you are ready, click **OK** to close the Appearance Settings dialog box.

CHANGE THE DESKTOP BACKGROUND

You can use any picture, color, or pattern you want for your desktop background. From the Personalization window:

1. Click **Desktop Background**. The Desktop Background window opens.

2. Click the down arrow in the text box in the upper-left, and select one of the options in the drop-down list. Click one of the pictures that appears and it will be displayed in the background, as shown in Figure 2-4.

–Or–

Click **Browse**, locate a picture of your own to use, and click **Open** to display the selected photo in the background in the Desktop Background window.

3. Click **OK** to close the Desktop Background window.

PICK A NEW SCREEN SAVER

When the computer is left on but not in use, the unchanging image on the screen can be burned into the face of a cathode-ray tube (CRT) monitor. The newer, thin, flat-screen liquid crystal display (LCD) monitors are not as affected by this, but plasma displays can be. To prevent this damage, you can choose to use a *screen saver*, which constantly changes the image on the screen when

---

Effects

☑ Use the following method to smooth edges of screen fonts:

ClearType

☑ Show shadows under menus
☑ Show window contents while dragging

OK   Cancel

NOTE

By default, Windows smoothes the edges of screen fonts using ClearType. You can change this by clicking **Effects** in the Appearance Settings dialog box (the Effects dialog box will then appear). ClearType is only effective if you are using a notebook computer or a flat-panel display.

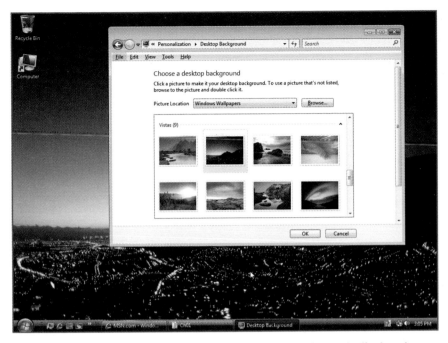

Figure 2-4: Selecting a background picture causes it to be instantly displayed as your background.

the computer is not in use. Windows Vista provides a number of alternative screen savers you can use. From the Personalization window:

1. Click **Screen Saver**. The Screen Saver dialog box appears.

2. Click the **Screen Saver** down arrow, and select one of the options in the drop-down list. It will be displayed in the preview area.

3. Click a screen saver option to see it previewed in the dialog box (see Figure 2-5).

4. Click **Preview** to see the screen saver on your full screen. Press ESC to return to the dialog box.

5. Click the up or down arrow on the **Wait** spinner to set the time to wait before enabling the screen saver.

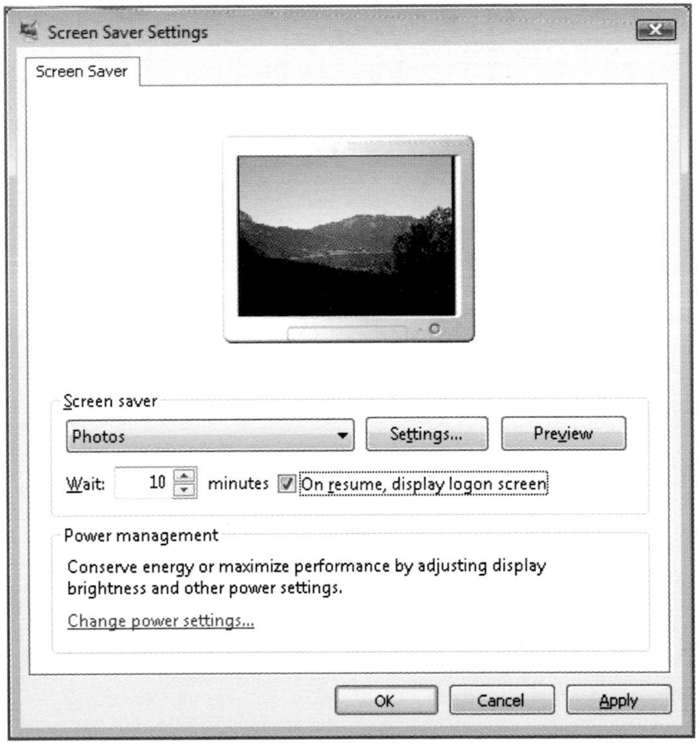

Figure 2-5: You can use your own photos with the Photos screen saver option.

6. When you have the screen saver you want, click **Settings**, if it is enabled, to see what settings are available for your screen saver. With the Photos option, you can select the folder, such as your Pictures, from which to display photos.

7. When you are ready, click **OK** to close the dialog box.

SELECT THE SOUNDS VISTA PLAYS

You can select the sounds that are played when various events occur, such as a critical stop or Windows shutdown, in the Sound dialog box. From the Personalization window:

1. Click **Sounds**. The Sound dialog box will open displaying the Sounds tab, as shown in Figure 2-6.

2. Click the **Sound Scheme** down arrow, and select one of the options.

3. Double-click a **Program** option to hear its current sound played.

4. Click the **Sounds** down arrow to select a different sound for the selected event. Click **Test** to hear the sound.

5. When you have made all the changes you want to the association of sounds and events, click **Save As** to save your changes. Type a name for the new scheme and click **OK**.

6. When you are ready, click **OK** to close the Sound dialog box.

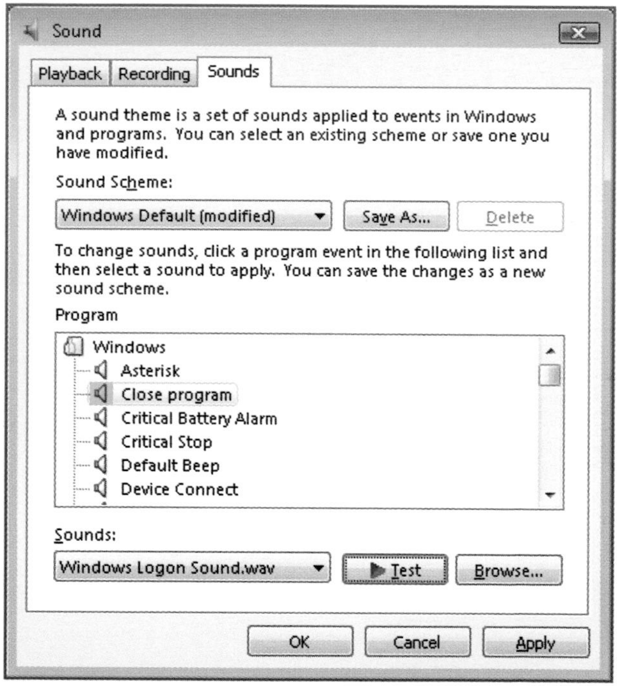

USE A DIFFERENT MOUSE POINTER

If it is difficult for you to see the mouse pointer, you can change how it looks and behaves in the Mouse Properties dialog box. From the Personalization window:

1. Click **Mouse Pointers**. The Mouse Properties dialog box will appear with the Pointers tab displayed, as shown in Figure 2-7.

2. Click the **Scheme** down arrow, and choose the scheme you want to use.

3. If you want to customize a particular mouse pointer, select that pointer, click **Browse**, locate and select the pointer you want to use, and click **Open**.

4. Click **OK** to close the Mouse Properties dialog box.

SELECT A THEME

A *theme* controls not only the look of Windows Vista, but also the sounds, icons, and other elements. To change the theme you are using, from the Personalization window:

Figure 2-6: Your sounds can be associated with various events.

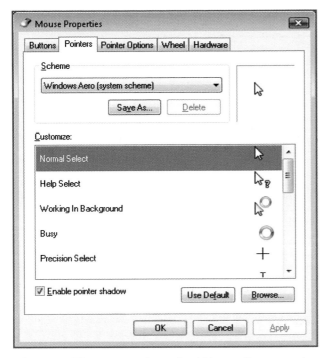

Figure 2-7: The mouse pointer should be easily seen and instantly informative for you.

You can select a new theme and within the dialog box see the changes in the preview area. If you don't like the changes, select a different theme or click **Cancel**. Your actual screen will remain unchanged.

Figure 2-8: The Themes tab allows you to control many facets of Windows Vista just by changing the theme.

1. Click **Theme**. The Theme Settings dialog box will appear with the Themes tab displayed, as shown in Figure 2-8.

2. Click the **Theme** drop-down list, and click your desired theme; or click **Browse**, select a theme stored on your computer, and click **Open**.

3. Click **OK** to close the Theme Settings dialog box.

CREATE A THEME

When you have set up the Windows Vista display features the way you want them, you can save those settings as a theme of your own and transfer them to another computer.

1. Use the features in the Personalization window to give Windows Vista the look and behavior you want. Then, from the Personalization window, click **Theme** to open the Theme Settings dialog box. The theme should be "Modified Theme."

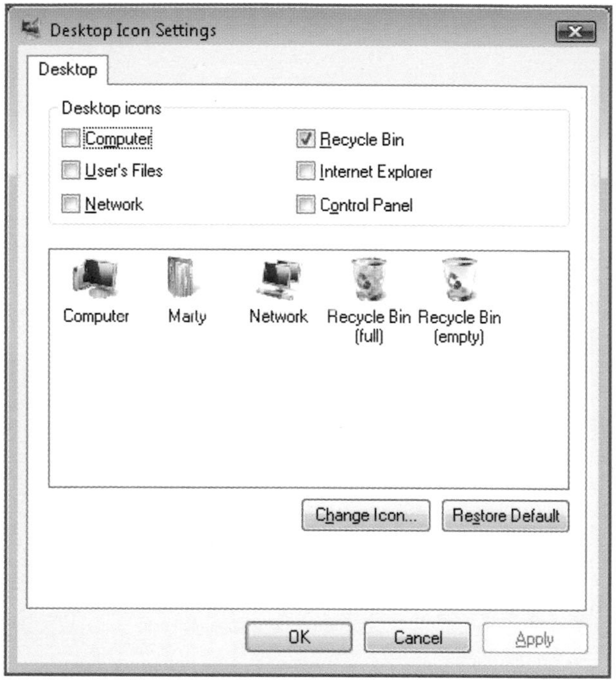

Figure 2-9: Add the icons to the desktop for the programs you use most often.

2. Click **Save As**, type the file name you want to use, select the folder you want to store the file in (this is optional), and click **Save**.

3. Click **OK** to close the Theme Settings dialog box.

Add Windows Program Icons

When you first install and start up Windows Vista, you will only have a couple icons on the desktop including the Recycle Bin, although some computer manufacturers may have additional icons. The purpose of having program icons on the desktop, called *shortcuts*, is to be able to easily start the programs by double-clicking their icons. To add Windows program icons, such as Windows Explorer and Internet Explorer, to the desktop and customize them:

1. Right-click a blank area of the desktop, and click **Personalize** to open the Personalization window.

2. Click **Change Desktop Icons** in the Tasks pane on the left to open the Desktop Icon Settings dialog box, shown in Figure 2-9.

3. In the **Desktop Icons** area, click one to six icons that you want to have on the desktop. For example, you might want icons for Computer and Internet Explorer. The others you might use less often, and they can be quickly accessed from the Start menu.

4. To customize a Windows program icon, click the icon and click **Change Icon**. A dialog box will appear displaying alternate icons.

5. Select the alternative you want, and click **OK**.

6. When you are satisfied with the Windows program icons you have selected and/or changed, click **OK**.

7. Click the **Close** button to close the Personalization window.

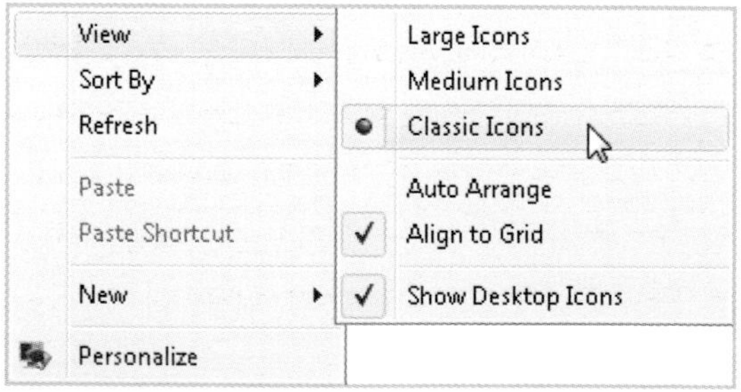

Change Desktop Icons

When you have the icons that you want on the desktop, you can change the size of the icons, their order, and their alignment through the desktop context menu:

Right-click a blank area of the desktop to open the context menu, and click **View** to open the View submenu.

QUICKSTEPS

ADDING OTHER PROGRAM ICONS TO THE DESKTOP

The method for adding other program icons, or shortcuts, to the desktop depends on where the icons are.

ADD ICONS FROM THE START MENU

Click **Start** to open the menu, and drag the icon from the menu to the desktop.

ADD ICONS FROM THE PROGRAM MENU

1. Click **Start**, and click **All Programs**.

2. Locate and point to the icon, hold down the right mouse button, and drag the icon to the desktop. (This is called *right-drag*.)

3. Click **Copy Here**.

ADD ICONS FROM OTHER MENUS

1. Click **Start**, click **All Programs**, and open additional folders as needed.

2. Point to the icon, hold down the right mouse button, and right-drag the icon to the desktop.

3. Click **Copy Here**.

ADD ICONS NOT ON A MENU

1. Click **Start**, and click **Computer**.

2. In the Computer window, if it is not already open, click **Folders** in the left pane.

3. Click the drive and folder(s) needed to locate the program.

4. Right-drag the program icon to the desktop, and click **Create Shortcut Here**.

RESIZE ICONS

Windows Vista gives you the choice of three different sizes of icons. The size you choose is a function of both the resolution you are using on your display and your personal preference. By default (the way Windows is set up when you first install and/or start it), your icons will be medium size. From the **View** submenu:

Click each of the sizes to see which is best for you.

ALIGN ICONS

You can drag desktop icons where you want them; but, by default, Windows Vista will align your icons to an invisible grid. If you don't like that, from the **View** submenu:

Click **Align To Grid** to clear the check mark and allow any arrangement on the desktop that you want.

If you should move your icons around and then change your mind, reopen the **View** submenu, and:

Click **Align To Grid** to reselect it. Your icons will jump to the invisible grid and be aligned.

ARRANGE ICONS

By default, there is no particular order to the icons on the desktop, and you can drag them into the order that suits you. However, you can have

TIP

The Recycle Bin cannot be renamed.

Windows arrange and sort the icons in several ways. From the **View** submenu:

> Click **Auto Arrange**. By default, the icons will be placed in a column alphabetically by name, except that the *system* icons (Computer, Recycle Bin, Internet Explorer, User's Files, Control Panel, and Network) will be at the top.

If you want to change the order in which Windows Vista arranges desktop icons:

1. Right-click a blank area of the desktop to open the context menu, and click **Sort By** to open that submenu.
2. Click one of the options to have the icons sorted in that manner.

RENAME DESKTOP ICONS

When you add program icons to the desktop, they may have the word "Shortcut" in their names, or they may have names that are not meaningful to you. To rename desktop icons:

1. Right-click an icon name you want to change, and click **Rename**.
2. Type the new name that you want to use, and press **ENTER**.

Change the Start Menu

The Start menu has several areas you can customize, including its overall look, the size of the icons, the number of programs on it, the programs to use for the Internet and for e-mail, and how the Start menu operates.

CHANGE THE LOOK OF THE START MENU

You have a choice between the "Classic," or Windows 98, look, shown on the left, and the newer Windows Vista look, which has more emphasis on using the Internet.

1. Right-click **Start**, and click **Properties** to open the Taskbar And Start Menu Properties dialog box (see Figure 2-10).
2. Click **Start Menu** or **Classic Start Menu**. If you choose Start Menu, you can also choose to store and display recently opened files and programs.
3. When you are done changing the Start menu, click **OK**.

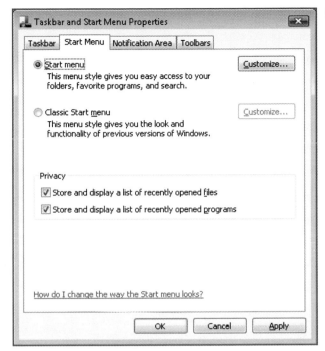

Figure 2-10: *The customization of the Start menu begins with choosing its look.*

NOTE

Changing the size of icons only affects the icons on the left of the Start menu. The purpose of smaller icons is to list more programs.

CHANGE WHAT IS DISPLAYED ON THE START MENU

Windows Vista gives you considerable flexibility as to what is displayed on the Start menu and how those items work.

1. Right-click **Start** and click **Properties** to open the Taskbar And Start Menu Properties dialog box.

2. With Start Menu selected, click **Customize**. The Customize Start Menu dialog box will appear (see Figure 2-11).

3. Scroll through the list of links, icons, and submenus. Select the ones you want included on the Start menu and indicate how they should operate. The last option lets you change the size of the icons on the Start menu.

4. Use the **Number Of Recent Programs To Display** spinner to select the number displayed in the lower-left of the start menu.

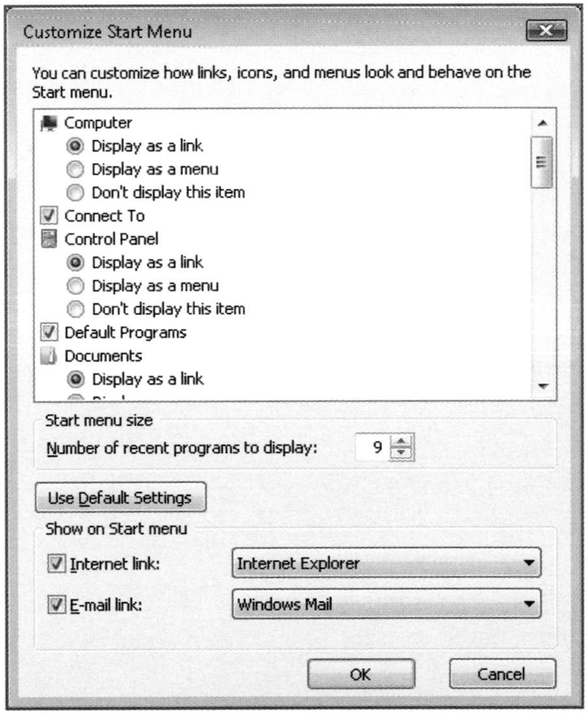

Figure 2-11: *You can customize what is displayed on the Start menu and how those items work.*

5. To return to the original default settings, click **Use Default Settings**.

6. When you have made the changes you want, click **OK** twice.

CHANGE THE START MENU PROGRAMS USED FOR THE INTERNET

The Windows Vista Start menu has spots for icons for an Internet browser (a program to access the World Wide Web) and an Internet e-mail program. Initially, clicking these icons opens Internet Explorer and Windows Mail. However, you can change the programs opened, or you can turn off the icons.

1. Right-click **Start** and click **Properties** to open the Taskbar And Start Menu Properties dialog box.

2. Click **Customize**. The Customize Start Menu dialog box will appear.

3. If you want to change your Internet browser, click the **Internet Link** drop-down list, and select the browser you want to use.

4. If you want to change your Internet mail program, click the **E-Mail Link** drop-down list, and select the program you want to use.

☑ E-mail link:	Windows Mail ▾
	Windows Live Mail
	Microsoft Office Outlook
	Windows Mail

5. If you don't want to display a browser and/or an e-mail program, click the check box to the left of the option to clear it.

6. When you have made the changes you want, click **OK** twice.

ADD PROGRAMS TO THE START MENU

You can add programs to the upper-left of the Start menu (where they will remain unless you remove them).

Open
Pin to Start Menu
Add to Quick Launch
Restore previous versions
Send To ▸
Cut
Copy
Delete
Rename
Properties

1. Click **Start**, click **All Programs**, and open the appropriate folders to display the program you want on the Start menu.

2. Right-click the program and click **Pin To Start Menu**. The program will appear on the Start menu.

3. Click outside the Start menu to close it.

TIP

To remove a program you have added to the Start menu, click Start, right-click the program, and click **Unpin From Start Menu**. Then click outside the Start menu to close it.

NOTE

The picture that is displayed on the Start menu comes from your user account, as described in Chapter 8.

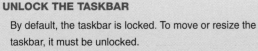

NOTE

You can turn on a second optional area on the taskbar that lets you open the Tablet PC Input Panel to enter text on the screen without a keyboard. Instead, you write with a mouse or stylus or click a keyboard layout on the screen. See the "Changing Taskbar Properties" QuickSteps to see how to turn this on.

QUICKSTEPS

CHANGING TASKBAR PROPERTIES

A number of the features of the taskbar can be changed through the Taskbar And Start Menu Properties dialog box.

OPEN TASKBAR PROPERTIES

Right-click an open area of the taskbar, and click **Properties**. The Taskbar And Start Menu Properties dialog box appears with the Taskbar tab selected.

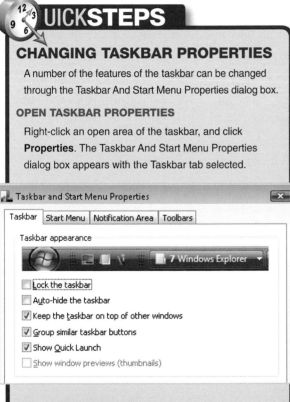

UNLOCK THE TASKBAR

By default, the taskbar is locked. To move or resize the taskbar, it must be unlocked.

Continued . . .

Figure 2-12: A Start menu with a number of the changes described in this chapter.

Figure 2-12 shows a changed Start menu, which you can compare with Figure 1-3 in Chapter 1.

Change the Taskbar

The taskbar at the bottom of the Windows Vista screen has three standard areas: the Start button on the left, the task list in the middle, and the notification area on the right. In addition, there is an optional area called the Quick

CHANGING TASKBAR PROPERTIES

(Continued)

Click **Lock The Taskbar** to remove the check mark and unlock the taskbar.

HIDE THE TASKBAR

Hiding the taskbar means that it is not displayed unless you move the mouse to the edge of the screen containing the taskbar. By default, it is displayed.

Click **Auto-Hide The Taskbar** to select the check box and hide the taskbar.

KEEP THE TASKBAR ON TOP

Keeping the taskbar on top means that it is always visible—nothing can cover it. By default, it is kept on top.

Click **Keep The Taskbar On Top Of Other Windows** to remove the check mark and not keep the taskbar on top.

GROUP SIMILAR BUTTONS

Grouping similar items puts, for example, all Microsoft Word documents in one icon or all Internet pages in one icon so that they take less room on the taskbar. By default, similar buttons are grouped.

Click **Group Similar Taskbar Buttons** to remove the check mark and disable this option.

SELECT TOOLBARS TO DISPLAY

You can display several toolbars on the taskbar. By default the Quick Launch toolbar is displayed, but other toolbars, such as the Tablet PC Input Panel and the Windows Media Player can also be displayed. You can choose which toolbars you want displayed in the Toolbars tab of the Taskbar And Start Menu Properties dialog box.

Continued . . .

Launch toolbar. You can change the taskbar by moving and sizing it and by changing its properties.

MOVE AND SIZE THE TASKBAR

You can move the taskbar to any of the four sides of the screen. Do this by dragging any empty area of the taskbar to another edge. For example, Figure 2-13 shows the taskbar moved to the right edge of the screen.

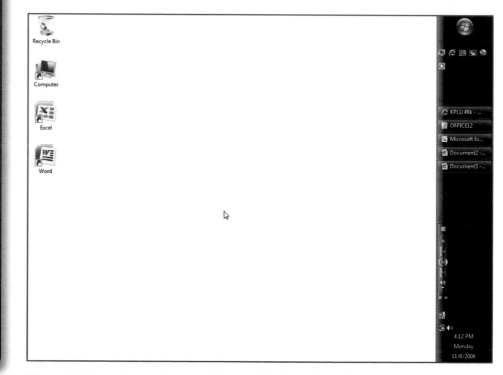

Figure 2-13: A taskbar can be moved to any of the four sides of the screen.

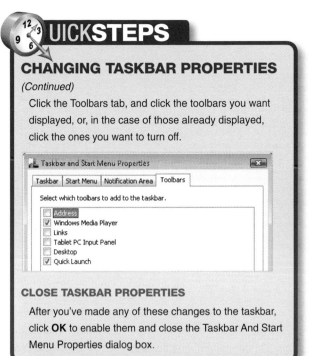

QUICKSTEPS

CHANGING TASKBAR PROPERTIES

(Continued)

Click the Toolbars tab, and click the toolbars you want displayed, or, in the case of those already displayed, click the ones you want to turn off.

CLOSE TASKBAR PROPERTIES

After you've made any of these changes to the taskbar, click **OK** to enable them and close the Taskbar And Start Menu Properties dialog box.

QUICKSTEPS

CHANGING THE NOTIFICATION AREA

The notification area on the right of the taskbar can also be changed through the Taskbar And Start Menu Properties dialog box (see the "Changing Taskbar Properties" QuickSteps for instructions on displaying the dialog box). The notification area, which can get crowded at times, contains program icons put there by Windows and other programs. You can control which icons are displayed, in the notification area but hidden, or not there at all (see Figure 2-14). To change the notification area:

Click the **Notification Area tab**.

Continued . . .

You can size the taskbar by dragging the inner edge (top edge when the taskbar is on the bottom) in or out. Here is a taskbar at double its normal size:

In either case, you must first unlock the taskbar. See the "Changing Taskbar Properties" QuickSteps to do this.

Use the Quick Launch Toolbar

The Quick Launch toolbar may be turned off on your computer, although in Windows Vista, it is turned on by default. When it is turned on, it is placed next

Figure 2-14: Turn off the notification area icons that are not useful to you.

QUICKSTEPS

CHANGING THE NOTIFICATION AREA *(Continued)*

HIDE INACTIVE ICONS

Hiding inactive icons removes icons that have not been recently used from the notification area. By default, inactive icons are hidden.

Click **Hide Inactive Icons** to remove the check mark and display the inactive icons.

SHOW SYSTEM ICONS

Four system icons—Clock, Volume, Network, and Power (on mobile computers)—are shown in the notification area by default.

Click the icon name to remove the check mark next to it and not display it.

CUSTOMIZE THE NOTIFICATION AREA

You can customize the behavior of other icons in the notification area, in addition to the changes you can make to the system icons.

1. Click **Customize**. The Customize Icons dialog box appears.

2. Click a program icon whose appearance you want to change.

3. Click the drop-down list that appears, and select the behavior you want (see Figure 2-15).

4. When you have made the changes you want, click **OK**.

CLOSE TASKBAR PROPERTIES

After you've made any of these changes to the notification area, click **OK** to enable them and close the Taskbar And Start Menu Properties dialog box.

Customize Notification Icons

Click an icon behavior to change it.

Icon	Behavior
Past Items	
Windows Sidebar	Hide when inactive
Windows Error Reporting	Hide when inactive
Safely Remove Hardware	Hide when inactive
Problem Reports and Solutions	Hide when inactive
SnagIt	Hide when inactive

Default Settings

OK   Cancel

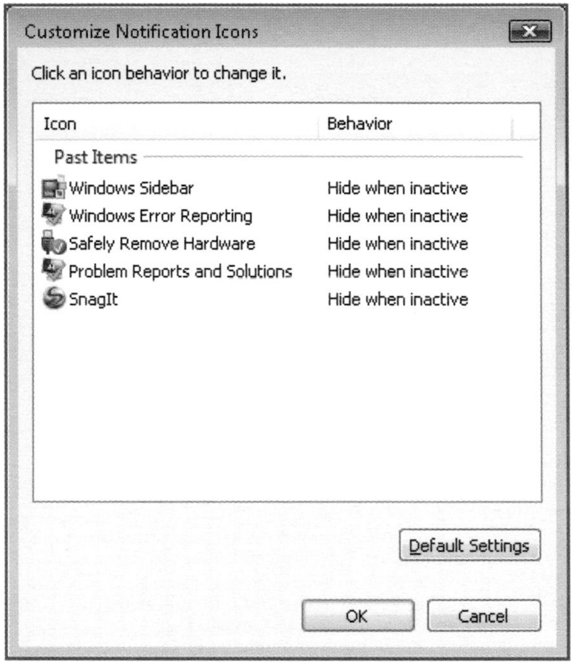

Figure 2-15: You can hide or show programs and system icons in the notification area.

to the Start menu and holds frequently used icons, which, with a single click, you can use to easily start a program or open a folder.

TURN ON THE QUICK LAUNCH TOOLBAR

If the Quick Launch toolbar is turned off, you can turn it on in two ways:

Right-click a blank area of the taskbar, click **Properties** to open the Taskbar And Start Menu Properties dialog box, and click **Show Quick Launch**.

-Or-

Right-click a blank area of the taskbar, click **Toolbars**, and click **Quick Launch**.

NOTE

The vertical column of dots on either side of the Quick Launch toolbar isn't available if "Lock The Taskbar" is enabled. Right-click the taskbar and click **Lock The Taskbar** to unlock it (remove the check mark).

Toolbars ▶	Address
Cascade Windows	✓ Windows Media Player
Show Windows Stacked	Links
Show Windows Side by Side	Tablet PC Input Panel
Show the Desktop	Desktop
	✓ Quick Launch
Task Manager	New Toolbar...
Lock the Taskbar	
Properties	

QUICKSTEPS

REARRANGING THE QUICK LAUNCH TOOLBAR

The Quick Launch toolbar can be expanded to display more icons and moved around the taskbar. Additionally, icons on the Quick Launch toolbar can be moved around and hidden.

SIZE THE QUICK LAUNCH TOOLBAR

Drag the vertical column of dots on the right of the toolbar to the right (to enlarge) or to the left (to reduce) the Quick Launch toolbar. As the toolbar is made smaller, icons may be hidden.

MOVE THE QUICK LAUNCH TOOLBAR

Drag the vertical column of dots on the left of the toolbar to move it to another location on the taskbar. To get around other icons on the taskbar, simply drag through them, use a two-row taskbar, or delete the other icons.

MOVE ICONS WITHIN THE QUICK LAUNCH TOOLBAR

Drag the Quick Launch icons where you want them on the toolbar.

ADD PROGRAMS TO THE QUICK LAUNCH TOOLBAR

When you first turn on the Quick Launch toolbar, it has two icons—one each for Show Desktop, and Switch Between Windows. (Show Desktop minimizes all the open windows so that you can see the icons on the desktop. Switch Between Windows allows you to choose which open window is on top, which can also be done by pressing ALT+TAB.) After you have used Vista for a while and use the Internet Explorer and Windows Media Player, icons for these products will automatically be added to the Quick Launch toolbar. You can add program, file, and folder icons to the Quick Launch toolbar in all the ways you add them to the desktop, except that you drag the icons to the toolbar instead of to the desktop. See the "Adding Other Program Icons to the Desktop" QuickSteps found earlier in this chapter.

REMOVE PROGRAMS FROM THE QUICK LAUNCH TOOLBAR

To remove a program icon from the Quick Launch toolbar:

Right-click the icon, click **Delete**, and click **Yes**.

Change How Windows Vista Operates

How Windows Vista operates is probably more important to you than how it looks. For that reason, Windows Vista has a number of facilities that allow you to customize its operation.

Set and Use the Date and Time

The time in the lower-right corner of the screen may seem simple enough, but significant capability lies behind these simple numbers.

1. Move the mouse until your cursor is on the time in the notification area. The current day and date will appear.

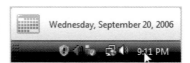

2. Click the time. The full calendar and clock appear.

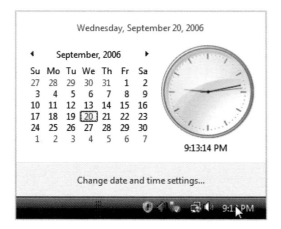

3. Click **Change Date And Time Settings**. The Date And Time dialog box will appear, as shown in Figure 2-16.

4. With the **Date And Time** tab selected, click **Change Date And Time**. The Date And Time Settings dialog box appears.

5. Use the arrows on the calendar to change the month. Or, click the month to display the year, use the arrows to change the year, click the month, and then click a day.

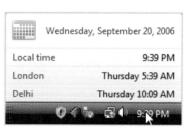

Figure 2-16: *Setting the date and time is normally automated using an Internet time server.*

6. Click an element of time (hour, minute, second, AM/PM), and use the spinner to change the selected time element. Click **OK** to close the Date And Time Settings dialog box.

7. Click **Change Time Zone**, click the **Time Zone** down arrow, and click your time zone.

8. Click **Automatically Adjust Clock For Daylight Saving Time** if it isn't already selected and you want Windows Vista to do that. Click **OK** to close the Time Zone Settings dialog box.

9. Click the **Additional Clocks** tab to add one or two clocks with different time zones. Click **Additional Clock 1**, open the drop-down list box, and click a time zone. Enter a display name, and repeat for a second additional clock, if desired.

	Wednesday, September 20, 2006
Local time	9:39 PM
London	Thursday 5:39 AM
Delhi	Thursday 10:09 AM

10. Click the **Internet Time** tab, and see how your computer's time is currently being synchronized. If you want to change that, click **Change Settings**.

11. Click **Synchronize With An Internet Time Server** if it isn't already selected, open the drop-down list, click a time server, and click **Update Now**. Once turned on, Windows will check the time every seven days. Click **OK** to close the Internet Time Settings dialog box.

12. Click **OK** to close the Date And Time dialog box.

Change Ease of Access Settings

Ease of Access settings provide alternatives to the normal way the mouse and keyboard are used, as well as some settings that make the screen more readable and sounds more understandable.

1. Right-click a blank area of the screen, click **Personalize**, and click **Ease Of Access** in the Tasks pane on the left. The Ease Of Access Center window will open, as shown in Figure 2-17.

   –Or–

   Press and hold the **Windows Flag** key while pressing **U**.

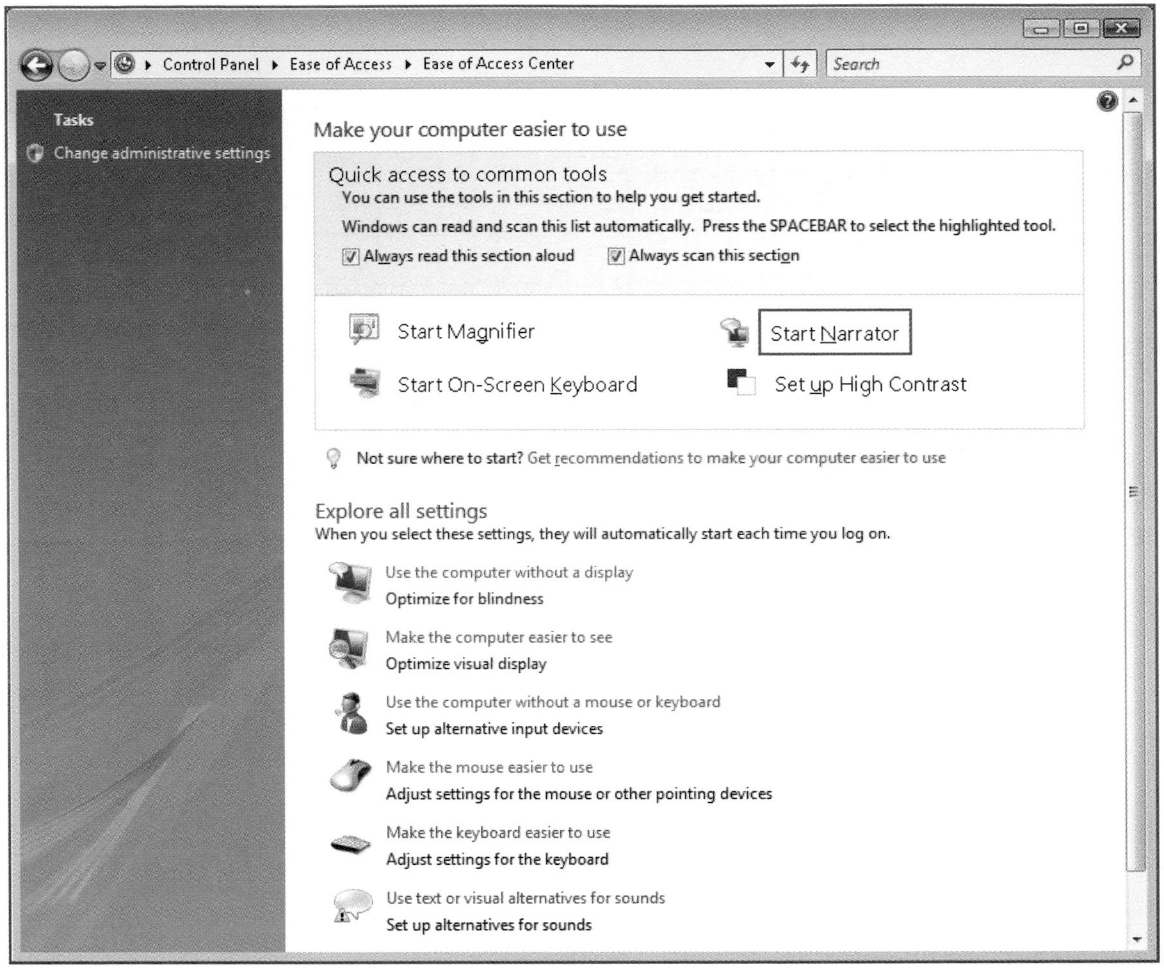

*Figure 2-17: **Ease of Access settings let you work with Windows Vista and your programs in ways that facilitate use with various physical limitations.***

NOTE

By default, and if you have speakers and a sound card, Windows Vista will scan and read aloud the four options in the Quick Access section.

2. Select the options you want to use in the common tools area at the top (see Table 2-1 for a description). You can also turn the options on or off using the keyboard shortcuts shown.

3. Click any of the blue text in the lower part of the window to review, and possibly change, the Ease of Access settings that apply to various areas of the computer.

4. When you have set up the accessibility options you want, click **Close**.

USING THE CONTROL PANEL

The Control Panel is a facility for customizing many of the functions available in Windows. The individual components of the Control Panel are discussed throughout this book (several in this chapter); this section is an introduction to the Control Panel itself.

OPEN THE CONTROL PANEL

Click **Start** and click **Control Panel**. The Control Panel is displayed. By default, it will be as shown in Figure 2-18. (Only mobile computers will show a Mobile PC category.)

SWITCH THE CONTROL PANEL VIEW

The Control Panel has two configurations: the default Control Panel Home, shown in Figure 2-18, and Classic View, shown in Figure 2-19. Classic View has icons for all the Control Panel components in one window.

When in Control Panel Home, click **Classic View** in the task pane on the left.

When in Classic View, click **Control Panel Home** in the task pane to switch back.

OPEN A CONTROL PANEL CATEGORY

Control Panel Home groups components into categories that must be opened to see the individual components, although some subcategories are listed.

Click a category to open a window for that category, where you can select either a task you want to do or open a Control Panel component represented by an icon.

OPEN A CONTROL PANEL COMPONENT

In both Classic View and in a Control Panel Home secondary window are icons for individual Control Panel components. To open a component:

Double-click (in Classic View) or click (in the secondary window from Control Panel Home) the component's icon.

OPTION	DESCRIPTION	KEYBOARD SHORTCUT
Magnifier	Enlarges a part of the screen around the mouse.	
On Screen Keyboard	Displays an image of a keyboard on the screen that you can click to select the appropriate keys.	
High Contrast	Uses high-contrast colors and special fonts to make the screen easy to use.	Press together left **SHIFT**, left **ALT**, and **PRINT SCREEN**.
Narrator	Reads aloud selected text on the screen	
Sticky Keys	Simulates pressing a pair of keys, such as **CTRL+A**, by pressing one key at a time. The keys **SHIFT**, **CTRL**, and **ALT** "stick" down until a second key is pressed. This is interpreted as two keys pressed together.	Press either **SHIFT** key five times in succession.
Filter Keys	Enables you to press a key twice in rapid succession and have it interpreted as a single keystroke; also slows down the rate at which the key is repeated if it is held down.	Hold down the right **SHIFT** key for eight seconds.

Table 2-1: Ease of Access Common Tools

Customize the Mouse

The mouse lets you interact with the screen and point at, select, and drag objects. You also can start and stop programs and close Windows using the mouse. While you can use Windows without a mouse, it is more difficult, making it important that the mouse operates in the most comfortable way possible. Change the way the mouse works through the Control Panel Mouse component:

1. Click **Start** and click **Control Panel**.
2. In Control Panel Home, under Hardware and Sound, click **Mouse**.

   –Or–

   In Classic View, double-click **Mouse**.

   Either way, the Mouse Properties dialog box will appear, as you can see in Figure 2-20.

Figure 2-18: *Control Panel Home provides a hierarchy of windows that leads you to the settings you want to change.*

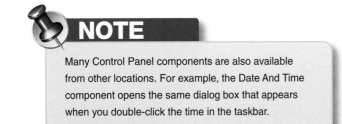

NOTE

Many Control Panel components are also available from other locations. For example, the Date And Time component opens the same dialog box that appears when you double-click the time in the taskbar.

3. If you want to use the mouse with your left hand, click **Switch Primary And Secondary Buttons**.

4. Double-click the folder in the middle-right of the **Buttons tab**. If the folder opens, your double-click speed is okay. If not, drag the **Speed** slider until the folder opens when you double-click it.

5. Select the options you want to use on the **Buttons, Pointer Options**, and **Wheel** tabs. Check marks indicate the options you want have been selected.

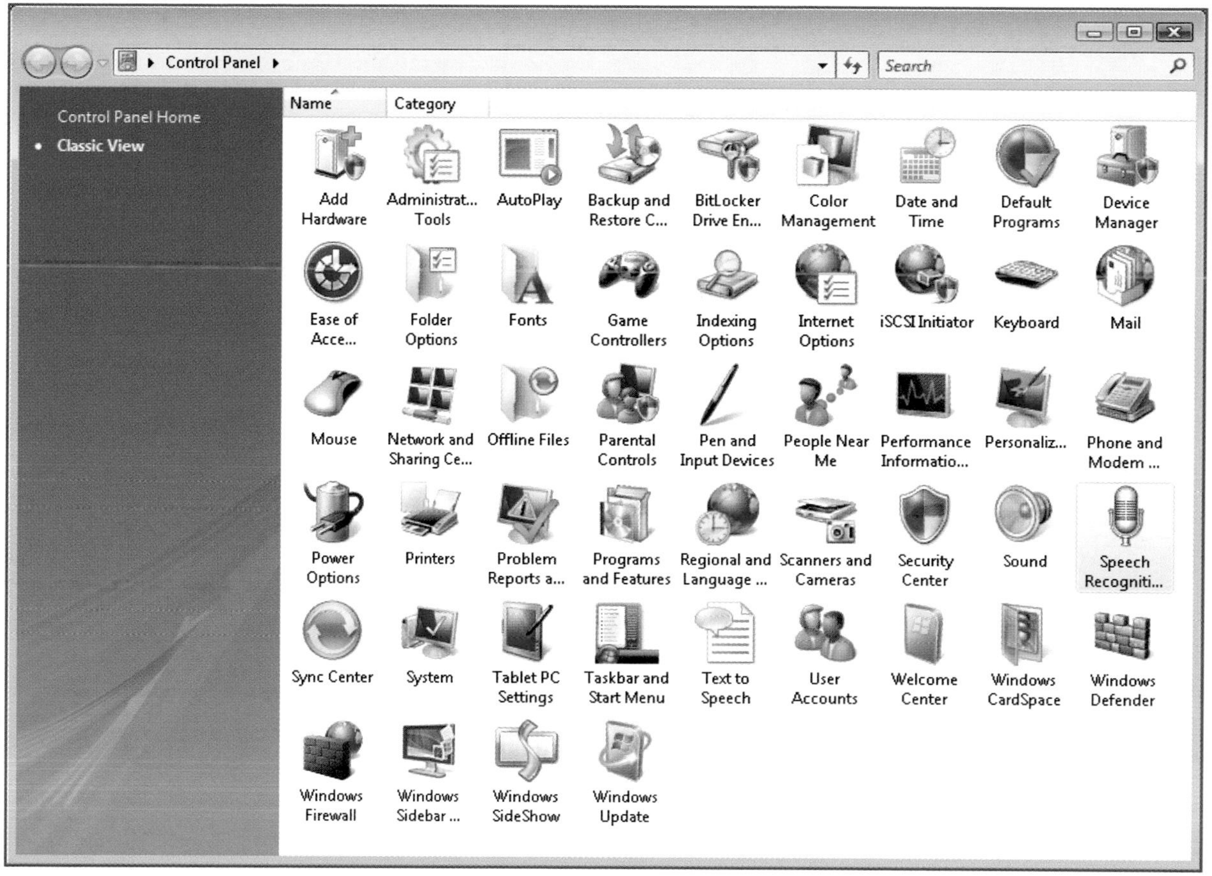

Figure 2-19: **The Control Panel's Classic View shows all of the components in the Control Panel.**

NOTE

If you have purchased a mouse separately from your computer and have installed its software, your tabs may be different and its features may not be as described here.

6. Click the **Pointers tab**. If you want to change the way the pointer looks, select a different scheme (see "Use a Different Mouse Pointer," earlier in the chapter).

7. When you have set up the mouse the way you want, click **OK**.

Customize the Keyboard

Windows requires a keyboard for textual communications. You can change the length of the delay before a key that is held down is repeated and the rate at which the key is repeated.

Keyboard

Mouse Properties

Buttons | Pointers | Pointer Options | Wheel | Hardware

Button configuration

☐ Switch primary and secondary buttons

Select this check box to make the button on the right the one you use for primary functions such as selecting and dragging.

Double-click speed

Double-click the folder to test your setting. If the folder does not open or close, try using a slower setting.

Speed: Slow ———□——— Fast

ClickLock

☐ Turn on ClickLock   [Settings...]

Enables you to highlight or drag without holding down the mouse button. To set, briefly press the mouse button. To release, click the mouse button again.

[OK] [Cancel] [Apply]

Figure 2-20: The mouse is the primary way you operate in Windows Vista.

1. Click **Start** and click **Control Panel**.

2. In Control Panel Home, click **Hardware And Sound**, and then click **Keyboard**.

   –Or–

   In Classic View, double-click **Keyboard**.

   Either way, the Keyboard Properties dialog box appears.

3. Click in the text box in the middle of the dialog box, and press a character key to see how long you wait before the key is repeated and how fast the repeated character appears.

4. Drag the **Repeat Delay** slider in the direction desired, and then test the repetition again.

5. Drag the **Repeat Rate** slider in the direction desired, and then test the repetition again.

6. Drag the **Cursor Blink Rate** slider in the direction desired and observe the blink rate.

7. When you have set up the keyboard the way you want, click **OK**.

Change Sounds

Windows Vista uses sounds to alert and entertain you. Through Control Panel's Sound component, you can select the sound scheme you want (see Figure 2-21).

Sound

1. Click **Start** and click **Control Panel**.

2. In Control Panel Home, click **Hardware And Sound**, and then click **Sound**.

   –Or–

   In Classic View, double-click **Sound Themes**.

   In either case, the **Sound** dialog box appears.

3. Click **Speakers**, click **Configure** in the lower-left, click the **Audio Channels** drop-down list, select your configuration, and click **Test** to test your setup. When you are ready, click **Next**.

4. Click the speakers that aren't present and click **Next**. Click the speakers that are full range speakers and click **Next**. When you are done, click **Finish**.

5. Double-click **Speakers** and click the **Levels** tab, and drag the sliders in the direction desired to set the volume. Click **OK** to close the Speakers Properties dialog box.

6. Click the **Sounds** tab, and if you want to change it, select a different sound scheme (see "Select the Sounds Vista Plays" earlier in the chapter).

7. When you have set up the sounds the way you want, click **OK**.

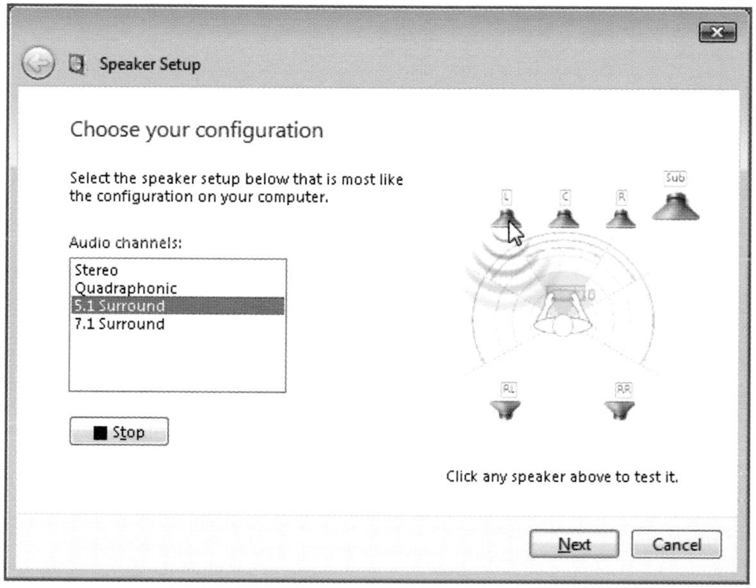

![Speaker Setup dialog box]

Speaker Setup

Choose your configuration

Select the speaker setup below that is most like
the configuration on your computer.

Audio channels:

Stereo
Quadraphonic
5.1 Surround
7.1 Surround

Stop

Click any speaker above to test it.

Next   Cancel

*Figure 2-21: Windows Vista can handle up to seven-speaker
surround sound.*

Change Regional Settings

Windows Vista lets you determine how numbers, dates, currency,
and time are displayed and used, as well as the languages that
will be used. Choosing a primary language and locale
sets all the other settings. You can customize these
options through the Regional And Language Options
component in the Control Panel.

Regional
and Lan...

1. Click **Start** and click **Control Panel**.

2. In Control Panel Home, click **Clock, Language, And Region**; and then
   click **Regional And Language Options**.

   –Or–

   In Classic View, double-click **Regional And Language Options**.

   In either case, the Regional And Language Options dialog box will
   appear, as you can see in Figure 2-22.

3. Click the **Current Format** drop-down list, and select the primary language and region
   in which the computer will be used. This changes the standards and formats that will
   be used by default.

4. Customize these settings by clicking **Customize This Format**. Then go to the
   individual tabs for numbers, currency, time, and date, and set how you want items
   displayed. Click **OK** when you are done.

5. When you have set up the regional settings the way you want, click **OK**.

Manage the Windows Sidebar

The Windows Sidebar is a new feature of Windows Vista. It displays a clock and
other gadgets on the side of the screen. To manage the sidebar:

1. Click **Start** and click **Control Panel**.

2. In Control Panel Home, click **Appearance And Personalization**, and then
   click **Windows Sidebar Properties**.

   Windows
   Sidebar ...

   –Or–

   In Classic View, double-click **Windows Sidebar Properties**.

   In either case, the Windows Sidebar Properties dialog box will appear.

CAUTION

Changing the format used for dates and times might
affect other Windows programs, such as Excel.

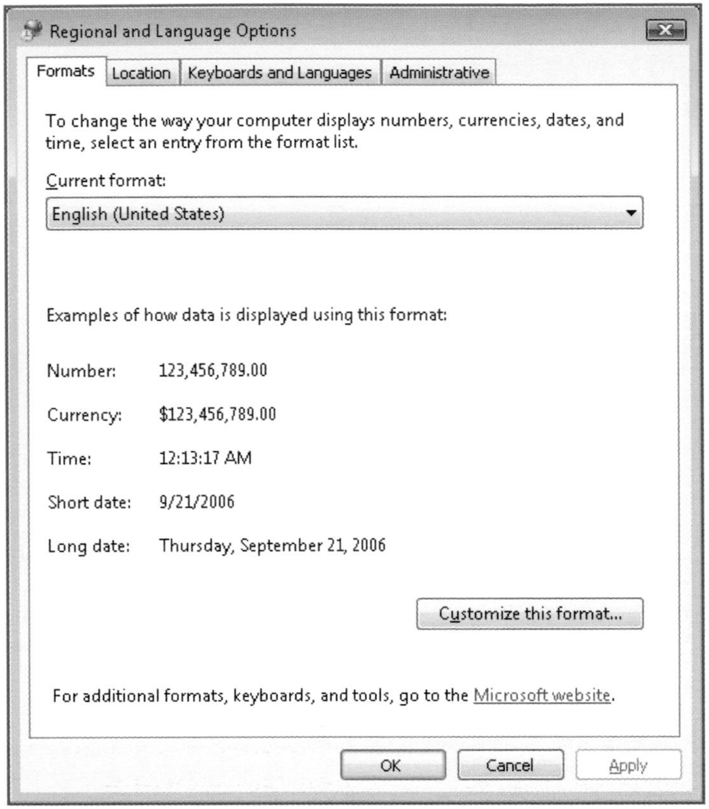

Figure 2-22: Regional and Language Options allow Windows Vista to operate almost anywhere in the world.

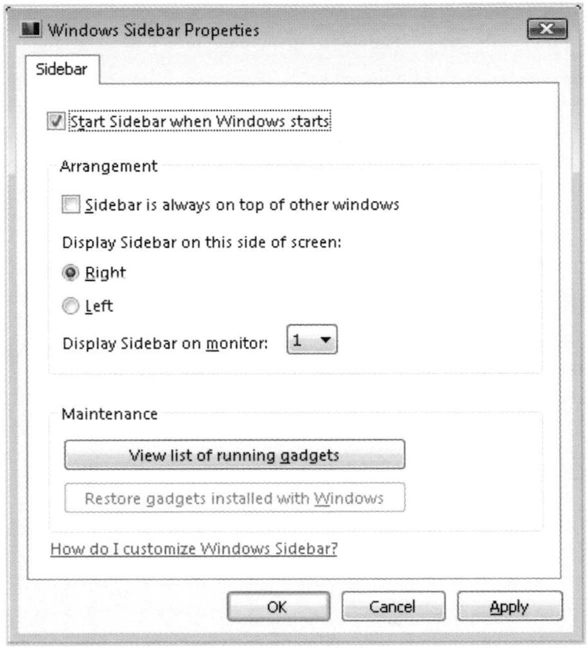

3. Click the respective check boxes if you want the Sidebar to always be on top of other windows and if you want it to start when Windows starts.

4. Click whether you want the sidebar on the right or left side of the screen, and select which monitor you want it displayed on if you have two or more monitors connected to your computer.

5. Click **View List Of Running Gadgets** (the Sidebar must be turned on), and select the gadgets that you want removed and click **Remove**. When you are ready, click **Close**.

6. Click **OK** when you have completed setting up the Sidebar the way you want.

How to...

- Open Windows Explorer
- Changing Windows Explorer Layout
- Customize Windows Explorer
- Use Windows Explorer Menus
- Identify Storage Devices
- Select and Open Drives and Folders
- Navigate Through Folders and Disks
- Renaming and Deleting Files and Folders
- Create New Folders
- Select Multiple Files and Folders
- Use the Recycle Bin
- Create Shortcuts
- Search for Files and Folders
- Copying and Moving Files and Folders
- Create Files
- Encrypt Files and Folders
- Change Other File and Folder Attributes
- Zipping Files and Folders
- Back Up Files and Folders
- Write Files and Folders to a CD or DVD
- Clean Up Disk
- Check for Errors
- Defragment a Disk

Chapter 3
Storing Information

The information on your computer—documents, e-mail, photographs, music, and programs—are stored in *files*. So that your files are organized and more easily found, they are kept in *folders*, and folders can be placed in other folders for further organization. For example, a folder labeled "Trips" contains separate folders for the years 2005, 2006, and 2007. The 2006 folder contains folders for Yellowstone and Disneyland. The Yellowstone folder contains folders of photos and sounds, as well as notes and expenses. Such a set of files and folders is shown in the Documents folder in Figure 3-1. In this chapter you'll see how to create, use, and manage files and folders like these. The term "objects" is used to refer to any mix of files, folders, and disk drives.

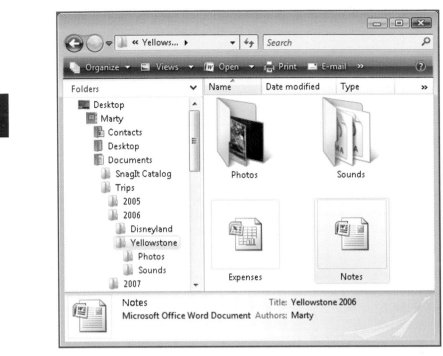

Figure 3-1: *Windows stores files in folders, which can be within other folders.*

Use the Windows File System

The tool that Windows Vista provides to locate and work with files and folders is *Windows Explorer* (often called "Explorer"). It has a number of components and features, most of which are shown in Figure 3-2 and described in Table 3-1. Much of this chapter is spent exploring these items and how they are used.

When you open Windows Explorer, you can choose what you want it to initially display from among the choices on the right of the Start menu. These choices give you access to (from top to bottom):

- Your personal folder, which contains your documents, pictures, music, and games
- Your documents
- Your pictures
- Your games
- The Search folder
- Recent files you have opened
- The computer on which you are working
- The network to which you are connected

NOTE

Depending on the permissions you have and whether or not you are connected to a network, you may not have Computer and/or Network on your Start menu.

Open Windows Explorer

To open Windows Explorer:

1. Start your computer, if it's not running, and log on to Windows if necessary.
2. Click **Start**. The Start menu will open and you'll see the Windows Explorer choices on the right of the menu.

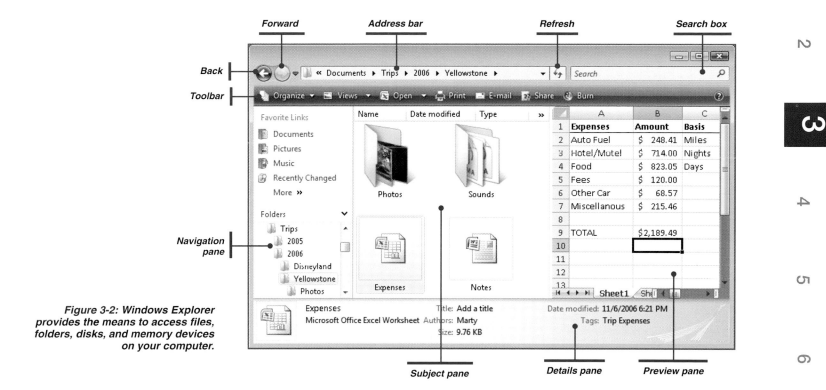

Figure 3-2: Windows Explorer provides the means to access files, folders, disks, and memory devices on your computer.

Table 3-1: Windows Explorer Components

AREA	FUNCTION
Back and Forward buttons	Displays an object previously shown
Address bar	Displays the location of what is being shown in the subject pane
Refresh	Updates what is displayed in the subject pane
Search box	Provides for the entry of text you want to search for
Preview pane	Displays the contents of the object selected in the subject pane
Details pane	Provides information about the object selected in the subject pane
Subject pane	Displays the objects stored at the address shown in the address bar
Navigation pane	Facilitates moving around among the objects you have available
Toolbar	Contains tools to work with objects in the subject pane

NOTE

If you are familiar with Windows XP, where Windows Explorer had a view with a task pane on the left, you might be wondering what happened to the task pane. The commands on the task pane have been moved to the toolbar, and the information on the task pane is now displayed on the details pane.

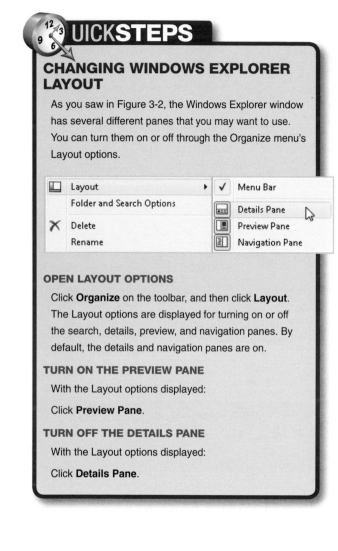

QUICKSTEPS

CHANGING WINDOWS EXPLORER LAYOUT

As you saw in Figure 3-2, the Windows Explorer window has several different panes that you may want to use. You can turn them on or off through the Organize menu's Layout options.

▢	Layout	▸	✓		Menu Bar
	Folder and Search Options			▦	Details Pane
✗	Delete			▦	Preview Pane
	Rename			▦	Navigation Pane

OPEN LAYOUT OPTIONS

Click **Organize** on the toolbar, and then click **Layout**. The Layout options are displayed for turning on or off the search, details, preview, and navigation panes. By default, the details and navigation panes are on.

TURN ON THE PREVIEW PANE

With the Layout options displayed:

Click **Preview Pane**.

TURN OFF THE DETAILS PANE

With the Layout options displayed:

Click **Details Pane**.

3. Click your personal folder. Explorer will open and display in the subject pane the files and folders that either come standard with Windows Vista or that have been placed there by you or somebody else. You can:

- Click an object in the subject pane to *select* it and get information about it in the details pane, preview it in the preview pane, or use the toolbar tools with that object.

  –Or–

- Double-click an object in the subject pane to *open* it so that you can see and work with its contents.

Customize Windows Explorer

You can customize how Windows Explorer looks and which features are available with the toolbar.

1. If Windows Explorer is not already open, click **Start** and click your personal folder.

2. Click **Pictures** in the navigation pane, and then double-click **Sample Pictures** in the subject pane. Windows Vista's sample pictures should open, as you can see in Figure 3-3.

Figure 3-3: Windows Explorer's toolbar changes to provide commands for what is selected in the subject pane.

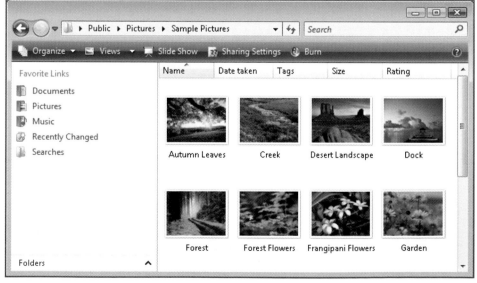

Click one of the pictures. The toolbar changes to something like this:

3. Click one of the pictures. The toolbar changes to something like this:

Organize ▼   Views ▼   Preview ▼   Slide Show   Print   E-mail   Share   Burn ?

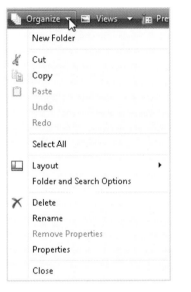

These toolbar options are specific to a picture. The selection of other types of files would have generated different options.

4. Click **Organize** to open the Organize menu. Here you can perform operations on the object you have selected, such as Cut, Paste, and Rename; and perform several folder-related operations such as New Folder, Layout, and Close.

5. Click the **Views** down arrow (not the Views button, which gives you another view of your folder). Drag the slider up and down to change the size of the objects in your folder.

6. Click the **Views** down arrow, and click **Details**, which is shown in Figure 3-4.

7. Click **Name** at the top of the left column in the subject pane. The contents of the subject pane will be sorted alphanumerically by name. Click **Name** again, and the contents will be sorted by name in the opposite direction.

	Extra Large Icons
	Large Icons
	Medium Icons
	Small Icons
	List
	Details
	Tiles

Figure 3-4: Folder Details view gives you further information about the objects in the folder.

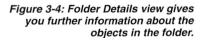

Name	Date taken	Tags	Size
Autumn Leaves	11/4/2005 5:12 PM		270 KB
Creek	4/30/2005 10:20 AM		259 KB
Desert Landscape	2/12/2004 4:30 PM		224 KB
Dock	6/22/2005 7:17 PM		310 KB
Forest	4/24/2005 11:00 PM		649 KB
Forest Flowers	4/26/2005 3:50 PM		126 KB
Frangipani Flowers	6/2/2005 2:41 PM		106 KB
Garden	4/9/2004 7:17 AM		505 KB
Green Sea Turtle	5/10/2005 9:45 AM		370 KB
Humpback Whale	11/30/2005 1:20 PM		257 KB
Oryx Antelope	4/22/2005 4:20 PM		291 KB
Toco Toucan	6/24/2005 11:22 AM		113 KB

8. Click one of the other column headings, and then click the same column heading again to see the contents sorted that way, first in one direction, and then in the other.

9. Click the **Close** button in the upper-right of the Explorer window to close it.

Use Windows Explorer Menus

The Windows Vista Explorer does not display the menu bar by default, although earlier versions of Windows Explorer did. Most of the menu commands are available on the toolbar, but, if you prefer, you can turn on and use the menus.

1. Click **Start**, click **Pictures**, and then click **Sample Pictures** to open the Windows Explorer window.

2. Click **Organize**, click **Layout**, and click **Menu Bar**. The Windows Explorer menu bar will appear between the address bar and the toolbar.

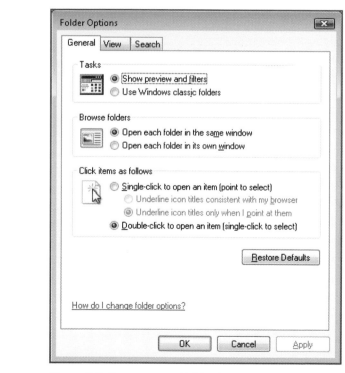

3. Click the **File**, **Edit**, and **View** menus, and review the available options. The toolbar's Organize and Views menus in Vista Explorer, along with the features of the column heading, replace the first three menus on the menu bar. The Help menu is equivalent to the Help icon on the toolbar.

4. Click the **Tools** menu. The first three options are discussed in Chapter 9. Click **Folder Options** (also available from the Organize menu). The Folder Options dialog box will appear with the General tab displayed, as shown in Figure 3-5. This allows you to:

- Disable the preview and details panes, similar to how it was in versions of Windows prior to Windows XP.
- Open a new window for each folder you open.
- Use a single click in place of a double-click to open a window
- If you choose single click you can also determine whether to permanently underline an icon title, as in an Internet browser, or underline an icon only when you point at it.

Figure 3-5: You can open Folder Options from either the Organize menu on the toolbar or the Tools menu on the menu bar.

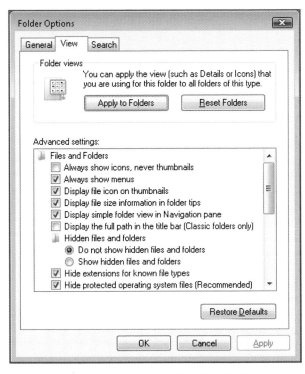

Figure 3-6: There are a number of options in the way that Windows Explorer can display folder and file information.

5. Click the **View** tab, which is shown in Figure 3-6. This gives you a number of options that determine what is displayed for the current folder and allow you to apply these changes to all folders. The default settings generally work for most people.

6. When you are ready, click **OK** to close the Folder Options dialog box. (The Search tab will be discussed under "Search for Files and Folders" later in this chapter.)

7. If you want to turn off the menu bar, click **Organize**, click **Layout**, and click **Menu Bar**.

8. Click **Close** to close the Explorer window.

Locate and Use Files and Folders

The purpose of a file system, of course, is to locate and use the files and folders on your computer, and possibly on other computers connected to your computer (accessing other computers is called *networking* and is discussed in Chapters 9 and 10). Within your computer, there is a storage hierarchy that starts with storage devices, such as disk drives, which are divided into areas called folders, each of which may be divided again into sub-areas called sub-folders. Each of these contains files, which can be documents, pictures, music, and other data. Figure 3-1 showed folders containing sub-folders and eventually containing files with information in them. Figure 3-7 shows a computer containing disk drives, which in turn contain folders. Windows Explorer contains a number of tools for locating, opening, and using disk drives, folders, and files.

Identify Storage Devices

Files and folders are stored on various physical storage devices, including disk drives, CD and DVD drives, memory cards and sticks, and USB flash memory. You will have some, but not necessarily all, of the following:

- Primary floppy disk, labeled "A:"
- Primary hard disk, labeled "C:"
- CD or DVD drive, labeled "D:"
- Other storage devices, labeled "E:" and then "F:" and so on

Figure 3-7: Your computer stores information in a hierarchy of disk drives and folders.

Your primary floppy drive is always labeled "A:." Your primary hard disk is always labeled "C:." Other drives have flexible labeling. Often, the CD or DVD drive will be drive "D:," but if you have a second hard disk drive, it may be labeled "D," as you can see in Figure 3-7.

Select and Open Drives and Folders

When you open Windows Explorer and display the items in Computer, you see the disk drives and other storage devices on your computer, as well as several folders, including Program Files, Users, and Windows, as you saw in Figure 3-7. To work with these drives and folders, you must select them; to see and work with their contents, you must open them.

1. Click **Start** and click **Computer** to open Windows Explorer and display the local disk drives.

Figure 3-8: Double-clicking a drive or folder will open it in the subject pane.

2. In the subject pane, click **Local Disk (C:)**. Local Disk (C:) will be highlighted and its characteristics will be displayed in the details pane.

3. Double-click **Local Disk (C:)**. Local Disk (C:) will open and its folders will be displayed in the subject pane. Double-click **Users** to open that folder and display your folder along with a Public folder.

4. Double-click your personal folder (the folder with your name on it). The subject pane displays the files and folders in your folder. This will include Contacts, Desktop, Documents, Music, and Pictures. You will probably have others as well, as shown in Figure 3-8.

5. Keep double-clicking each folder to open it until you see the contents you are looking for.

Navigate Through Folders and Disks

Opening Windows Explorer and navigating through several folders—beginning with your hard disk—to find a file you want is fine. However, if you want to quickly go to another folder or file, you won't want to have to start with your hard disk every single time. The Windows Vista Explorer gives you three ways to do this: by clicking the links in the navigation pane, by using a folder tree similar to previous versions of Windows, or by using the address bar in a way new to Windows Vista.

TIP

The links in the navigation pane are contained in the Links folder within your personal folder. You can change the links in the navigation pane by adding and removing shortcuts to folders and drives. See "Create Shortcuts" later in this chapter. Compare this set of links with ones shown earlier.

NAVIGATE USING THE NAVIGATION PANE

By default, the navigation pane contains links to the folders within your personal folder. By clicking a link in the navigation pane and then double-clicking folders within the subject pane, you can move around the folders and files within your personal folder.

NAVIGATE USING THE ADDRESS BAR

Windows Vista gives you a slick new way to quickly navigate through your drives and folders by clicking segments of a folder address in the address bar, which looks like this:

| « Win Vista (C:) ▶ Users ▶ Marty ▶ Documents ▶ Trips ▶ 2006 ▶ Yellowstone ▶ | ▼ |

By clicking the down arrow on the far right of the address bar, you can see how this same address looked in previous versions of Windows and use the address bar as it was in the past:

C:\Users\Marty\Documents\Trips\2006\Yellowstone

With Windows Vista, if you click any segment of the address, you will open that level in the subject pane. If you click the arrow to the right of the segment, it displays a drop-down list of sub-folders that you can jump to. By successively clicking segments and their subordinate folders, you can easily move throughout the storage space on your computer and beyond to any network you are connected to.

2006 | Yellowstone ▶
Disneyland
Yellowstone

TIP

The small down arrow between the Forward button and the address bar displays a list of disks and folders that you recently displayed.

Folders   ✓
▲ 🖥 Marty
   📇 Contacts
   📁 Desktop
▲ 📁 Documents
   ▷ 📁 Marty
   ▷ 📁 SnagIt Catalog
   ▲ 📁 Trips
      📁 2005
      ▲ 📁 2006
         📁 Disneyland
         ▲ 📁 Yellowstone
            📁 Photos
            📁 Sounds
      📁 2007
   📁 Downloads

NAVIGATE USING FOLDERS

The method of navigation prior to Windows Vista (which is still available) is to use a folder tree in the navigation pane. By default, the folder tree is not displayed, but you can display it and use it to navigate through your storage space. With Windows Explorer open and the navigation pane displayed:

1. Click **Folders** at the bottom of the navigation pane. The folder tree will open and, by default, take up only part of the navigation pane.

2. If you want, drag the top of the folder bar to the top of the navigation pane.

3. Click the clear triangle to the right of a folder to display the sub-folders within a folder in the folder tree. The triangle rotates down 45 degrees and turns dark.

4. Click a folder in the tree to display its contents in the subject pane.

5. Click the folder bar to close the folder tree.

QUICKSTEPS

RENAMING AND DELETING FILES AND FOLDERS

Sometimes, a folder needs to be renamed (whether it was created by you or by an application) because you may no longer need it or for any number of reasons.

RENAME A FILE OR FOLDER

With the file or folder in view but not selected, to rename it:

Slowly click the name twice, type the new name, and press **ENTER**.

–Or–

Right-click the name, click **Rename**, type the new name, and press **ENTER**.

DELETE A FILE OR FOLDER TO THE RECYCLE BIN

With the file or folder in view, to delete it:

Click the icon for the file or folder to select it, press **DELETE**, and click **Yes** to confirm the deletion.

–Or–

Right-click the icon, click **Delete**, and click **Yes** to confirm the deletion.

Continued . . .

Create New Folders

While you could store all your files within one of the ready-made folders in Windows Vista—such as Documents, Music, and Pictures—you will probably want to make your files easier to find by creating several sub-folders.

For example, to create the Trips folder discussed earlier:

1. Click **Start** and click **Documents**. Make sure nothing is selected.

2. Click **Organize** on the toolbar, and click **New Folder**. A new folder will appear with its name highlighted.

3. Type the name of the folder, such as Trips, and press **ENTER**. Double-click your new folder to open it.

As an alternative to using the Organize menu, right-click the open area in the subject pane of Windows Explorer. Click **New** and click **Folder**. Type a name for the folder, and press **ENTER**.

Select Multiple Files and Folders

Often, you will want to do one or more operations—such as copy, move, or delete—on several files and/or folders at the same time. To select several files or folders from the subject pane of an Explorer window:

Move the mouse pointer to the upper-left, just outside of the top and leftmost object. Then drag the mouse to the lower-right, just outside of the bottom and rightmost object, creating a shading across the objects, as shown in Figure 3-9.

–Or–

Click the first object, and press and hold **CTRL** while clicking the remaining objects, if the objects are noncontiguous (not adjacent to each other). If the objects are contiguous, click the first object, press and hold **SHIFT**, and click the last object.

UICKSTEPS

RENAMING AND DELETING FILES AND FOLDERS *(Continued)*

RECOVER A DELETED FILE OR FOLDER

To recover a file or folder that has been deleted:

Click the **Organize** menu, and click **Undo**. This only works if you do the undo immediately after the deletion.

–Or–

Double-click the **Recycle Bin** on the desktop (or click **Recycle Bin** in Folders in the Explorer navigation pane) to display the Recycle Bin. Right-click the file or folder icon, and choose **Restore**.

PERMANENTLY DELETE A FILE OR FOLDER

If you're sure you want to permanently delete a file or folder:

Click the icon to select it, press and hold **SHIFT** while pressing **DELETE**, and click **Yes** to confirm the deletion.

–Or–

Right-click the icon, press and hold **SHIFT** while clicking **Delete**, and click **Yes** to confirm the deletion.

TIP

To select all objects in the subject pane, click **Organize** and click **Select All**; or click any object in the subject pane, and press **CTRL+A**.

Figure 3-9: Drag across multiple objects to select all of them.

Use the Recycle Bin

If you do a normal delete in Explorer or the desktop, the item or items deleted will go into the Recycle Bin. Should you change your mind about the deletion, you can reclaim an item from the Recycle Bin, as explained in the "Renaming and Deleting Files and Folders" QuickSteps earlier in this chapter.

The Recycle Bin is a special folder and it can contain both files and folders. You can open it and see its contents as you would any other folder, by double-clicking

![Recycle Bin window showing deleted items: '05 Marketing Plan (File Folder), List (Microsoft Office Word 97, 49.0 KB), 2006 Inventory (Microsoft Office Excel 97-20..., 59.0 KB), SnagIt 8 (Shortcut, 1.83 KB). 4 items. Toolbar includes Organize, Views, Empty the Recycle Bin, Restore all items.]

Figure 3-10: The Recycle Bin holds deleted items so that you can recover them until you empty it.

![Recycle Bin Properties dialog box, General tab. Recycle Bin Location / Space Available: Local Disk (C:) 23.1 GB, Local Disk (D:) 32.7 GB. Settings for selected location: Custom size: Maximum size (MB): 2367. Do not move files to the Recycle Bin. Remove files immediately when deleted. Display delete confirmation dialog checkbox checked. OK, Cancel, Apply buttons.]

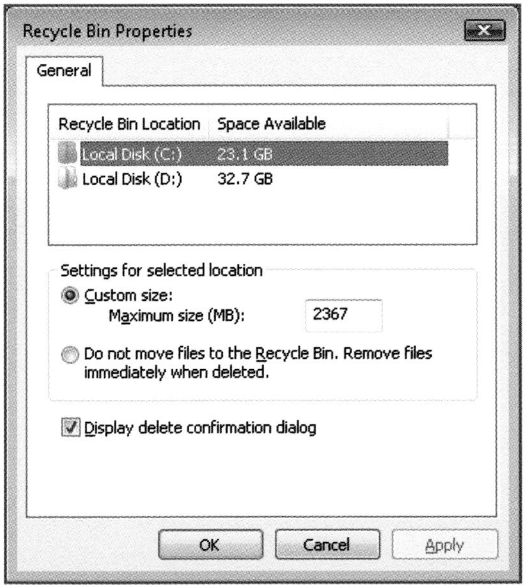

Figure 3-11: The amount of space used by the Recycle Bin is set independently for each drive.

its desktop icon or clicking it in Folders in the navigation pane. Figure 3-10 shows a Recycle Bin after deleting several files and folders. What makes the Recycle Bin special are the two special tasks in the toolbar:

- **Empty The Recycle Bin** permanently removes all of the contents of the Recycle Bin.
- **Restore All Items** returns all the contents to their original folders, in effect, "undeleting" all of the contents.

Obviously, there is a limit to how much the Recycle Bin should hold. You can limit the amount of space it takes so that it doesn't take over your hard disk. That and other settings are configured in the Recycle Bin's Properties dialog box.

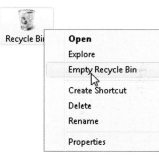

1. Right-click the **Recycle Bin** on the desktop, and click **Properties**. The Recycle Bin Properties dialog box will appear, as you can see in Figure 3-11.

2. If you have multiple hard disks, click the drive you want to set. In any case, make sure **Custom Size** is selected, select the size, and type the number of megabytes you want to use ("2367" megabytes is 2.367 gigabytes).

3. If you don't want to use the Recycle Bin, click **Do Not Move Files To The Recycle Bin**. (This is strongly discouraged.)

4. If you don't need to see the deletion confirmation message, click that check box to deselect it. (Again this is discouraged.)

5. When you are ready, click **OK** to close the dialog box.

Create Shortcuts

Shortcuts allow you to quickly open files and folders from places other than where the files are stored. For example, you can start a program from the desktop even though the actual program file is stored in some other folder. To create a shortcut:

1. In Windows Explorer, locate the folder or file for which you want to create a shortcut.

2. If it is a program file (one identified as an "application" or with an .exe extension), drag it to a different folder (as from a folder to the desktop).

3. If it is any other file or folder, hold down the right mouse button while dragging the file or folder to a different folder, and then click **Create Shortcuts Here**.

| Copy Here |
| Move Here |
| Create Shortcuts Here |
| Cancel |

–Or–

1. In Windows Explorer, open the folder in which you want to create a shortcut.

2. Right-click a blank area in the subject pane of the folder, click **New**, and click **Shortcut**.

| New ▸ | | Folder |
| Personalize | | Shortcut |

3. In the dialog box that appears, click **Browse**, and use the folder tree to locate and select the file or folder for which you want to make a shortcut.

4. Click **OK**, and click **Next**. Type a name for the shortcut, and click **Finish**.

Search for Files and Folders

With large and, possibly, several hard disks, it is often difficult to find files and folders on a system. Windows Explorer's Search feature addresses that problem.

1. Click **Start** and click **Search**. Windows Explorer will open the Search Results window.

2. Type all or part of the folder name, file name, or keyword or phrase in a file in the Search box. As you type, Windows Vista will start locating files and folders that match your criteria, as shown in Figure 3-12.

TIP

You may want to have the folders tree visible in the navigation pane and have the destination folder visible so you can drag the shortcut to it.

NOTE

You can tell if an object is a shortcut in two possible ways: "Shortcut" is in its title (unless you've renamed it), and an upward-pointing arrow is in the lower-left corner of the icon, like the one in the right.

TIP

You can also use the Cut, Copy, and Paste commands from the Organize menu in Windows Explorer.

COPYING AND MOVING FILES AND FOLDERS

Copying and moving files and folders are similar actions, and can be done with the mouse alone, with the mouse and a menu, and with the keyboard.

COPY WITH THE MOUSE

To copy with the mouse, hold down **CTRL** while dragging any file or folder from one folder to another on the same disk drive, or drag a file or folder from one disk drive to another.

MOVE NON-PROGRAM FILES ON THE SAME DISK WITH THE MOUSE

Move non-program files from one folder to another on the same disk with the mouse by dragging the file or folder.

MOVE NON-PROGRAM FILES TO ANOTHER DISK WITH THE MOUSE

Move non-program files to another disk by holding down **SHIFT** while dragging them.

MOVE PROGRAM FILES WITH THE MOUSE

Move program files to another folder or disk by holding down **SHIFT** while dragging them.

COPY AND MOVE WITH THE MOUSE AND A MENU

To copy and move with a mouse and a menu, hold down the right mouse button while dragging the file or folder. When you release the right mouse button, a context menu opens and allows you to choose whether to copy, move, or create a shortcut (see "Create Shortcuts" in this chapter).

| **Copy Here** |
| Move Here |
| Create Shortcuts Here |
| Cancel |

Continued . . .

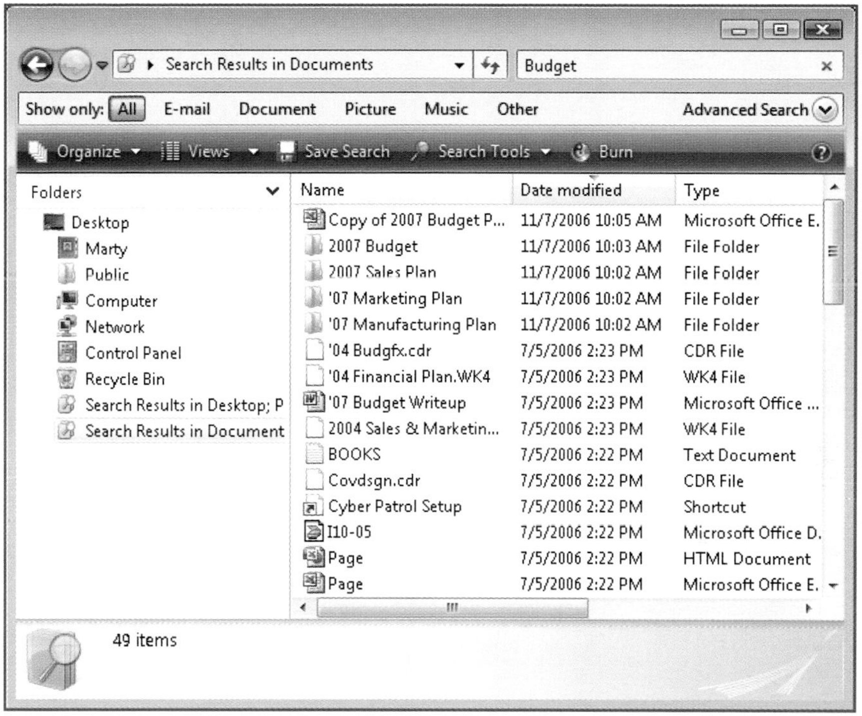

Figure 3-12: Your search criteria, in the upper-right text box, may need to be refined to give you only the files you are looking for.

3. Initially, the search will be of all indexed files (Windows Vista, by default, will index your files and folders automatically) and will show all results. If you want to click one of the alternative document types.

4. If you want a more defined search, click **Search Tools** on the toolbar, and click **Search Options**. The File Options dialog box will appear with the Search tab displayed. Make any change to settings that you want, and click **OK**.

5. For an even more refined search, click **Advanced Search** on the right of the search pane to show the advanced search criteria entry. Click the **Location** down arrow and select a location to search. Select or enter any further criteria you want to use in the search. When you are ready, click **Search**.

QUICKSTEPS

COPYING AND MOVING FILES AND FOLDERS *(Continued)*

COPY AND MOVE WITH THE KEYBOARD

Copying and moving with the keyboard is done with three sets of keys:

- **CTRL+C** ("Copy") copies the selected item to the Windows Clipboard

- **CTRL+X** ("Cut") moves the selected item to the Windows Clipboard, deleting it from its original location.

- **CTRL+V** ("Paste") copies the current contents of the Windows Clipboard to the currently open folder. You can repeatedly paste the same clipboard contents to any additional folders you want to copy to by opening them and pressing **CTRL+V** again.

To copy a file from one folder to another using the keyboard:

1. In Windows Explorer, open the disk and folder containing the file to be copied.

2. Select the file and press **CTRL+C** to copy the file to the Clipboard.

3. Open the disk and folder that is to be the destination of the copied item.

4. Press **CTRL+V** to paste the file into the destination folder.

---

6. If you want to save the search results, click **Save Search** on the toolbar, type the file name, and click **Save**. Saved searches are available in the Searches folder.

7. When you are done, close Windows Explorer.

Create Files

Files are usually created by applications or by copying existing files; however, Windows has an additional file-creation capability that creates an empty file and opens the application to allow work on the file.

1. Click **Start**, click **Documents**, and open the folder in which you want to create the new file.

2. Right-click a blank area of the subject pane in Windows Explorer, and choose **New**. A menu of all the file types that can be created by the registered applications on your computer will appear.

3. Click the file type you want to create.

Encrypt Files and Folders

Windows Vista Business, Enterprise, and Ultimate editions, but not Vista Home Basic or Home Premium editions, have the ability to encrypt files and folders so that they cannot be read without the key to decrypt them. The key is attached to the person who performed the encryption. When she or he logs on to the computer, the files can be used as if they were not encrypted. If someone else logs on, the files cannot be accessed. Even if someone takes the disk to another computer, all that will be displayed is gibberish. To encrypt a file or folder:

1. Click **Start**, click **Computer**, and click **Folders** in the navigation pane.
2. In the folders tree, open the drive and folders necessary to display the files or folders you want to encrypt in the subject pane.
3. Right-click the file or folder, and choose **Properties**. In the General tab, click **Advanced**. The Advanced Attributes dialog box appears.

Advanced Attributes

Choose the settings you want for this folder.

File attributes

☑ File is ready for archiving

☑ Index this file for faster searching

Compress or Encrypt attributes

☐ Compress contents to save disk space

☑ Encrypt contents to secure data   Details

OK   Cancel

4. Click **Encrypt Contents To Secure Data**.
5. Click **OK** twice.

If you are encrypting a file, you will see an Encryption Warning dialog box stating that the file is not in an encrypted folder, which means that when you

TIP

It is recommended that folders rather than files be the encrypting container, because many applications save temporary and secondary files during execution.

NOTE

Windows Vista Enterprise and Ultimate versions have the ability, called BitLocker, to encrypt an entire drive so that if someone takes a drive out of a computer and tries to access it with a different operating system, he or she will not be able to read anything on the drive. BitLocker requires a complex setup of a computer and can use a USB Flash memory device for a key. To use BitLocker, access Windows Help, make sure you are connected to the Internet, type BitLocker Drive Encryption, and press ENTER. Click **Learn More About BitLocker Drive Encryption**, and then click **Windows Vista BitLocker Drive Encryption Step By Step Guide**.

NOTE

Using the attribute to compress a file or folder is seldom done since the advent of zipping a file (see the "Zipping Files and Folders" QuickSteps later in this chapter), which is more efficient (makes smaller files) and can be more easily "unzipped" or decompressed by most people. Also, a file or folder that has been compressed with attributes cannot also be encrypted and vice versa.

edit the file, temporary or backup files might be created that are not encrypted. Options include whether to encrypt the file and its parent folder or just the file.

If you are encrypting a folder, you will see a Confirm Attribute Changes dialog box that asks if the change applies to this folder only or applies to this folder and its subfolders and files.

6. Choose the option you want, and click **OK**. You may see a message from the Encrypting File System that you should back up your encryption key. Click the icon in the notification area to choose how you want to back up your key. The title under the file or folder icon turns a different color, normally green.

Change Other File and Folder Attributes

Encryption, described in the previous section, is one of five or six file or folder attributes. The others are shown in Table 3-2.

To set the additional attributes:

1. Click **Start**, click **Computer**, and, if it isn't open already, click **Folders** in the navigation pane.

2. In the folders tree, navigate to the files or folders whose attributes you want to set in the subject pane.

QUICKSTEPS

ZIPPING FILES AND FOLDERS

Windows Vista has a way to compress files and folders called "zipping." *Zipped* files have the extension .zip and are compatible with programs like WinZip. Zipped files take up less room on a disk and are transmitted over the Internet faster.

CREATE A ZIPPED FOLDER

You can create a new zipped folder and drag files to it.

1. Click **Start** and click **Computer**. Click **Folders**.

2. Navigate to the folder that you want to contain the zipped folder.

3. Right-click in a blank area of the subject pane, click **New**, and click **Compressed (Zipped) Folder**. The zipped folder will appear.

New Compressed (zipped) Folder

4. Type a name for the folder, and drag files and folders into it to compress them.

SEND FILES OR FOLDERS TO A ZIPPED FOLDER

1. In Windows Explorer, select the files and/or folders you want zipped.

2. Right-click the selected objects, click **Send To**, and click **Compressed (Zipped) Folder**. A new zipped folder will appear containing the original files and/or folders, now compressed.

Continued . . .

ATTRIBUTE	DESCRIPTION
Read-Only	The file or folder cannot be changed.
Hidden	The file or folder cannot be seen unless Show Hidden Files And Folders is selected in Folder Options View tab.
File Or Folder Is Ready For Archiving	This serves as a flag to backup programs that the file or folder is ready to be backed up.
Index This Folder For Faster Searching	This allows the Windows Indexing Service to index the file or folder so that searching for the file can be done quickly. (See Chapter 6 for how to use the Indexing Service.)
Compress Contents To Save Disk Space	The file or folder is rewritten on the disk in compressed format. The file can still be read, but it will take a little longer while it is decompressed.

Table 3-2: Additional File and Folder Attributes

3. Right-click the file or folder, and choose **Properties**. In the General tab, you can click **Read-Only** and **Hidden**. Do that if you wish, and click **OK**.

4. If you want to set archiving or indexing, click **Advanced**. The Advanced Attributes dialog box appears.

5. Click the attribute you want to set, and click **OK** twice.

Back Up Files and Folders

Backing up copies important files and folders on your disk and writes them on another device, such as a recordable CD or DVD, a USB Flash drive, or to another hard disk. To start the backup process:

Click **Start**, click **All Programs**, click **Accessories**, click **System Tools**, and click **Backup Status And Configuration**.

SCHEDULE A BACKUP

If this is the first time you are doing a backup and you are using any version of Windows Vista except Home Basic, you will be asked to configure an automatic file backup, as you can see in Figure 3-13.

ZIPPING FILES AND FOLDERS

(Continued)

EXTRACT ZIPPED FILES AND FOLDERS

To unzip a file or folder, simply drag it out of the zipped folder, or you can extract all of a zipped folder's contents.

1. Right-click a zipped folder, and click **Extract All**. The Extraction Wizard will appear.

2. Enter or browse to the location of where you want the extracted files and folders, and click **Extract**.

3. Close Windows Explorer when you are done.

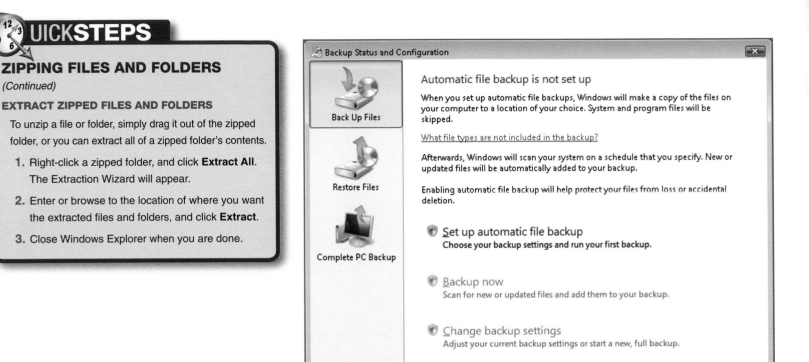

Figure 3-13: Most versions of Windows Vista encourage you to set up an automatic scheduled backup.

1. Click **Set Up Automatic File Backup**.

2. Click either **On A Hard Disk, CD, Or DVD**, or **On A Network**. Either select a local drive by clicking the down arrow, or click **Browse** and select a network drive where you want the backup. Click **Next**.

3. Select the drives you want to back up, and click **Next**. Select the file types you want to back up, and again click **Next**.

4. Select how often and when you want to do the backup, and click **Save Settings And Start Backup**. Click **Yes** to confirm starting the backup.

NOTE

System and program files will not be backed up in an automatic scheduled backup.

NOTE

If you back up to a CD or DVD, you will need the number of blank disks that it will take to do the backup. As the backup progresses, you will be prompted when you need to insert a disk.

Your next backup will be scheduled and the current backup will begin. You can stop the backup if you wish. You can now allow the automatic backup to run when it is scheduled or run an additional backup, as you choose.

5. Click the **Close** button to close the Backup Status And Configuration dialog box.

RUN IMMEDIATE FILE BACKUP

If you have Windows Vista Home Basic, you can run an immediate file backup.

1. Click **Run A File Backup Now**. Click the down arrow to select the local drive on which you want to do a backup (Home Basic does not allow a backup on a network drive).

2. Select the drives you want to back up, and click **Next**. Select the file types you want to back up, and again click **Next**.

3. Click **Save Settings And Start Backup**. Click **Yes** to confirm starting the backup. Your backup will begin. You can stop the backup if you wish.

4. Click the **Close** button to close the Backup Status And Configuration dialog box.

Write Files and Folders to a CD or DVD

Windows Vista allows you to copy ("burn" or record) files to a writable or rewritable CD or DVD. You must have a CD or DVD writing drive and blank media.

1. Place a blank recordable disc in the drive. You will be asked if you want to burn a CD or DVD using Windows or Windows Media Player, or possibly other programs on your computer.

Figure 3-14: It is important to choose the correct format when writing to a CD or DVD.

2. Click **Burn Files To Disc**. Type a name for the disc. Click **Show Formatting Options** to enlarge the dialog box and see your two choices (see Figure 3-14):

- **File System (UDF)**, which is the default. This format can only be read on a computer with Windows XP, Windows Server 2003 or 2007, Windows Vista, or future Windows operating systems. UDF allows you to add one file or folder to the CD or DVD at a time, like you would with a hard disk, a floppy disk, or a USB Flash drive. You can leave the disc in the drive and drag data to it whenever you want. The default format is UDF 2.01. If you want to read the disc with Windows 98 and later Windows operating systems or with Apple computers, use UDF 1.02. If you are going to read the disc only with Windows Vista or Windows Server 2007, use UDF 2.5.

- **Mastered (ISO)** can be read by most computers, including older Windows and Apple computers and most standalone CD and DVD players. To use this format, you must gather all the files in one place and then burn them all at one time. Use this format for music and video files that you want to play on automobile or stand-alone devices, such as MP3 and video players.

3. Click the file system you want to use, and click **Next**. The disc will be formatted and a Windows Explorer window will open for the CD/DVD drive.

4. Open another Windows Explorer window, locate the files and folders you want on the CD or DVD, and drag them to the CD/DVD drive subject pane:

- If you are using the File System (UDF) format, as you drag the objects to the drive, they will be immediately written on the disc. When you have written all the files you want to the disc, right-click the drive and click **Close Session**. After you see the message "Disc Ready" you can remove the disc from the drive and insert it at a later time to resume adding or removing files and folders.

- If you are using the Mastered (ISO) format, drag all the objects you want written on the disc to the drive. When all files and folders are in the drive's subject pane, click **Burn To Disc**. You are asked to confirm the title, select a recording speed, and click **Next**. When the burn is complete, the disc will be ejected and you can choose to burn the same  files to another disc. In any case, click **Finish**.

5. When you are done, click **Close** to close Windows Explorer.

Managing Disks

Windows Vista provides three tools to help manage the files and folders stored on hard disks.

Clean Up a Disk

Disk Cleanup helps you get rid of old files on your hard disk. Windows looks through your hard disk for types of files that can be deleted and lists them, as shown in Figure 3-15. You can then select the types of files you want to delete.

1. Click **Start**, click **Computer**, right-click a disk drive you want to work on, and click **Properties**.

2. Click **Disk Cleanup**. Choose whether you want to clean up your files only, or files from all users on your computer. Windows Vista will then calculate how much space you could save.

3. Select the types of files to delete, and click **OK**. You are asked if you want to permanently delete these files. Click **Delete Files** to delete them.

4. Click **More Options**. Under Programs And Features, click **Clean Up** to remove any programs that you are not using. Under System Restore, click **Clean Up** to remove all but the latest restore point.

5. When you are ready, close the Properties dialog box.

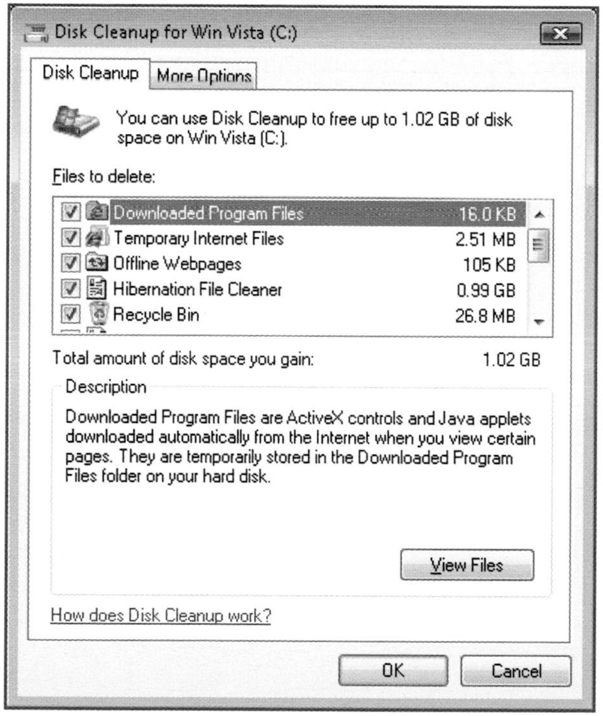

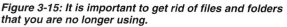

Figure 3-15: It is important to get rid of files and folders that you are no longer using.

Check for Errors

Error Checking tries to read and write on your disk, without losing information, to determine if bad areas exist. If it finds a bad area, that area is flagged so that the system will not use it. Error Checking automatically fixes file system errors and attempts recovery of bad sectors.

1. Click **Start**, click **Computer**, right-click a disk drive you want to work on, and click **Properties**.

2. Click **Tools**, and click **Check Now**. Select whether you want to automatically fix errors, and/or attempt recovery of bad sectors, and click **Start**. You will be told you have to restart Windows to do use Error Checking. Close any open applications,

> **NOTE**
>
> Unlike earlier versions of Windows, Windows Vista, by default, automatically defragments your drives on a periodic basis, so under most circumstances you won't need to do it.

click **Schedule Disk Check** to do a disk check the next time you start your computer, and then restart your computer. Error Checking will automatically begin when Windows restarts.

You will be shown the status of the Error Checking operation and told of any problems that could not be fixed. When Error Checking is complete, your computer will finish restarting.

Defragment a Disk

When files are stored on a hard disk, they are broken into pieces (or *fragments*) and individually written to the disk. As the disk fills, the fragments are spread over the disk as space allows. To read a file that has been fragmented requires extra disk activity and can slow down the performance of your computer. To fix this, Windows has a defragmentation process that rewrites the contents of a disk, placing all of the pieces of a file in one contiguous area.

1. Click **Start**, click **Computer**, right-click a disk drive you want to work on, and click **Properties**.
2. Click **Tools**, and click **Defragment Now**. The Disk Defragmenter will open, as shown in Figure 3-16. You can choose to turn off the automatic defragmentation or to modify the schedule.
3. If you wish to go ahead manually, click **Defragment Now**. The process will take up to a couple of hours. Some fragments may remain, which is fine.

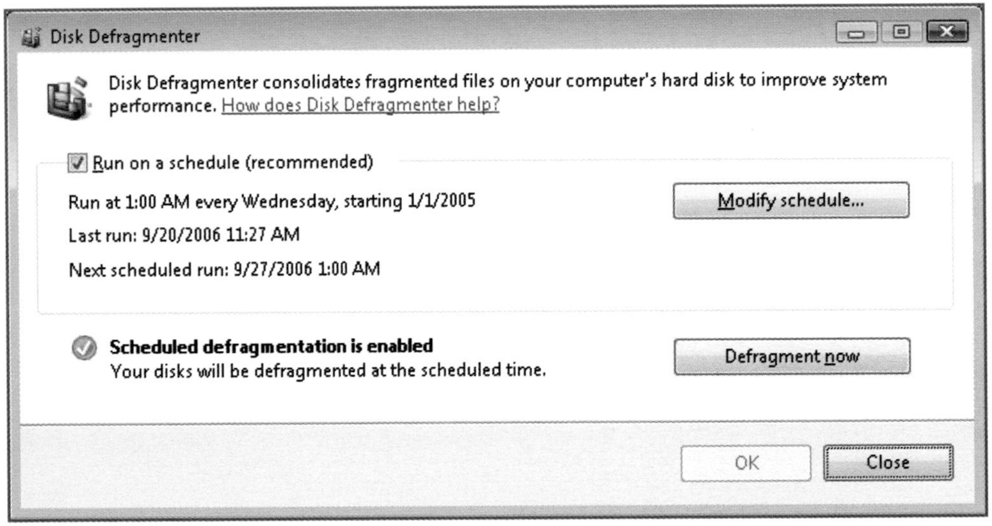

Figure 3-16: Defragmenting brings pieces of a file together into one contiguous area.

How to...

- *Set Up Communications*

- *Configure an Internet Connection*

- *Browsing the Internet*

- *Search the Internet*

- *Keep a Favorite Site*

- *Use Tabs*

- *Organizing Favorite Sites*

- *Change Your Home Page*

- *Access Web History*

- *Controlling Internet Security*

- *Copy Internet Information*

- *Play Internet Audio and Video Files*

- *Establish an E-Mail Account*

- *Create and Send E-Mail*

- *Receive E-Mail*

- *Using the Contacts List*

- *Respond to E-Mail*

- *Use Stationery*

- *Apply Formatting*

- *Using Web Mail*

- *Attach Files to E-Mail*

- *Participate in Newsgroups*

Chapter 4
Using the Internet

The Internet provides a major means for worldwide communication between both individuals and organizations, as well as a major means for locating and sharing information. For many, having access to the Internet is the primary reason for having a computer. To use the Internet, you must have a connection to it using a dial-up connection, a broadband connection, or a wireless connection. You then can send and receive e-mail, access the World Wide Web, and participate in newsgroups, among many other things.

FEATURE	DIAL-UP	DSL
Cost	Average $10/month	Average $30/month
Speed	Up to 48 Kbps* download***, 33 Kbps upload****	Most common: 1.54 Mbps** download, 256 Kbps upload
Connection	Dial up each time	Always connected
Use of line	Ties up line; may want a second line	Line can be used for voice and FAX while connected to the Internet
Availability	Almost everywhere	Metropolitan and suburb areas (within 3.5 miles of phone company switch)

*Kbps is Kilobits (thousands of bits) per second.

**Mbps is Megabits (millions of bits) per second **Download is receiving information from the Internet on your computer.

***Upload is sending information from your computer to the Internet.

Table 4-1: Comparison of Dial-Up and DSL Connections

Connect to the Internet

You can connect to the Internet using a telephone line, a cable TV cable, a satellite link, or a land wireless link. With a telephone line, you can connect with either a *dial-up* connection or a *DSL* (digital subscriber line) connection (see comparison in Table 4-1). DSL, cable, satellite, and some wireless connections are called *broadband* connections because of their higher (than dial-up) speed and the fact they are always on (see comparison in Table 4-2). You must have access to at least one of these forms of communication in order to connect to the Internet. You must also set up the Internet connection itself.

SERVICE	DOWNLOAD SPEED*	UPLOAD SPEED*	MONTHLY COST**	RELIABILITY
Dial-up	48 Kbps	33.6 Kbps	$10	Fair
DSL	1.54 Mbps	256 Kbps	$30	Very Good
Cable Internet	3.0 Mbps	512 Kbps	$40	Good
Satellite Internet	1.0 Mbps	200 Kbps	$70	Good***

*Speeds are maximum possible and normal operation is generally slower, especially cable.

**Costs are representative averages and can vary by area and service levels. All but dial-up may require installation and equipment charges.

***Satellite service can be affected by weather and requires a southern sky exposure.

Table 4-2: Representative Speeds, Costs, and Reliability for Internet Connections

Set Up Communications

Communications is the link between your computer and the Internet. To set up communications, you must first choose a type of connection link. With a dial-up connection, you must set up a modem.

NOTE

As you perform the steps in this and other chapters, you may see a User Account Control (UAC) dialog box appear and tell you that Windows needs your permission to continue. When you see these dialog boxes and if you are an administrator and, in fact, want to continue, click **Continue**. If you are not logged on as an administrator, you will need to enter a password. If you don't want to do whatever is being requested, click **Cancel**. The UAC dialog box and its associated steps are not included in the steps here to simplify them. When you see the UAC dialog box, process it as you want and continue with the instructions. UAC is discussed in Chapter 8.

INSTALL A MODEM

If a modem came with your computer, or if one was already installed when you upgraded to Windows Vista, your modem was probably automatically installed and you don't need to do anything more. In that case skip to "Set Up a Dial-Up Connection." Otherwise, if you need to install a modem:

1. Make sure a modem is either physically installed in your computer or, if you have an external modem, that it is connected to your computer, plugged in, and turned on.

2. Click **Start** and click **Control Panel**.

3. In Control Panel Home, click **Hardware And Sound**, and then click **Phone And Modem Options**.

   —Or—

   In Classic view, double-click **Phone And Modem Options**.

4. If this is the first time you've set up a modem, you need to enter location information. Select your country, enter your area or city code, and, if necessary, your carrier code and the number to access an outside line. If needed, click **Pulse Dialing** (with old phone systems only), and click **OK**. The Phone And Modem Options dialog box will appear.

5. Click the **Modems** tab. If it shows a modem, as shown next, your modem is installed and you can skip to "Set Up a Dial-Up Connection."

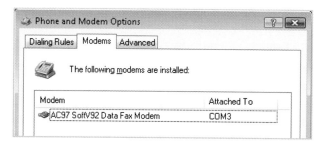

6. If you don't see a modem but you know you have one installed, close the Phone And Modem Options dialog box, and return to the Hardware And Sound component of Control Panel. Click **Device Manager**. You'll see a list of all your hardware in

alphabetical order. You should not see a Modem listing, but hopefully, under Other Devices, you'll see a modem with an exclamation point, like this:

```
⊞ 🖥 Monitors
⊞ 🖥 Network adapters
⊟ 📷 Other devices
         📄 PCI Modem
⊞ 🖥 PCMCIA adapters
⊞ 🖨 Ports (COM & LPT)
```

7. If you do not see a modem, it is a good bet that one is not installed and you need to do that. If you do see a modem with an exclamation point, then it needs a device driver installed. In that case, double-click the modem to open its Properties dialog box.

8. Click **Reinstall Driver**. Click **Search Automatically For Updated Driver Software**. At the completion of the search, you will be told whether it was successful. If it was successful, click **Close** and skip to "Set Up a Dial-Up Connection."

9. If the search does not find a driver and you have an installation disk for your modem or know where on your computer or network one could be, return to the Device Manager window and again double-click the modem. Click **Reinstall Driver**. Click **Browse My Computer For Driver Software**.

10. If you have a CD for the modem driver, put it in the drive. Click **Browse**, select the drive and, if needed, the folder, and click **OK**. Click **Include Subfolders** (if it isn't already selected), and click **Next**. When you are told that your modem has been installed successfully, click **Close**. Close the Device Manager window and Control Panel.

SET UP A DIAL-UP CONNECTION

With a modem installed and working, you can set up a *dial-up connection* that uses the modem to dial and connect to another computer at the other end of a phone line.

1. If your Control Panel isn't open, click **Start** and then click **Control Panel**. If your Control Panel is already open, click **Back**.

2. In Control Panel Home, click **Network And Internet**, and then click **Network And Sharing Center**.

   –Or–

   In Classic view, double-click **Network And Sharing Center**.

   In either case, click **Set Up A Connection Or Network** in the Tasks pane on the left. The Set Up A Connection Or Network dialog box will appear.

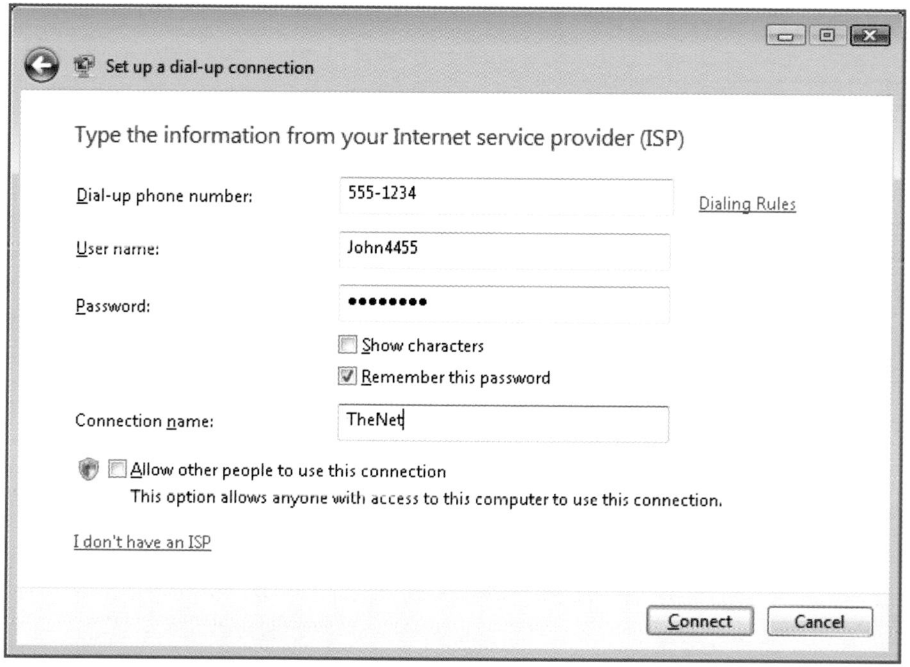

Type the information from your Internet service provider (ISP)

Dial-up phone number: 555-1234   Dialing Rules

User name: John4455

Password: ●●●●●●●●

☐ Show characters
☑ Remember this password

Connection name: TheNet

🛡 ☐ Allow other people to use this connection
This option allows anyone with access to this computer to use this connection.

I don't have an ISP

[Connect] [Cancel]

Figure 4-1: You will need a user name and a password, as well as other information from your ISP, in order to connect with them. See the accompanying Note.

NOTE

To connect to the Internet, you need to have an existing account with an Internet service provider (ISP) and you need to know your ISP's phone number for your modem to dial. You also must have the user name and password for your account. If you want to use Internet mail, you need to know your e-mail address, the type of mail server (POP3, IMAP, or HTTP), the names of the incoming and outgoing mail servers, and the name and password for the mail account. This information is provided by your ISP when you establish your account.

3. Click **Set Up A Dial-Up Connection**, and click **Next**. The Set Up A Dial-Up Connection dialog box will appear.

4. Enter the phone number to dial, enter the user name and password given to you by your Internet service provider (ISP), choose whether to show the password and whether to remember the password or require it to be entered each time you connect, and then enter a name for this connection (see Figure 4-1).

5. Choose whether anyone else can use this user name and password. When you are done, click **Connect**.

6. You will be told when you are connected to the Internet.

7. Click **Browse The Internet Now** to do that. You will be asked if this network is in a home, work, or a public location. Click **Public Location**. This will be explained further in Chapter 9. Click **Close**.

8. Internet Explorer (Windows Vista's integral Web browser) will open for your use. See, "Use the World Wide Web" later in this chapter. When you are done, click **Close** on Internet Explorer.

9. To disconnect, right-click the connection icon in the notification area, click **Disconnect From**, and click the name of your connection. Click **Close** to close the Network And Sharing window.

SET UP A BROADBAND CONNECTION

A broadband connection—made with a DSL phone line, a TV cable, a satellite connection, or a high speed wireless connection—is normally made with a device that connects to your local area network (LAN) and allows several computers on the network to use the connection. (See Chapter 9 to set up a network.) With a network set up, your computer connected to the network, and a broadband service connected to the network, your computer is connected to the broadband service. There is nothing else you need to do to set up a broadband connection.

NOTE

Sometimes, a DSL or TV cable connecting device is called a "modem," but it is not an analog-to-digital converter, which is the major point of a **mo**dulator-**dem**odulator. Therefore, that term is not used for those devices in this book.

NOTE

For the sake of writing convenience and because Windows Vista comes with Internet Explorer, this book assumes you are using Internet Explorer to access the Internet.

Configure an Internet Connection

In the process of establishing either a dial-up connection or a broadband connection, you may have also configured an Internet connection. The easiest way to check that is to try to connect to the Internet by clicking **Start** and clicking **Internet**. If an Internet Web page is displayed, like the MSN page shown in Figure 4-2, then you are connected and you need do no more. If you did not connect to the Internet and you know that your dial-up or broadband and network connections are all working properly, you need to configure your Internet connection.

1. If Internet Explorer did not connect to the Internet, click **Start** and click **Control Panel**.

2. In Control Panel Home, click **Network And Internet**, and click **Network And Sharing Center**.

–Or–

In Classic view, double-click **Network And Sharing Center**.

In either case, click **Set Up A Connection Or Network** in the left pane. The Set Up A Connection Or Network dialog box will appear (see Figure 4-3).

3. Click **Connect To The Internet**, and click **Next** again. Click your choice between broadband and dial-up, and, if needed, click **Next**.

4. Enter your user name and password, choose whether to display the password and if it is to be remembered by the system, enter a name for the connection, and choose whether to allow others to use this user name and password. When you are done, click **Connect**.

5. Once more, click **Start** and click **Internet**. If asked, click **Connect** and then click **Dial**. If you still do not connect to the Internet, you may need to reinstall your modem, in which case you should go to "Install a Modem" earlier in this chapter. If you are using a broadband connection, you may need to go to Chapter 9 and look at potential network problems.

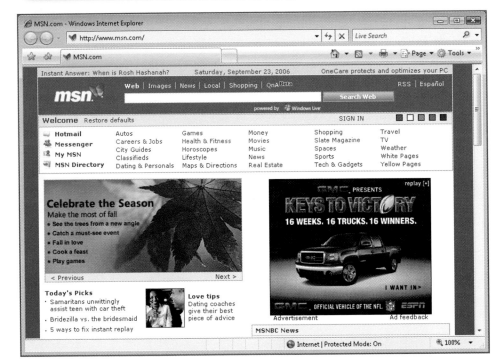

Figure 4-2: The easiest way to see if you have an Internet connection is to try to connect to the Internet.

QUICKSTEPS

BROWSING THE INTERNET

Browsing the Internet refers to using a browser, like Internet Explorer, to go from one Web site to another to see the sites' contents. You can browse to a site by directly entering a site address, by navigating to a site from another site, or by using the browser controls. First, of course, you have to start the browser.

START A BROWSER

To start your default browser (assumed to be Internet Explorer) open **Start** and click **Internet**.

ENTER A SITE DIRECTLY

To go directly to a site:

1. Start your browser and click the existing address, or URL (uniform resource locator), in the address bar.

2. Type the address of the site you want to open, and either click **Go To** (the right-pointing arrow) next to the address bar or press **ENTER**.

USE SITE NAVIGATION

Site navigation is using a combination of links and menus on one Web page to locate and open another Web page, either in the same site or in another site:

- **Links** are words, phrases, sentences, or graphics that always have an open hand displayed when

Continued . . .

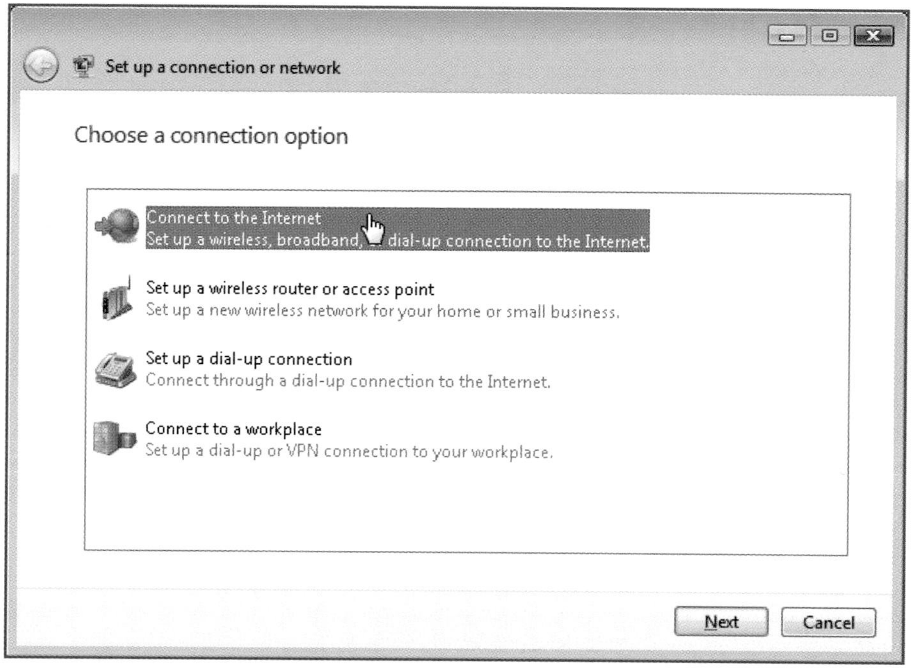

Choose a connection option

Connect to the Internet
Set up a wireless, broadband, or dial-up connection to the Internet.

Set up a wireless router or access point
Set up a new wireless network for your home or small business.

Set up a dial-up connection
Connect through a dial-up connection to the Internet.

Connect to a workplace
Set up a dial-up or VPN connection to your workplace.

Figure 4-3: Most broadband connections are always on and don't require a user name and password.

Use the World Wide Web

The *World Wide Web* (or just the *Web*) is the sum of all the Web sites in the world—examples of which are CNN, eBay, and MSN (which was shown in Figure 4-2). The World Wide Web is what you can access with a *Web browser*, such as Internet Explorer, which comes with Windows Vista.

Search the Internet

You can search the Internet in two ways: by using the search facility built into Internet Explorer and by using an independent search facility on the Web.

BROWSING THE INTERNET (Continued)

the mouse pointer is moved over them and, when clicked, take you to another page. They are often underlined—if not initially, then when you move the mouse pointer to them.

ONLY ON CNN

- I-Report: Funnel cloud hovers in Kansas
- 'Tis the season to be seeing: Fall in full spectrum
- The end of the road for the car?

- **Menus** contain one or a few words, in either a horizontal or vertical list, that always have an open hand displayed when the mouse pointer is moved over them and, when clicked, take you to another page.

| Home | World | U.S. | Weather | Business | Sports |

USE BROWSER NAVIGATION

Browser navigation is using the controls within your browser to go to another Web page. Internet Explorer has two controls not discussed elsewhere that are used for navigation:

- **Back** and **Forward** buttons take you to the next or previous page in the stack of pages you have viewed most recently.

- **Recent Pages** allows you to open a list of the recent pages you have viewed, click one, and quickly return to that page.

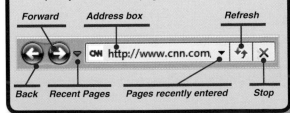

Forward   Address box   Refresh

Back   Recent Pages   Pages recently entered   Stop

SEARCH FROM INTERNET EXPLORER

To use Internet Explorer's search facility:

1. Click **Start** and click **Internet** to open Internet Explorer.

2. Click in the search box on the right of the address bar, type what you want to search for, and click **Search** on the right end of the search box. The Windows Live search site will open with the results of the search, as you can see in Figure 4-4.

3. Click the link of your choice to go to that site.

Figure 4-4: The results of a search using Internet Explorer's search box.

TIP

If you are using the Quick Launch toolbar (see Chapter 2), you can quickly start Internet Explorer by clicking its icon on the Quick Launch toolbar.

TIP

When you enter search criteria, place quotation marks around certain keywords or phrases to get only results that match those words exactly (see Figure 4-5).

SEARCH FROM AN INTERNET SITE

There are many independent Internet search sites. The most popular is Google.

1. Click **Start** and click **Internet** to open Internet Explorer.

2. Drag over to highlight the current address in the address bar, type www.google.com, and either click **Go To** or press ENTER.

3. In the text box, type what you want to search for, and click **Google Search**. The resulting Web sites are shown in a full Web page, as illustrated in Figure 4-5.

4. Click the link of your choice to go to that site.

Figure 4-5: The results of a search using Google.

Keep a Favorite Site

Sometimes, you visit a site that you would like to return to quickly or often. Internet Explorer has a memory bank called Favorite Sites to which you can save sites for easy retrieval.

SAVE A FAVORITE SITE

To add a site to Favorite Sites:

1. Click **Start** and click **Internet** to open Internet Explorer.
2. Open the Web page you want in your favorites list, and make sure its correct address or URL is in the address bar.
3. Click the **Add To Favorites** icon on the tab row, and then click **Add To Favorites** in the drop-down menu.
4. Adjust the name as needed in the text box (you may want to type a name you will readily associate with that site), and click **Add**.

OPEN A FAVORITE SITE

To open a Favorite Site you have saved:

1. Click **Start** and click **Internet** to open Internet Explorer.
2. Click the **Favorites** Center in the tab row, and click the site you want to open.

Use Tabs

Internet Explorer 7 (IE7), which comes with Windows Vista, has added the ability to have several Web pages open at one time and easily switch between them by clicking the tab associated with the page. The tabs reside on the *tab row*, immediately below the address bar, along with the Favorites Center and Add To Favorites, as shown in Figure 4-6. Under normal circumstances, only one page is open at a time, as in earlier versions of Internet Explorer. If you open a second page, it replaces the first page. IE7, however, gives you the ability to open multiple pages as separate tabs that you can switch among by clicking their tabs.

TIP

If the status bar is turned on (click the **Tools** menu, click **Toolbars**, and click **Status Bar**), there is a Zoom button and menu in the lower-right corner of the Internet Explorer window. Click the down arrow to open the menu, and select a level of magnification, or click the button to iterate through the levels.

Zoom In	Ctrl +
Zoom Out	Ctrl -
400%	
200%	
150%	
125%	
100%	
75%	
50%	
Custom...	

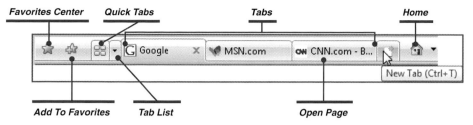

Favorites Center | Quick Tabs | Tabs | Home

Add To Favorites | Tab List | Open Page

Figure 4-6: Tabs allow you to quickly switch among several Web sites.

Figure 4-7: Through the Quick Tabs button, you can see thumbnails of all your open pages side-by-side.

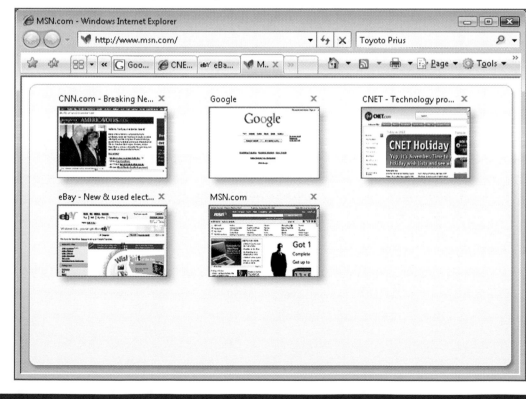

OPEN PAGES IN A NEW TAB

To open a page in a new tab:

1. Click **Start** and click **Internet** to open Internet Explorer.

2. Open your first Web page in any of the ways described earlier in this chapter.

3. Click **New Tab** on the right end of the tab row, or press **CTRL+T**, and open a second Web page in any of the ways described earlier in this chapter.

   –Or–

   Type a Web address in the address bar, and press **ALT+ENTER**.

   –Or–

   Type a search request in the search box, and press **ALT+ENTER**.

   –Or–

   Hold down **CTRL** while clicking a link in open page.

   –Or–

   Click the arrow on the right of a site in your Favorites Center.

4. Repeat any of the alternatives in step 3 as needed to open further pages.

SWITCH AMONG TABS

To switch among open tabs:

Click the tab of the page you want to open.

–Or–

Click **Quick Tabs** in the tab row, or press **CTRL+Q**, and click the thumbnail of the page you want to open (see Figure 4-7).

–Or–

Click **Tab List** in the tab row, and click the page you want to open.

–Or–

Press **CTRL+TAB** to switch to the next tab to the right, or press **CTRL+ SHIFT+TAB** to switch to the next tab to the left.

–Or–

Press **CTRL+***n*, where *n* is a number from 1 to 8 to switch to one of the first eight tabs numbered from the left in the order they were opened. You can also press **CTRL+**9 to switch to the last tab that was opened, shown on the right of the tab row.

CLOSE TABS

To close one or more tabs:

Right-click the tab for the page you want to close, and click **Close** on the context menu, or click **Close Other Tabs** to close all of the pages except the one you clicked.

–Or–

Press **CTRL+W** to close the current page.

–Or–

Click the middle mouse button (if your mouse has one) on the page you want to close.

TIP

Press just the **ALT** key to view Internet Explorer's menus.

NOTE

To use **CTRL+***n* to switch among Internet Explorer's tabs, you need to use a number key on the main keyboard, *not* on the numeric keypad.

–Or–

Press **ALT+F4** to close all tabs, or click **CTRL+ALT+ F4** to close all tabs except the currently selected one.

Change Your Home Page

When you first start Internet Explorer, a given Web page is automatically displayed. This page is called your *home page*. When you go to other Web pages, you can return to this page by clicking the **Home** page icon on the tab row. To change your home page:

1. Click **Start** and click **Internet** to open Internet Explorer.

2. Directly enter or browse to the site you want as your home page.

3. Click the **Home** page down arrow, and click **Add Or Change Home Page**. The Add Or Change Home Page dialog box will appear.

4. Click:
   - **Use This Webpage As Your Only Home Page** if you wish to have only a single home page.
   - **Add This Webpage To Your Home Page Tabs** if you wish to have several home pages on different tabs.
   - **Use The Current Tab Set As Your Home Page** if you want all the current tabs to appear when you click the **Home** page icon.

5. Click **Yes** to complete your home page selection and close the dialog box.

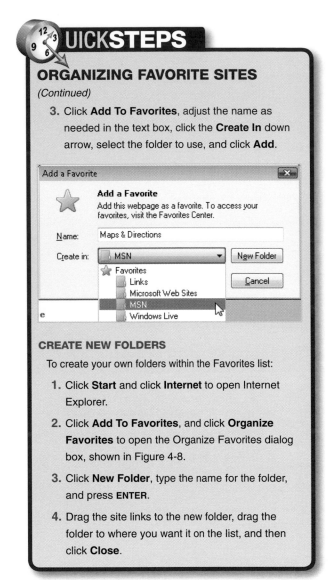

QUICKSTEPS

ORGANIZING FAVORITE SITES

(Continued)

3. Click **Add To Favorites**, adjust the name as needed in the text box, click the **Create In** down arrow, select the folder to use, and click **Add**.

Add a Favorite

⭐ **Add a Favorite**
Add this webpage as a favorite. To access your favorites, visit the Favorites Center.

Name: Maps & Directions

Create in: MSN ▼   New Folder

⭐ Favorites
   Links
   Microsoft Web Sites
   MSN
   Windows Live

Cancel

CREATE NEW FOLDERS

To create your own folders within the Favorites list:

1. Click **Start** and click **Internet** to open Internet Explorer.

2. Click **Add To Favorites**, and click **Organize Favorites** to open the Organize Favorites dialog box, shown in Figure 4-8.

3. Click **New Folder**, type the name for the folder, and press **ENTER**.

4. Drag the site links to the new folder, drag the folder to where you want it on the list, and then click **Close**.

Access Web History

Internet Explorer keeps a history of the Web sites you visit, and you can use that history to return to a site. You can set the length of time to keep sites in that history, and you can clear your history.

USE WEB HISTORY

To use the Web History feature:

1. Click **Start** and click **Internet** to open Internet Explorer.

2. Click the **Favorites Center** on the left of the tab row, and click **History**, or press **CTRL+H**, to open the History pane.

3. Click how you want the history sorted, then click the day, Web site, and Web page you want to open, as shown in Figure 4-9.

Organize Favorites

Links
Microsoft Websites
MSN Websites
Windows Live
88.5 FM Jazz24 48k Win Media Abacast
98.1 FM Classical KING
98.9 FM Smooth Jazz
CNET
Google
MSN.com
USBANK
CNN
Radio

New Folder
Favorites Folder

Modified:
9/24/2006 10:10 PM

New Folder   Move...   Rename   Delete...

Close

Figure 4-8: Like any files, organizing your favorite Web sites helps you easily find what you want.

Figure 4-9: The Web History feature allows you to find a site that you visited in the recent past.

DELETE AND SET HISTORY

You can set the length of time to keep your Internet history, and you can clear this history.

1. Click **Start** and click **Internet** to open Internet Explorer.

2. Click **Tools** at the right end of the tab row, and click **Internet Options**.

3. In the General tab, under Browsing History, click **Delete** to open the Delete Browsing History dialog box. Opposite History, click **Delete History**, confirm your deletion, and click **Close**.

–Or–

In the General tab, under Browsing History, click **Settings**. Under History, at the bottom of the dialog box, use the **Days** spinner to set the number of days to keep your Web history. Click **OK**.

4. Click **OK** again to close the Internet Options dialog box.

UICKSTEPS

CONTROLLING INTERNET SECURITY

Internet Explorer allows you to control three aspects of Internet security. You can categorize sites by the degree to which you trust them, determine how you want to handle *cookies* placed on your computer by Web sites, and set and use ratings to control the content of Web sites that can be viewed. These controls are found in the Internet Options dialog box.

1. Click **Start** and click **Internet** to open Internet Explorer.

2. Click **Tools** on the tab row, and click **Internet Options**.

CATEGORIZE WEB SITES

Internet Explorer allows you to categorize Web sites into zones: Internet (sites that are not classified in one of the other ways), Local Intranet, Trusted Sites, and Restricted Sites (as shown in Figure 4-10).

From the Internet Options dialog box:

1. Click the **Security** tab. Click the **Internet** zone. Note its definition.

2. Click **Custom Level**. Select the elements in this zone that you want to disable, enable, or prompt you before using. Alternatively, select a level of security you want for this zone, and click **Reset**. Click **OK** when you are finished.

3. Click each of the other zones, where you can identify either groups or individual sites you want in that zone.

Continued . . .

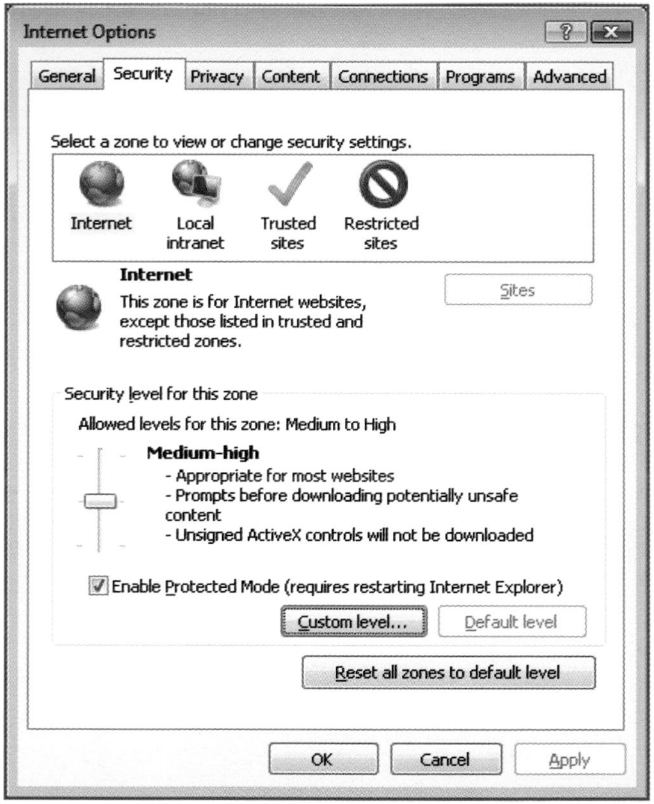

Figure 4-10: Internet Explorer allows you to categorize Web sites into zones and determine what can be done within those zones.

CONTROLLING INTERNET SECURITY *(Continued)*

HANDLE COOKIES

Cookies are small pieces of data that Web sites store on your computer so that they can remind themselves who you are. These can save you from having to constantly enter your name and ID. Cookies can also be dangerous, however, letting people into your computer where they can potentially do damage.

Internet Explorer lets you determine the types and sources of cookies you will allow and what those cookies can do on your computer (see Figure 4-11).

From the Internet Options dialog box:

1. Click the **Privacy** tab. Select a privacy setting by dragging the slider up or down.

2. Click **Advanced** to open the Advanced Privacy Settings dialog box. If you wish, click **Override Automatic Cookie Handling**, and select the settings you want to use.

3. Click **OK** to return to the Internet Options dialog box.

4. At the bottom of the Privacy tab, you can turn off the pop-up blocker, which is on by default (it is recommended that you leave it on). If you have a site that you frequently use that needs pop-ups, click **Settings**, enter the site address (URL), click **Add**, and click **Close**.

CONTROL CONTENT

You can control the content that will be displayed by Internet Explorer.

Continued . . .

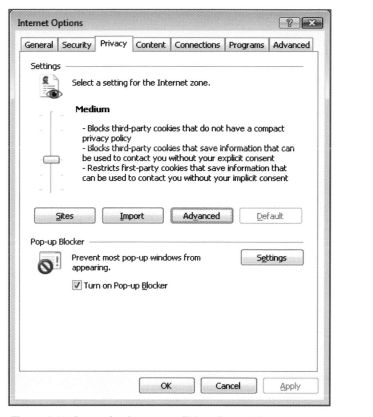

Figure 4-11: Determine how you will handle cookies that Web sites want to leave on your computer.

Copy Internet Information

You may occasionally find something on the Internet that you want to copy—a picture, some text, or a Web page.

COPY A PICTURE FROM THE INTERNET

To copy a picture from an Internet Web page to a folder on your hard disk:

1. Open Internet Explorer and locate the Web page containing the picture you want.

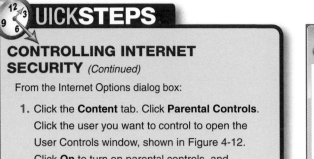

UICKSTEPS

CONTROLLING INTERNET SECURITY *(Continued)*

From the Internet Options dialog box:

1. Click the **Content** tab. Click **Parental Controls**. Click the user you want to control to open the User Controls window, shown in Figure 4-12. Click **On** to turn on parental controls, and configure any other settings you want to use. Click **OK** when you are done.

2. Click **Enable** to open the Content Advisor dialog box. Individually select each of the categories, and drag the slider to the level you want to allow. Detailed descriptions of each area are shown in the lower half of the dialog box.

3. Click **OK** to close the Content Advisor dialog box.

When you are done, click **OK** to close the Internet Options dialog box.

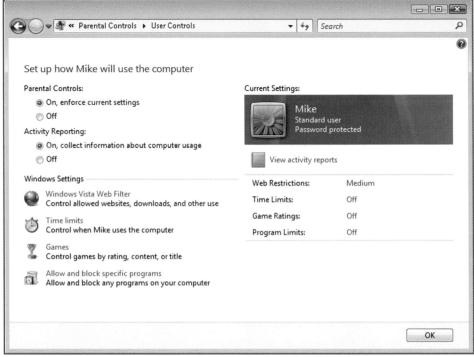

Figure 4-12: You can place a number of controls on what a particular user can do on a computer using the Parental Controls feature.

CAUTION

Material you copy from the Internet is normally protected by copyright; therefore, what you can do with it is limited. Basically, you can store it on your hard disk and refer to it. You cannot put it on your own Web site, sell it, copy it for distribution, or use it for a commercial purpose without the express, written permission of the owner.

2. Right-click the picture and click **Save Picture As**. Locate the folder in which you want to save the picture, and click **Save**.

3. Close Internet Explorer if you are done.

COPY TEXT FROM THE INTERNET

To copy text from a Web page to a Microsoft Word document:

1. Open Internet Explorer and locate the Web page containing the text you want.

2. Drag across to highlight the text, right-click the selection, and click **Copy**.

NOTE

Chapter 7 discusses working with audio and video files in depth, including how to play audio and video files using Windows Media Player.

TIP

To enjoy audio and video files from the Internet, you should have a broadband connection.

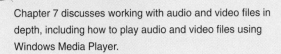

3. Open Microsoft Word and the document (or new document) in which you want to paste the text. Right-click where you want the text, and click **Paste**.
4. Save the Word document and close Internet Explorer and Microsoft Word if you are done with them.

COPY A WEB PAGE FROM THE INTERNET

To make a copy of a Web page and store it on your hard disk:

1. Open Internet Explorer and locate the Web page you want to copy.
2. Click **Page** on the tab row, and click **Save As**. In the Save Webpage dialog box, select the folder in which to save the page, enter the file name you want to use, and click **Save**.
3. Close Internet Explorer if you are done.

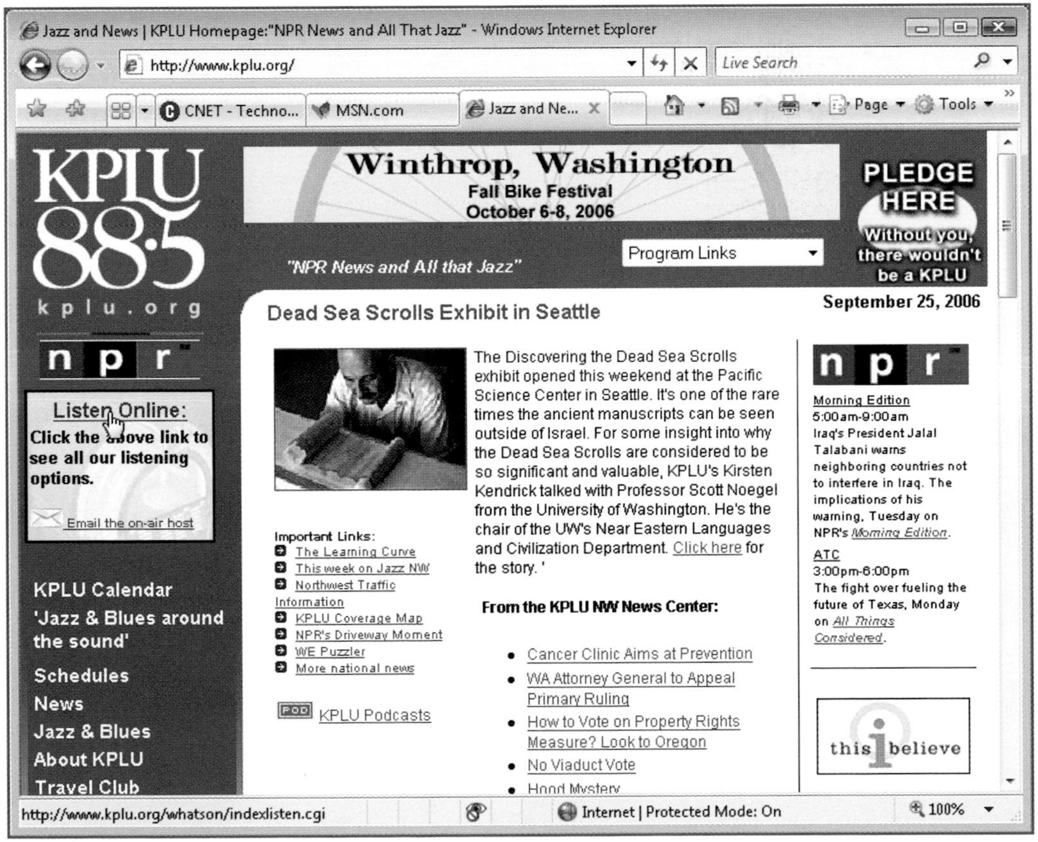

Play Internet Audio and Video Files

You can play audio and video files on the Internet with Internet Explorer directly from a link on a Web page. Many Web pages have links to audio and video files, such as the one shown in Figure 4-13. To play these files, simply click the links. If you have several audio players installed (for example, Windows Media Player and Real Player), you will be asked which one you want to use. Make that choice, and the player will open to play the requested piece.

Figure 4-13: Play an audio or video file on a Web page by clicking the link.

Use Internet E-Mail

Windows Vista includes Windows Mail that allows you to send and receive e-mail and to participate in newsgroups. You can also send and receive e-mail through a Web-mail account using Internet Explorer. This section will primarily describe using Windows Mail. See the "Using Web Mail" QuickSteps for a discussion of that subject.

Establish an E-Mail Account

To send and receive e-mail with Windows Mail, you must have an Internet connection, an e-mail account established with an Internet service provider (ISP), and that account must be set up in Windows Mail.

For an e-mail account, you need:

- Your e-mail address, for example: mike@anisp.com
- The type of mail server the ISP uses (POP3, IMAP, or HTTP—POP3 is the most common)
- The names of the incoming and outgoing mail servers, for example: mail.anisp.com
- The name and password for your mail account

With an Internet connection established and with the above information, you can set up an account in Windows Mail.

1. Click **Start** and click **E-mail**. (This assumes that Windows Mail is your default e-mail application. If it isn't, click **Start**, click **All Programs**, and click **Windows Mail**.) If Windows Mail has not been previously set up, the first new account dialog box will appear; if it doesn't, click the **Tools** menu, click **Accounts**, click **Add**, click **E-mail Account**, and click **Next** to open it.

2. Enter the name you want people to see when they get your e-mail, and click **Next**.

3. Enter your e-mail address, and click **Next**.

4. Select the type of mail server used by your ISP (commonly POP3), enter the names of your ISP's incoming and outgoing mail servers, whether your outgoing server requires authentication (most don't, but your ISP will tell you if it does and how to handle it), and click **Next**.

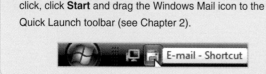

TIP

To be able to quickly start Windows Mail with a single click, click **Start** and drag the Windows Mail icon to the Quick Launch toolbar (see Chapter 2).

E-mail - Shortcut

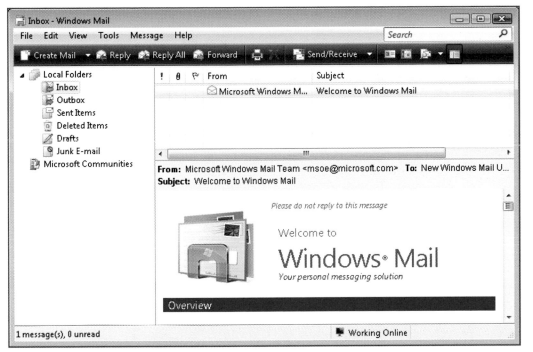

Figure 4-14: Windows Mail provides access to e-mail and newsgroups.

5. Enter your e-mail user name and your password and whether you want Windows to remember your password so that you don't have to enter it each time you sign on to the mail server.

6. When you have completed these steps click **Next**. Click **Do Not Download My E-Mail At This Time** if that is what you want, and then click **Finish**. You will see a Welcome to Windows Mail message in Windows Mail, as shown in Figure 4-14.

Use the next two sections, "Create and Send E-Mail" and "Receive E-Mail," to test your setup.

Create and Send E-Mail

To create and send an e-mail message:

1. Open Windows Mail and click **Create Mail** on the toolbar. The New Message window will open, similar to the one in Figure 4-15.

2. Start to enter a name in the **To** text box. If the name is in your Contact List, (see the "Using the Contacts List" QuickSteps in this chapter) it will be automatically completed and you can press **ENTER** to accept that name. If the name is not automatically completed, finish typing a full e-mail address (such as **billg@microsoft.com**).

3. If you want more than one addressee, place a semi-colon (;) and a space after the first address, and then type a second one as in step 2.

4. If you want to differentiate the addressees to whom the message is principally being sent from those for whom it is just information, press **TAB** and put the second or subsequent addressees in the **Cc** text box as you did in the **To** text box.

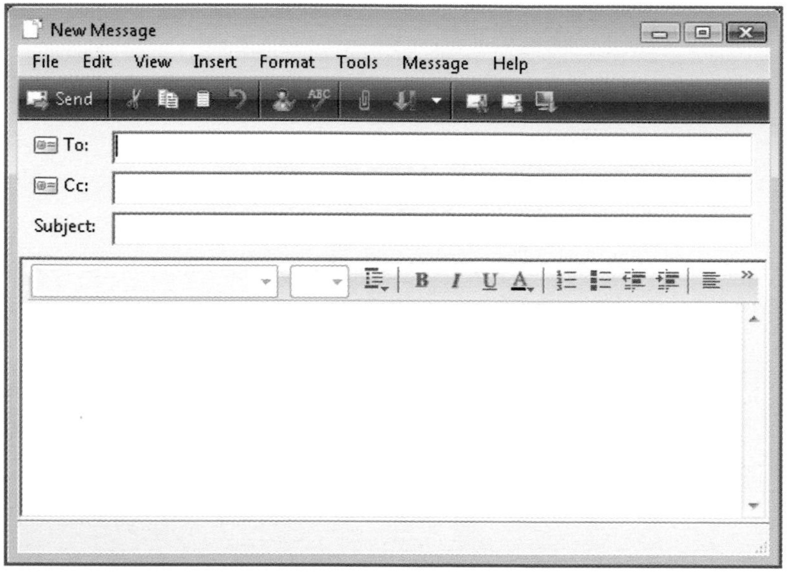

![New Message window]

Figure 4-15: Sending e-mail messages is an easy and fast way to communicate.

5. Press **TAB**, type a subject for the message, press **TAB** again, and type your message.

6. When you have completed your message, click **Send** 🖂 Send . For a brief moment, you will see a message in your Outbox and then, if you look, you will see the message in your Sent Items folder. If you are done, close Windows Mail.

Receive E-Mail

Depending on how Windows Mail is set up, it may automatically receive any e-mail you have when you are connected to your ISP. If not, or if you need to dial in to your ISP, click **Send/Receive**. In any case, the mail you receive will go to your Inbox. To open and read your mail:

🖂 Send/Receive ▾

1. Open **Windows Mail** and click **Inbox** in the Folders list to open your Inbox, which contains all of the messages you received and haven't deleted or organized in folders.

2. Click a message in the Inbox to read it in the Preview pane at the bottom of the window, as shown in Figure 4-16, or double-click a message to open the message in its own window, similar to the Create A New Message window.

TIP

Normally, the contents of your Inbox are sorted by the date in the Received column, with the most recent message at the top. You can sort on any of the columns by clicking the column heading, as shown in Figure 4-16. The first time you click, the column is sorted alphabetically; the second time, it is sorted in inverse alphabetical order.

Figure 4-16: Work with a message you have received in the Inbox or in its own window and sort the Inbox by who sent them, their subject, or the date they were sent.

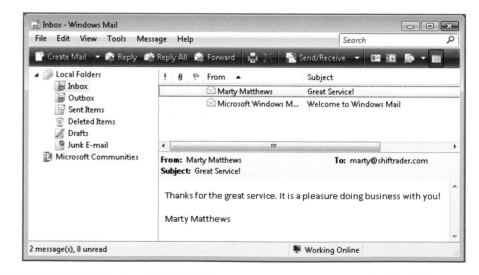

USING THE CONTACTS LIST

The Contacts list, shown in Figure 4-17, allows you to collect e-mail addresses and other information about the people with whom you correspond or otherwise interact.

OPEN THE CONTACTS LIST

To open the Contacts list:

Click **Contacts** on the Windows Mail toolbar.

ADD A NEW CONTACT

To add a new contact to the Contacts list:

1. With the Contacts list open, click **New Contact**. The contact's Properties dialog box appears.

2. Enter as much of the information as you have or want. For e-mail, you need a name and an e-mail address. You can have several e-mail addresses for each contact. For each one, type it in the **E-Mail Address** text box, and click **Add**.

3. When you are done, click **OK** to close the Properties dialog box.

ADD A GROUP OF CONTACTS

To add a group of contacts that you want to send a single message to:

1. Click **New Contact Group**. The group's Properties dialog box appears.

2. Enter the group name, and click **Add To Contact Group**. The Add Members To Contact Group opens. Hold **CTRL** while clicking the names you want on the list. When you have selected all the names, click **Add**.

Continued . . .

3. Print or delete a message in either the Inbox or its own window by clicking the relevant button on the toolbar. Close Windows Mail if you are finished with it.

Respond to E-Mail

You can respond to messages you receive in three ways. First, click the message in your Inbox, and then:

- Click **Reply** to return a message to just the person who sent the original message.

  –Or–

- Click **Reply All** to return a message to all the people who were addressees (both To and Cc) in the original message.

  –Or–

- Click **Forward** to relay a message to people not shown as addressees on the original message.

In all three cases, a window similar to the New Message window opens and allows you to add or change addressees and the subject, and add a message.

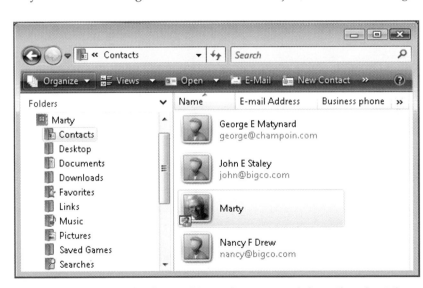

Figure 4-17: The Contacts list provides a place to store information about the people with whom you correspond.

QUICKSTEPS

USING THE CONTACTS LIST *(Continued)*

3. Alternatively, click **Create New Contact** and enter a new name as described in Add A New Contact, and click **OK** to have it added to the group.

4. When you are done, click **OK** to close the Properties dialog box. Click **Close** to close the Contacts list.

TIP

While you can have several e-mail addresses in a single contact's Properties dialog box, there is not an easy way to select any but the default address. A better solution is to have several contacts with the same name but different e-mail addresses. That way, when you send an e-mail to that person, you will be asked which address you want to use.

TIP

If you see an e-mail address in an e-mail message that you want to add to your Contacts list, right-click the address and choose **Add To Contacts**. This creates a new contact and opens its Properties dialog box so that you can make changes and add other information.

Use Stationery

If you would like to add some character to your e-mail messages, you can include a background image with them. You can do this individually for each message or for all your messages.

APPLY STATIONERY TO INDIVIDUAL MESSAGES

1. Open **Windows Mail** and click the **Create Mail** down arrow on the toolbar.

2. Choose one of the ten preselected backgrounds, or click **Select Stationery** for additional options, select one, and then click **OK**. The New Message window will open with your stationery displayed.

3. Address, enter, and send the message as you otherwise would, and then close Windows Mail.

Create Mail ▾ Reply
1 Stars
2 Soft Blue
3 Shades of Blue
4 Roses
5 Peacock
6 Orange Circles
7 Hand Prints
8 Green Bubbles
9 Garden
10 Bears
Select Stationery...
No Stationery
Web Page...

APPLY STATIONERY TO ALL MESSAGES

1. Open Windows Mail, click the **Tools** menu, and click **Options.**

2. Click the **Compose** tab, and, under **Stationery**, click **Mail**.

3. Click **Select**, select the stationery that you want to apply to all your e-mail, click **OK** twice, and then close Windows Mail.

Apply Formatting

The simplest messages are sent in plain text without any formatting. These messages take the least bandwidth and are the easiest to receive. If you wish, you can send messages with formatting using HTML, the Internet's Hypertext Markup Language with which many Web sites have been created. You can do this for an individual message and for all messages.

APPLY FORMATTING TO INDIVIDUAL MESSAGES

1. Open **Windows Mail** and click the **Create Mail** button on the toolbar.

2. Click the **Format** menu, and click **Rich Text (HTML)** if it is not already selected.

3. Address, create, and send the message as you otherwise would, and then close Windows Mail.

APPLY FORMATTING TO ALL MESSAGES

1. Open Windows Mail, click **Tools**, and click **Options**.

2. Click the **Send** tab. Under **Mail Sending Format**, click **HTML**.

3. Click **OK**, and then close Windows Mail.

SELECT A FONT AND A COLOR FOR ALL MESSAGES

To use a particular font and font color on all of your e-mail messages (you must send your mail using HTML in place of plain text—see "Apply Formatting to All Messages"):

1. Open Windows Mail, click **Tools**, and click **Options**.

2. Click the **Compose** tab. Under **Compose Font**, click **Font Settings** opposite Mail.

3. Select the font, style, size, effects, and color that you want to use (see Figure 4-18) with all your e-mail, click **OK** twice, and then close Windows Mail.

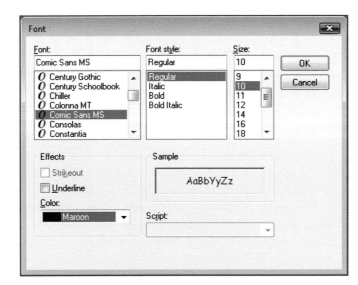

Figure 4-18: If you send your mail using HTML in place of plain text, you can apply fonts and color and do many other things not available with plain text.

USING WEB MAIL

Web mail is the sending and receiving of e-mail over the Internet using a browser, such as Internet Explorer, instead of an e-mail program, such as Windows Mail. There are a number of Web mail programs, such as MSN's Hotmail (www.hotmail.com), Yahoo Mail (mail.yahoo.com), and Google's Gmail (mail.google .com—you must first get an invitation over a cell phone or from a friend who has a Gmail account). So long as you have access to the Internet, you can sign up for one or more of these services. The basic features (simple sending and receiving of e-mail) are often free. For example, to sign up for MSN Hotmail:

1. Open Internet Explorer. In the address bar, type www.hotmail.com, and press **ENTER**.

2. Click **Sign Up**, click **Get It Free** or select one of the other services, fill in the requested information, and click **I Accept** the terms of use, select any newsletters you want (this gets you lots of marketing e-mail, and click **Continue**.

3. When you are done, click **Mail**. The MSN Hotmail page will open and display your mail, as shown in Figure 4-20.

4. Click the link under From to open and read a message.

5. Click **New** on the toolbar to write an e-mail message. Enter the address, a subject, and the message. When you are done, click **Send**.

6. When you are finished with Hotmail, close Internet Explorer.

ATTACH A SIGNATURE

To attach a signature (a closing) on all of your e-mail messages:

1. Open Windows Mail, click **Tools**, and click **Options**.

2. Click the **Signatures** tab, and click **New**. Under **Edit Signature**, enter the closing text you want to use, or click File and enter or browse to the path and file name you want for the closing. The file could be a graphic image if you wished.

3. Click **Add Signatures To All Outgoing Messages**, as shown in Figure 4-19, and click **OK**. Then close Windows Mail.

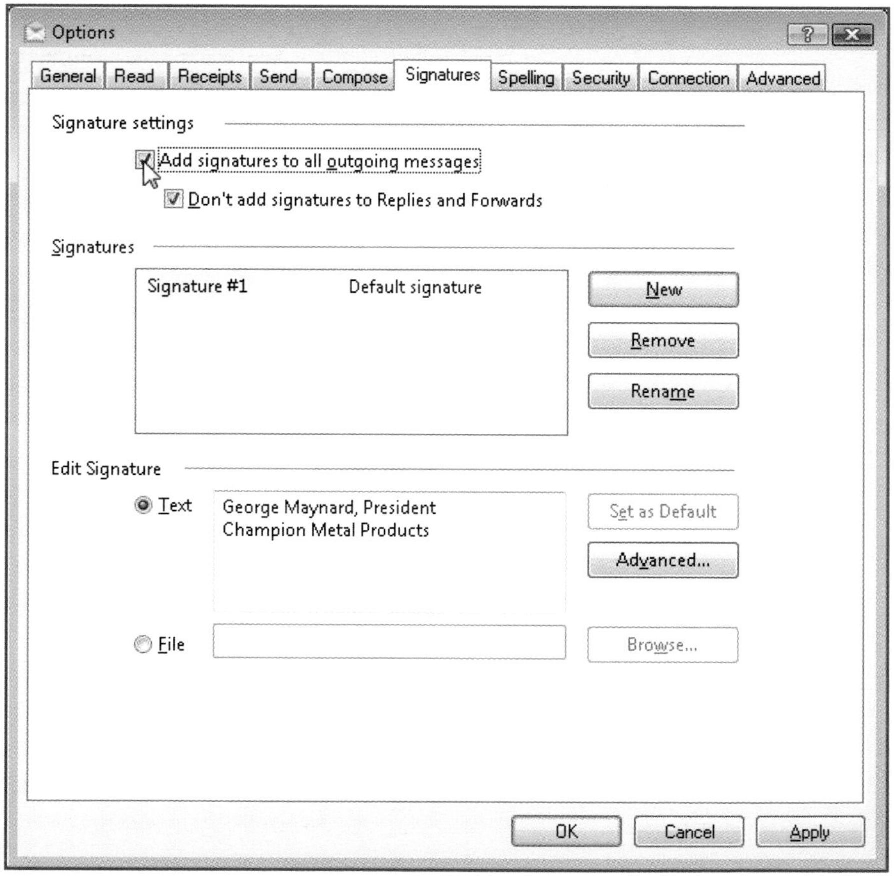

Figure 4-19: A "signature" in Windows Mail is really a closing.

NOTE

If you have several e-mail accounts, you can click **Advanced** in the Signatures tab of the Options dialog box and select the account(s) with which to use a selected signature.

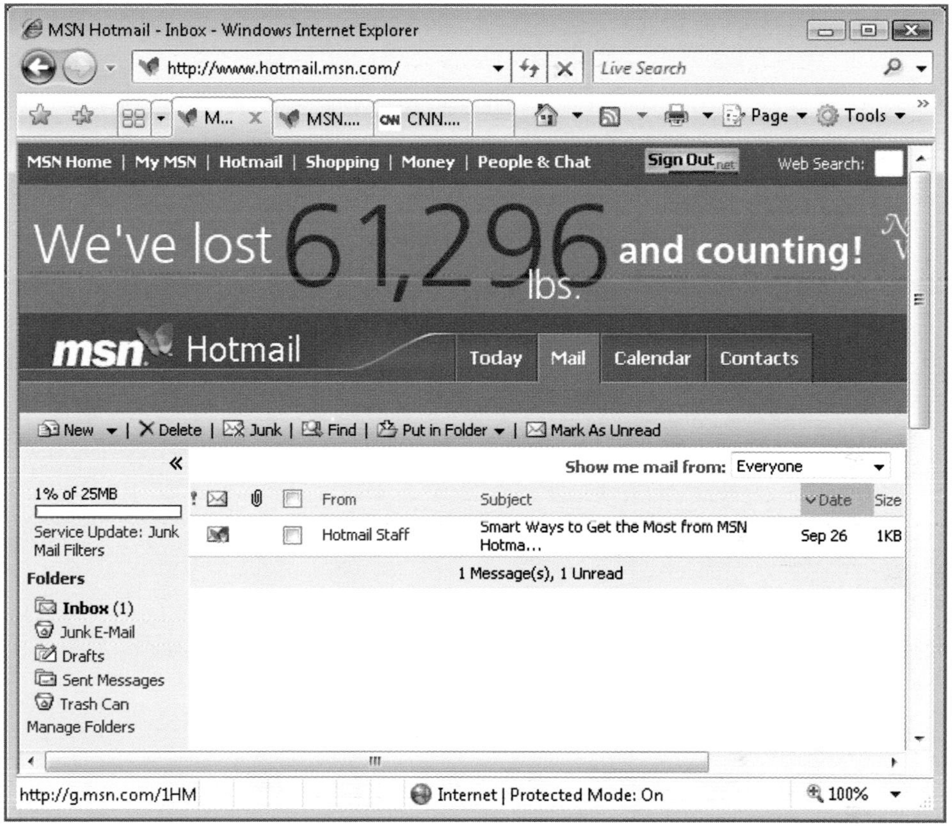

Figure 4-20: Web mail accounts are a quick and free way to get one or more e-mail accounts.

Attach Files to E-Mail

You can attach and send files, such as documents or images, with e-mail messages:

1. Open Windows Mail and click **Create Mail** to open a new message.

2. Click **Attach** on the toolbar. Select the folder and name of the file you want to send, and click **Open**.

3. Address, enter, and send the message as you normally would, and then close Windows Mail.

TIP

With a New Message window open, you can drag a file from Windows Explorer or the desktop to the message, and it will automatically be attached and sent with the message.

Participate in Newsgroups

Newsgroups are organized chains of messages on a particular subject. Newsgroups allow people to enter new messages and respond to previous ones. To participate in one or more newsgroups, you need to set up a newsgroup account, then locate and open a particular newsgroup, and finally send and receive messages within the newsgroup.

SET UP A NEWSGROUP ACCOUNT

Setting up a new account for a newsgroup is similar to setting up the account for your e-mail. To set up a newsgroup account, you need the name of the news server and, possibly, an account name and password.

1. Open Windows Mail, click **Tools**, and click **Accounts**.

2. Click **Add**, click **Newsgroup Account**, and click **Next**. Enter the name you want displayed, and click **Next**. Enter your e-mail address if not already displayed, and click **Next**.

Figure 4-21: A list of newsgroups to which you can subscribe.

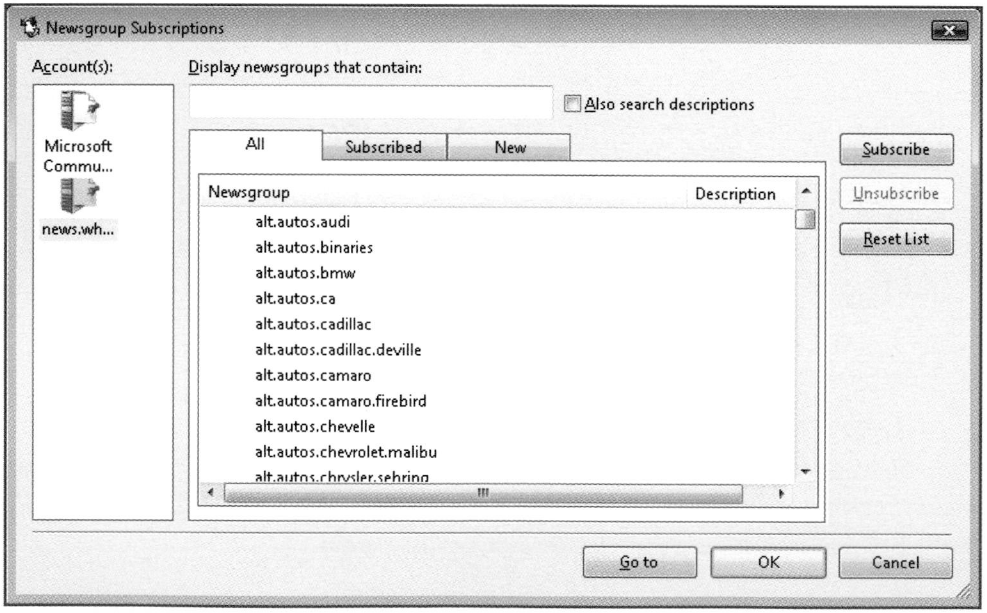

3. Enter the name of your news server. Your ISP or sponsoring organization will give you this. If you do not need to enter an account name and password, your ISP or sponsoring organization will tell you this and you can skip to step 5.

4. To enter an account name and password, click **My News Server Requires Me To Log On**, and click **Next**. Enter your account name and password, click **Remember Password** (if desired).

5. Click **Next**, click **Finish**, and click **Close**. A new folder will appear in the Folders pane of Windows Mail.

6. Click **Yes** to subscribe to one or more news group and download the newsgroups from the news account you just set up. If necessary, click **Connect** to connect to the Internet. If all of your entries are okay, you will be connected. If your account name and password are in error, you are told so and given a chance to fix them. A list of newsgroups will be displayed, as shown in Figure 4-21.

SUBSCRIBE TO A NEWSGROUP

Most general-purpose news servers, such as those maintained by ISPs, have many newsgroups, probably only some of which might interest you. To subscribe to a newsgroup (meaning to read and reply to messages they contain):

1. If you have just come from setting up a newsgroup account, skip to step 2. Otherwise, open Windows Mail and click your news server in the Folders pane. If you have not subscribed to a newsgroup, you will be asked if you want to. Click **Yes**. If you have subscribed to a newsgroup and want to subscribe to more, click **Newsgroups** in the right pane. In either case, the Newsgroup Subscriptions dialog box will appear.

2. To search for a particular newsgroup, type a keyword (such as BMW) in the **Display Newsgroups That Contain** text box, and press ENTER (newsgroups start popping up as you type your search keywords and you may not need to press ENTER).

3. Double-click the newsgroups to which you want to subscribe. An icon appears to the left of the newsgroup. After you have selected the newsgroups, click **OK**. You are returned to Windows Mail.

READ AND POST MESSAGES IN A NEWSGROUP

For newsgroups to which you have subscribed, you can read and send messages like e-mail messages, but with two differences. You can choose to reply to the newsgroup or to the individual, and a new message is called a Write Message. If someone replies to this message, it gets added to the end of the original message, thereby creating a chain, or *thread*, of messages on a given subject.

Figure 4-22: A newsgroup provides a thread on a given topic to which you can add your comments.

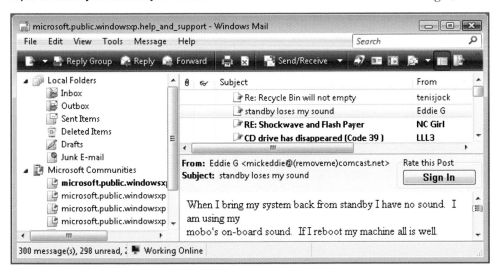

1. Open Windows Mail, open your news server in the Folders pane, and click a newsgroup you want to open. A list of messages will be displayed.

2. Click a message and click the plus icon (+) to its left (this identifies that there are replies) to have the message shown in the bottom pane, as shown in Figure 4-22. Or, double-click the message to have it displayed in its own window.

3. To respond to a newsgroup message:

- Click **Write Message** on the toolbar to create a public message that will begin a new thread.

  –Or–

- Click **Reply Group** on the toolbar to create a public message in the thread you have selected.

  –Or–

- Click **Reply** on the toolbar to create a private message to the person who wrote the message you have selected.

  –Or–

- Click **Forward** on the toolbar to send a copy of the message you have selected to one or more individuals.

5. Create and send the message as you would any e-mail message. When you are done, close Windows Mail.

How to...

- *Automatically Start Programs*
- *Start Programs Minimized*
- *Schedule Programs*
- *Switching Programs*
- *Control with the Task Manager*
- *Stopping Programs*
- *Start a Program in Run*
- *Start Older Programs*
- *Control Automatic Programs*
- *Control Windows Indexing*
- *Running Accessory Programs*
- *Update Windows Vista*
- *Restore Windows Vista*
- *Get System Information*
- *Set Power Options*
- *Add and Remove Software*
- *Add Hardware*
- *Use Remote Assistance*

Chapter 5
Managing Windows Vista

Running programs is one of Windows Vista's major functions. The managing of Windows Vista, the subject of this chapter, entails setting up the starting and stopping of programs in a number of different ways. Management also includes the maintenance and enhancement of Windows Vista and the setting up of remote assistance so that you can have someone help you without actually being in front of your computer.

Start and Stop Programs

Previous chapters discussed starting programs from the Start menu, through All Programs, through a shortcut on the desktop, and by locating the program with Windows Explorer. All of these methods of starting a program require a direct action by you. Windows also provides several ways to automatically start programs and to monitor and manage them while they are running.

Automatically Start Programs

Sometimes, you will want to start a program automatically and have it run in the background every time you start the computer. For example, you might automatically run an antivirus program or a screen-capture program (such as SnagIt), which was used to capture the figures and illustrations you see here. To automatically start a program, open a folder, or open a file in a program:

1. Click **Start**, click **All Programs**, right-click **Startup**, and click **Open All Users**. The Startup folder will open.

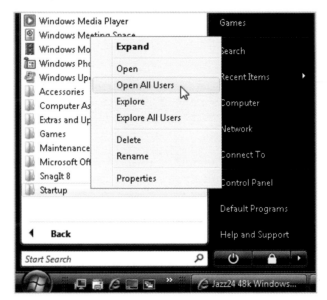

2. Click **Start** and click **Computer** to open Windows Explorer. Position the Explorer window so that you can see both it and the Startup window on the desktop at the same time (right-click the taskbar and click **Show Windows Side By Side** to arrange both windows).

3. In Explorer, open the drive and folders needed to display the program file you want to automatically start, or the folder or disk drive you want to automatically open, or the file you want to automatically start in its program.

4. Hold the right mouse button while dragging (right-drag) the program file, the folder, or the file to the open Startup folder, as you can see in Figure 5-1. When you reach the Startup folder, click **Create Shortcuts Here**.

5. Close the Startup folder and Windows Explorer. The next time you start your computer, the action you want will take place.

Start Programs Minimized

Sometimes, when you start programs automatically, you want them to run in the background, in other words, minimized. To do that:

1. Click **Start**, click **All Programs**, right-click **Startup**, and click **Open All Users** to open the Startup folder.

2. Right-click the program you want minimized, and click **Properties**. Click the **Shortcut** tab.

3. Click the **Run** down arrow, and click **Minimized**, as shown in Figure 5-2.

4. Click **OK** to close the Properties dialog box, and then close the Startup folder.

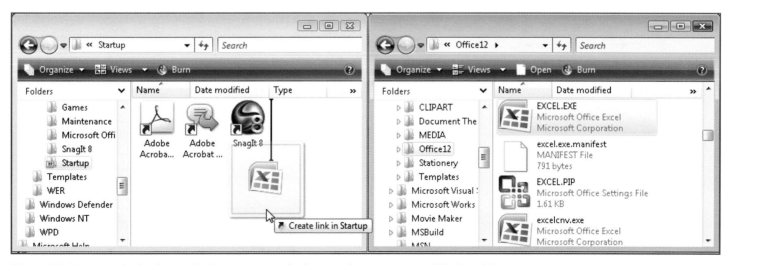

Figure 5-1: Programs in the Startup folder are automatically started when you start Windows Vista.

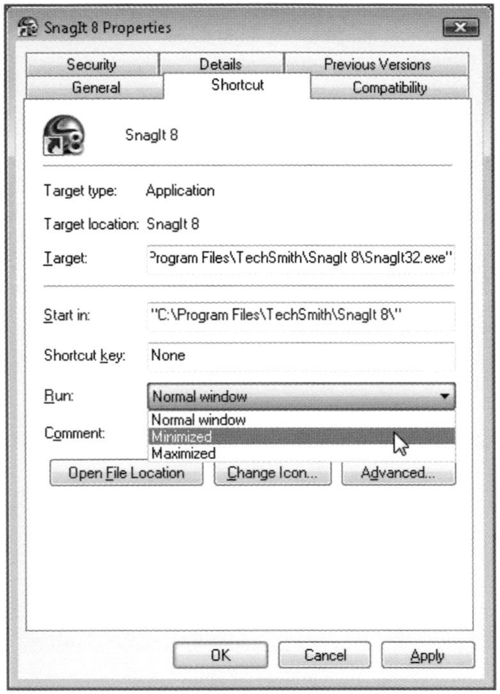

Figure 5-2: *Minimizing a program, when it has automatically started, lets it run in the background.*

NOTE

Many programs, such as Backup and antivirus programs, use their own scheduler to run automatically on a scheduled basis.

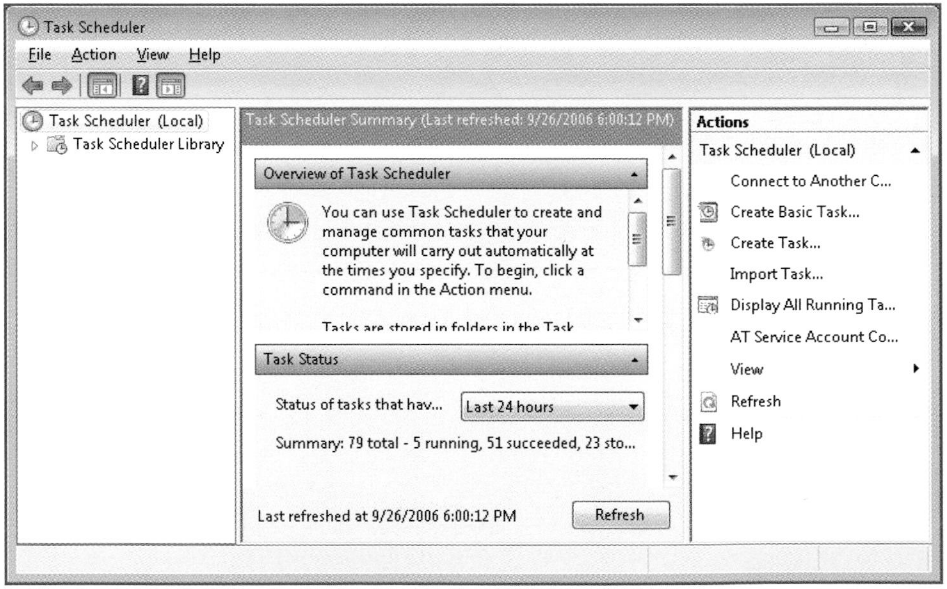

Figure 5-3: *The Task Scheduler is used by Windows Vista for many of its tasks, but you can also use it to repeatedly perform a task you want.*

Schedule Programs

You can schedule a program to run automatically using Windows Vista's Task Scheduler, although you may need to specify how the program is to run using command-line parameters. See how to use Help in step 2 of "Start Older Programs" later in this chapter to learn what parameters are available for the program you want to run.

1. Click **Start**, click **All Programs**, click **Accessories**, click **System Tools**, and click **Task Scheduler**. The Task Scheduler window will open, as you can see in Figure 5-3.

2. Click **Create Basic Task** in the Action pane or in the Action menu. The Create A Basic Task Wizard opens. Type a name and description, and click **Next**. Click what you want to use as a trigger, and again click **Next**.

3. Depending on what you choose for the trigger, you may have to select the start date and time and enter additional information, such as the day of the week for a weekly trigger. Click **Next**.

4. Choose whether you want to start a program, send an e-mail, or display a message, and click **Next**.

5. If you want to start a program, select it either from the list of programs or by browsing to it, add any arguments that are to be passed to the program when it starts, and indicate if you would like the program to be looking at a particular folder when it starts (Start In).

–Or–

If you want to send an e-mail, type the From and To e-mail addresses, the subject and text; browse to and select an attachment; and type your SMTP e-mail server (this your outgoing mail server that you entered when you set up Windows Mail—see Chapter 4).

–Or–

If you want to display a message, type a title and the message you want it to contain.

6. Click **Next**. The Summary dialog box will appear, as shown in Figure 5-4. Click **Open The Properties Dialog For This Task When I Click Finish**, and click **Finish**. The Task Properties dialog box will appear.

7. Look at each of the tabs, review the information you have entered, and determine if you need to change anything.

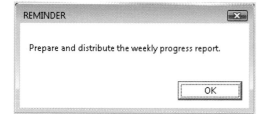

NOTE

The Task Scheduler Properties dialog box can be directly used to set up a scheduled task in place of using the Task Scheduler Wizard. Click **Create Task** instead of clicking **Create Basic Task**.

TIP

Right-click a task in the center pane of the Task Scheduler to work with it. Click **Properties** to edit the task's settings.

Figure 5-4: The Task Scheduler can be used to send e-mail messages and display a message on your screen, as well as to start a program.

UICKSTEPS

SWITCHING PROGRAMS

You can switch programs that are running on the desktop, on the taskbar, and on the task list. You can also switch them using the Task Manager (see "Control with the Task Manager" on the right).

SWITCH PROGRAMS ON THE DESKTOP

If you have several programs running and arranged so that you can see all of them, switch from one to another by clicking the program you want to be active. However, if you have more than two or three programs running, it may be hard to see them on the desktop and, therefore, to select the one you want.

SWITCH PROGRAMS ON THE TASKBAR

If you have up to five or six programs running, you should be able to see their tasks on the taskbar. Here, again, clicking the task will switch to that program.

If you have more than five or six tasks (or even seven or eight, with a large monitor at high resolution), they will be grouped into similar items. For example, on the following illustration of a taskbar, there are three instances each of Windows Explorer, Microsoft Word, Adobe Acrobat, and Microsoft Excel.

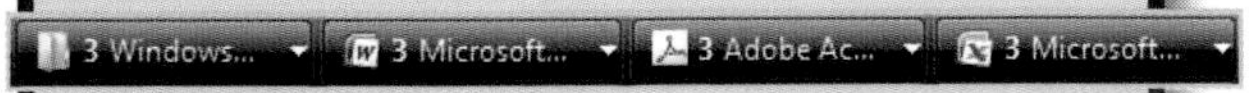

[3 Windows... ▾][3 Microsoft... ▾][3 Adobe Ac... ▾][3 Microsoft... ▾]

Continued . . .

8. When you are done reviewing the scheduled task, click **OK**. Click **Task Scheduler Library** in the left pane (called the console tree). You should see your scheduled task in the middle pane. Close the Task Scheduler window.

Control with the Task Manager

The Windows Task Manager, shown in Figure 5-5, performs a number of functions, but most importantly, it allows you to see what programs and processes (individual threads of a program) are running and to unequivocally stop both. A display of real-time graphs and tables also shows you what is

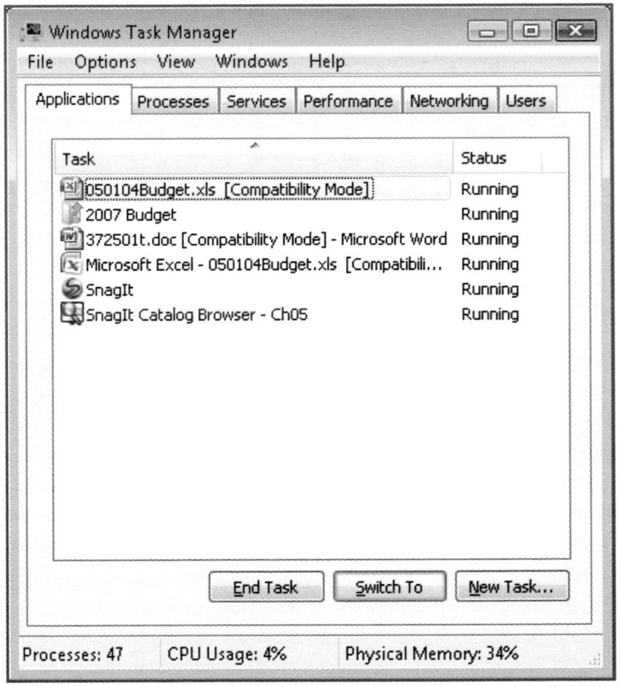

Figure 5-5: The Task Manager shows you what programs are running and allows you to stop them.

QUICKSTEPS

SWITCHING PROGRAMS *(Continued)*

To select a particular instance of a program when there are multiple instances running, click the task on the taskbar to open a menu of the several instances, and select the one you want.

SWITCH PROGRAMS ON THE TASK LIST

The oldest method of switching programs, which predates Windows 95 and the taskbar, is using the task list.

1. Press **ALT+TAB** and hold down **ALT**. The task list will appear.

2. While continuing to hold down **ALT**, press **TAB** repeatedly until the highlight moves to the program you want. Then release **ALT** or click an icon to select the program you want.

CAUTION

It is generally not a good idea to end a process. Instead, stop the program in the Applications tab that is generating the process.

happening at any second on your computer, as you can see in Figure 5-6. To work with the Task Manager:

1. Press **CTRL+ALT+DELETE** and click **Start Task Manager**. Alternately, you can right-click a blank area of the taskbar, and click **Task Manager**.

2. Click the **Applications** tab. You'll see a list of the programs you are running, as shown in Figure 5-5.

3. Click a program in the list. Click **End Task** to stop the program, or click **Switch To** to activate that program.

4. Click **New Task** to open the Run command, where you can enter a program you want to start. See "Start a Program in Run," next.

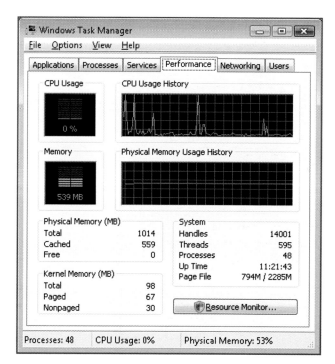

Figure 5-6: Under most circumstances, on a personal computer, only a small fraction of the computer's resources are being used.

QUICKSTEPS

STOPPING PROGRAMS

Stopping a program may be simply because you are done using it or an attempt to keep a program from harming your data or other programs.

USE THE CLOSE BUTTON

One of the easiest ways to close a program is to click the Close button on the upper-right corner of all windows.

USE THE EXIT COMMAND

Almost all programs have an Exit command on the menu on the far left of the menu bar; often, this is the File menu (in Microsoft Office 2007, the Office Button is the "menu" where the exit command is located). Open this menu and click **Exit**.

Game	Help	
New Game		F2
Select Game...		F3
Undo		Ctrl+Z
Hint		H
Statistics		F4
Options		F5
Change Appearance		F7
Exit		

CLOSE FROM THE TASKBAR

Right-click a task on the taskbar, and click **Close**.

⊡	**Restore**	
	Move	
	Size	
—	Minimize	
⊡	Maximize	
×	Close	Alt+F4

CLOSE FROM THE KEYBOARD

Press **ALT+F4**.

If none of these options work, see "Control with the Task Manager."

5. Click the **Processes** tab. Here you see a list of all the processes that are currently running and their CPU and memory usage. Most of these processes are components of Windows Vista.

6. Click the **Services** tab. This is a list of the Windows Vista services that are active and their status. There is nothing that you can do here except observe it.

7. Click the **Performance** tab. This tab graphically shows the CPU and memory usage (see Figure 5-6), while the Networking tab shows the computer's use of the network. The Users tab shows the users that are logged on to the computer. You can disconnect them if they are coming in over the network or log them off if they are directly logged on.

8. When you are done, close the Windows Task Manager.

Start a Program in Run

The Start menu has an option called "Run" that opens the Run dialog box. From this dialog box, you can start most programs if you know the path of the program, its name, and don't mind typing all that information.

1. Click **Start**, click **All Programs**, click **Accessories**, and click **Run**.

   –Or–

   Click **Start**, type <u>run</u> in the Start Search box, and press **ENTER**.

2. In either case, the Run dialog box will appear. Type the path and file name of the program you want to run, and press **ENTER**.

> **NOTE**
>
> Programs that are part of Windows Vista or that are in the root directory (C:\) do not require you to type the path. See "Control Automatic Programs" later in this chapter.

> **NOTE**
>
> If you open the Command Prompt window, you will see white text on a black background. For Figure 5-7, the text and background colors have been reversed by clicking the control menu in the upper-left corner, clicking **Properties**, clicking the **Colors** tab, and selecting black in the Screen Text field and white in the Screen Background field. Click **OK** to close the Properties dialog box.

Start Older Programs

While you can start most programs from the desktop or Start menu, older, less-sophisticated programs (often called "16-bit programs"), especially games, require that they be run in their own isolated window named Command Prompt (also called a DOS, or Disk Operating System, window). Here, you can type DOS commands at the flashing underscore, which is called the *command prompt*.

1. Click **Start**, click **All Programs**, click **Accessories**, and click **Command Prompt**. The Command Prompt window will open.
2. Type help and press **ENTER**. A list of commands that can be used at the command prompt will be displayed, as shown in Figure 5-7 (the colors of the background and text have been switched for printing purposes).
3. To run a program in the Games folder on the C: drive, type cd c:\games, press **ENTER**, type dir /p, press **ENTER** to see the name of the program, type the name of the program, and press **ENTER**. The program should run, although not all programs will run in Windows Vista.
4. When you are done with the Command Prompt window, type exit and press **ENTER**.

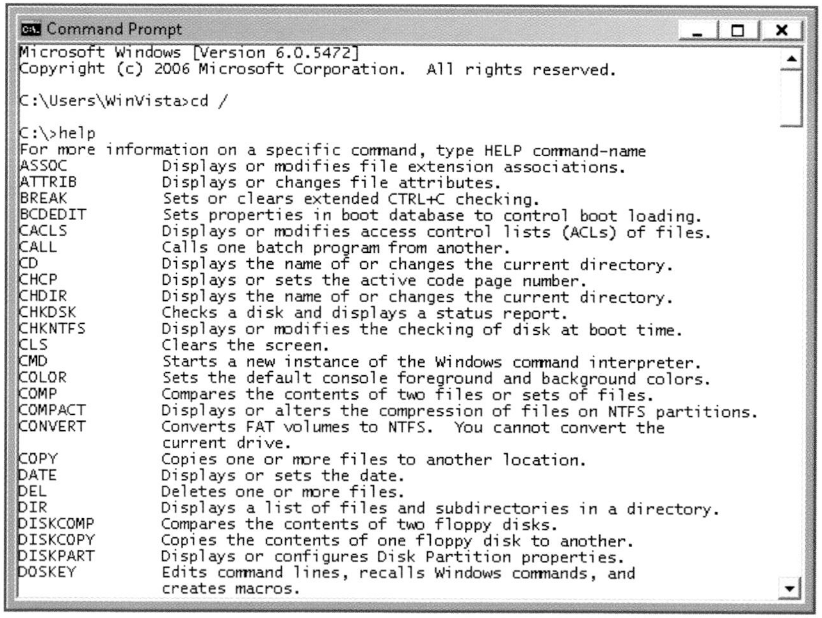

```
Command Prompt
Microsoft Windows [Version 6.0.5472]
Copyright (c) 2006 Microsoft Corporation.  All rights reserved.

C:\Users\WinVista>cd /

C:\>help
For more information on a specific command, type HELP command-name
ASSOC          Displays or modifies file extension associations.
ATTRIB         Displays or changes file attributes.
BREAK          Sets or clears extended CTRL+C checking.
BCDEDIT        Sets properties in boot database to control boot loading.
CACLS          Displays or modifies access control lists (ACLs) of files.
CALL           Calls one batch program from another.
CD             Displays the name of or changes the current directory.
CHCP           Displays or sets the active code page number.
CHDIR          Displays the name of or changes the current directory.
CHKDSK         Checks a disk and displays a status report.
CHKNTFS        Displays or modifies the checking of disk at boot time.
CLS            Clears the screen.
CMD            Starts a new instance of the Windows command interpreter.
COLOR          Sets the default console foreground and background colors.
COMP           Compares the contents of two files or sets of files.
COMPACT        Displays or alters the compression of files on NTFS partitions.
CONVERT        Converts FAT volumes to NTFS.  You cannot convert the
               current drive.
COPY           Copies one or more files to another location.
DATE           Displays or sets the date.
DEL            Deletes one or more files.
DIR            Displays a list of files and subdirectories in a directory.
DISKCOMP       Compares the contents of two floppy disks.
DISKCOPY       Copies the contents of one floppy disk to another.
DISKPART       Displays or configures Disk Partition properties.
DOSKEY         Edits command lines, recalls Windows commands, and
               creates macros.
```

Figure 5-7: ***At the command prompt, you can type DOS commands, which Windows Vista will carry out.***

> **CAUTION**
>
> Unless you are trying to diagnose a problem and have considerable experience doing that, you normally do not want to change the settings in the System Configuration utility.

Control Automatic Programs

Sometimes, when you install a program, it sets up itself or other programs to run in perpetuity, even if that is not what you had in mind. Many of these programs are not started from the Startup folder. To control these programs and prevent them from running, Windows Vista has a program named MSConfig, and the easiest way to start it is from the Run dialog box.

1. Click **Start**, click **All Programs**, click **Accessories**, and click **Run**.

   –Or–

   Click **Start**, type run in the Start Search box, and press **ENTER**.

2. Type msconfig and press **ENTER**. The System Configuration utility dialog box appears.
3. Click the **Startup** tab. You will see a list all of the programs that start when Windows Vista starts, as shown in Figure 5-8.
4. Click the checkbox to deselect a program so that it is not started the next time Windows Vista starts. When you are done, click **OK** to close the System Configuration utility dialog box. A System Configuration message box will appear. Click **Restart** to restart your computer and reflect the changes you have made.
5. Click **OK** when you are told that you have used the System Configuration utility to make changes to the way Windows Vista starts. The System Configuration utility dialog box will appear once more. Click **Close**. If you don't want to see the message or have MSConfig open automatically when you start Windows, click **Don't Show This Message Or Start System Configuration When Windows Starts**.

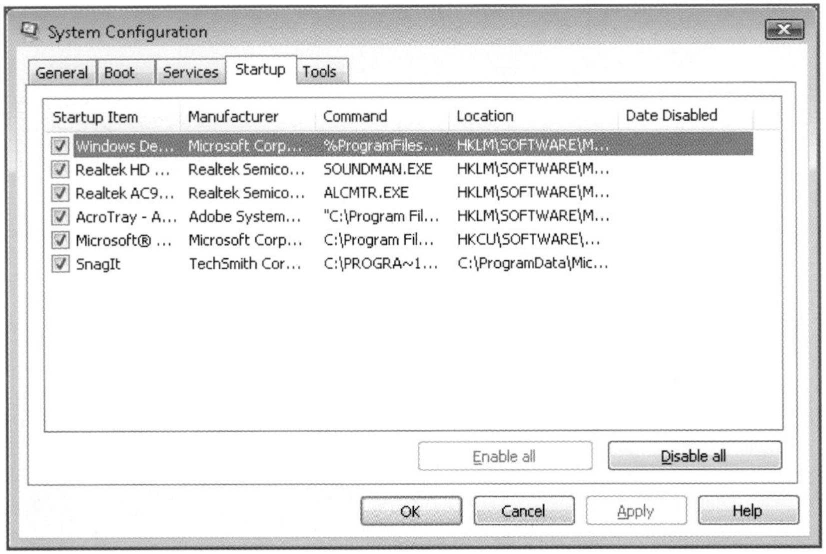

***Figure 5-8:** In the System Configuration utility (MSConfig) dialog box, you can see and stop from running all of the programs that Windows Vista starts.*

Control Windows Indexing

Windows Vista automatically indexes the files that are stored on a computer to substantially speed up your searches of files and folders.

Unlike earlier versions of Windows, in Windows Vista, you cannot turn off indexing—it is an integral part of the search facility. Windows indexing has become quite efficient and seldom affects the performance of the computer.

1. Click **Start**, click **Control Panel**, click **System And Maintenance** in Control Panel Home view, and click (double-click in Classic View) **Indexing Options** to open the Indexing Options dialog box.

2. If you want to change what is being indexed, click **Modify**, click the triangle icon to open the drives on your computer, and click the folders as shown in Figure 5-9. Then click **OK**.

3. If you want to change the types of files being indexed, click **Advanced**. Choose if you want encrypted files indexed, or if you want similar words that have different marks (such as the accent, grave, and umlaut) that change the sound and meaning of the word indexed differently. Click the **File Types** tab, and select the types of files you want included. When you are done, click **OK**.

4. Close the Indexing Options dialog box.

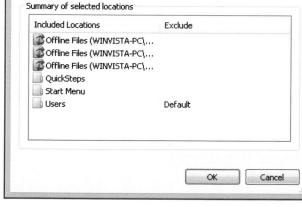

Figure 5-9: Windows indexing uses idle time to index your files and folders.

RUNNING ACCESSORY PROGRAMS

Windows Vista comes with a number of accessory programs. You can open these by clicking **Start**, clicking **All Programs**, choosing **Accessories**, and, where needed, clicking **System Tools**. Many of these programs are discussed elsewhere in this book, but Calculator, Character Map, Notepad, and Paint will be briefly looked at here.

CALCULATOR

The Calculator, started from Accessories, has two views: one shows a standard desktop calculator; the other, a comprehensive scientific one, shown in Figure 5-10. To switch from one view to the other, click **View** and click the other view. To use a calculator, click the numbers on the screen or type them on the keyboard.

CHARACTER MAP

The Character Map, which is in System Tools, allows selection of special characters that are not available on a standard keyboard.

1. Click the **Font** down arrow, and click the font you want for the special character.

2. Scroll until you find it, and then double-click the character to copy it to the Clipboard.

Continued . . .

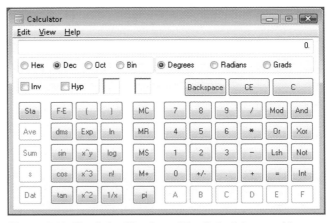

Figure 5-10: *The Scientific view of the Calculator provides a number of advanced functions.*

Figure 5-11: *Paint allows you to make simple line drawings or touch up other images.*

RUNNING ACCESSORY PROGRAMS

(Continued)

3. In the program where you want the character, click **Paste**.

NOTEPAD

Notepad is a simple text editor you can use to view and create unformatted text (.txt) files. If you double-click a text file in Windows Explorer, Notepad will likely open and display the file. If a line of text is too long to display without scrolling, click **Format** and click **Word Wrap**. To create a file, simply start typing in the Notepad window. Before printing a file, click **File**, click **Page Setup**, and select the paper orientation, margins, header, and footer.

PAINT

Paint lets you view, create, and edit bitmap image files in .bmp, .gif, .ico, .jpg, .png, and .tif formats. Several drawing tools and many colors are available to create simple drawings and illustrations (see Figure 5-11).

Maintain Windows Vista

Windows Vista maintenance consists of periodically updating for fixes and new features, restoring Windows Vista when hardware or other software damages it, getting information about it, and installing new hardware and software.

Update Windows Vista

Microsoft tries hard to encourage you to allow Windows Vista to update itself, from the point of installation, where you are asked to establish automatic updates, to periodically reminding you to do that. If you turn on Automatic Updates, on a regular basis, Windows will automatically determine if any updates are available, download the updates (which come from Microsoft) over the Internet, and install them. If Automatic Updates was not turned on during installation, you can do that at any time and control the updating process once it is turned on.

TURN ON AUTOMATIC UPDATES

1. If you get a message suggesting that you turn on Automatic Updates, click the message to open Windows Update.

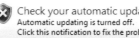

Check your automatic updates settings. ×
Automatic updating is turned off.
Click this notification to fix the problem.

–Or–

If the message is not available, click **Start** and click **Control Panel**. In Control Panel Home view, click **System And Maintenance**, and click (or double-click in Classic View) **Windows Update**.

2. Click **Change Settings**, determine the amount of automation you want, and click one of the following four choices (see Figure 5-12):

- The first and recommended choice, which is the default, automatically determines if there are updates that are needed, downloads them, and then installs them on a frequency and at a time you specify.

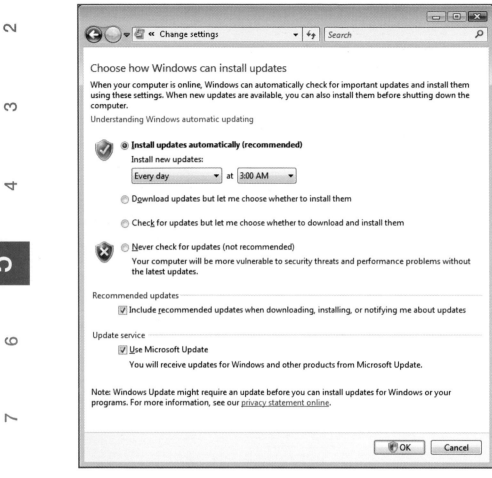

Figure 5-12: *Automatic Updates determines which updates you need and can automatically download and install them.*

- The second choice automatically determines if there are updates that are needed and downloads them; it then asks you whether you want to install them.
- The third choice automatically determines if there are updates that are needed, asks you before downloading them, and asks you again before installing them.
- The fourth choice, which is not recommended, never checks for updates.

3. Choose whether to include recommended updates when you are otherwise online with Microsoft and whether to use Microsoft Update Service to receive updates for other Microsoft products you have installed, like Microsoft Office.

4. Click **OK** when you are finished, and close Windows Update.

APPLY AUTOMATIC UPDATES

If you choose either the second or third option, you will see a notice when updates are ready to download and/or install.

When you click the notice, the Widows Updates dialog box appears. You can click View Available Update to see the specific updates being proposed. When you are ready, click either **Install** or **Install Updates.**

Restore Windows Vista

System Restore keeps track of the changes you make to your system, including the software you install and the settings you make. If a hardware change, a software installation, or something else causes the system not to load or not to run properly, you can use System Restore to return the system to the way it was at the last restore point.

NOTE

System Restore does not restore or make any changes to data files, only to system and application program files. Data files must be backed up, using either the Windows Vista backup program or a third-party backup program, and then restored from a backup.

NOTE

System Restore actually needs at least 300 MB on each hard drive that has System Restore turned on, and may use up to 15 percent of each drive. If a drive is smaller than 1 GB (gigabyte), System Restore cannot be used.

SET UP SYSTEM RESTORE

In a default installation of Windows Vista, System Restore is automatically installed. If you have at least 300 megabytes (MB) of free disk space after installing Windows Vista, System Restore will be turned on and the first restore point will be set. If System Restore is not enabled, you can turn it on and set a restore point:

1. Click **Start** and click **Control Panel**. In Control Panel Home view, click **System And Maintenance**, click (double-click in Classic View) **System**, and click **System Protection** in the left pane. The System Properties dialog box will appear with the System Protection tab displayed, as you can see in Figure 5-13.
2. By default, the disk on which Windows Vista is installed should have a check mark beside it, indicating that System Restore is automatically operating for that disk. If it does not have a check mark, it is recommended that you click the check box to turn it on.

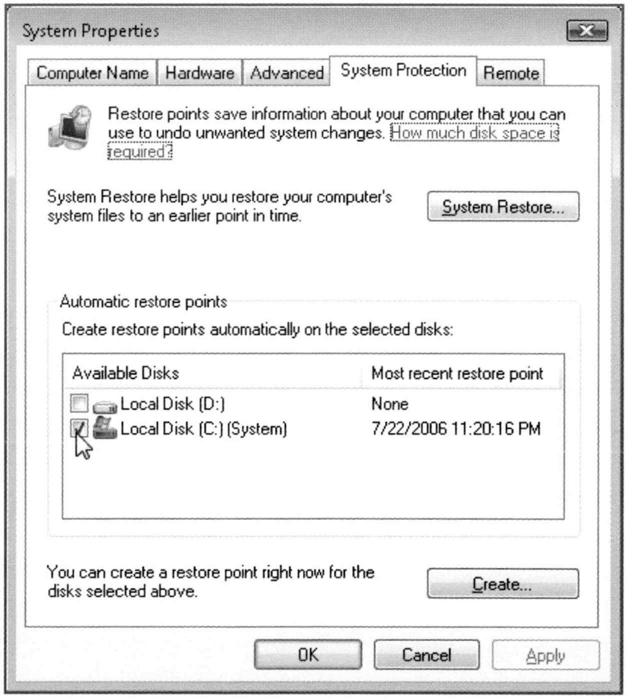

***Figure 5-13:* System Restore returns the system to a previous time when it was functioning normally.**

3. If you have other hard disk drives, click the check box for the drives on which you want to use System Restore.

4. When you have selected all the drives you want, click **OK**.

CREATE RESTORE POINTS

A *restore point* is an identifiable point in time when you know your system was working correctly. If your computer's settings are saved at that point, you can use those settings to restore your computer to that time. Normally, Windows Vista automatically creates restore points on a periodic basis. But if you know at a given point in time that your computer is operating exactly the way you want it to, you can create a restore point.

1. Click **Start** and click **Control Panel**. In Control Panel Home view, click **System And Maintenance**, click (double-click in Classic View) **System**, and click **System Protection** in the left pane. The System Properties dialog box will appear with the System Protection tab displayed.

2. Click **Create** and type a name for the restore point. The date and time are automatically added, and you cannot change the name once you create it.

3. Click **Create** again. You will be told when the restore point is created. Click **OK** and click **Close** to close the System Properties dialog box.

RUN SYSTEM RESTORE FROM WINDOWS

If you can start and operate Windows Vista normally, try to execute the following steps. If you can't make it through these steps without Windows Vista crashing, go to the next section.

1. Click **Start** and click **Control Panel**. In Control Panel Home view, click **System And Maintenance**, click (double-click in Classic View) **System**, and click **System Protection** in the left pane. The System Properties dialog box will appear with the System Protection tab displayed.

2. Click **System Restore** to open the System Restore dialog box shown in Figure 5-14. You can choose:

- **Recommended Restore** to restore your disk to the most recent incident or time that created a restore point

   –Or–

- **A Different Restore Point** to select one from a list

3. In either case click **Next**:

- If you choose Recommended Restore, you are asked to confirm the restore point the system will be returned to and given information about that point. If you do not want to restore to that point, click **Back** and return to step 2. If you want to restore to the described point, click **Finish**.

- If you want to use a different restore point, you are shown a list of restore points. Click one of the points, and click **Next**. You are asked to confirm the restore point. If you do not want to restore to that point, click **Back** and return to step 2. If you want to restore to the described point, click **Finish**.

4. A confirmation dialog box appears, telling you that the restore process cannot be interrupted or undone until it has completed and that you should save documents and shut down programs. Click **Yes** to continue. Some time will be spent saving files and settings for a new restore point, and then the computer will be restarted.

5. When the restore is completed, you will be told that it was successful. Click **Close**.

TIP

You can restore from a System Restore. Immediately before doing a System Restore, a restore point is created and can be used to return to the point the system was at prior to System Restore. Simply re-run System Restore as described in either of the System Restore sections in this chapter, and choose **Undo System Restore**.

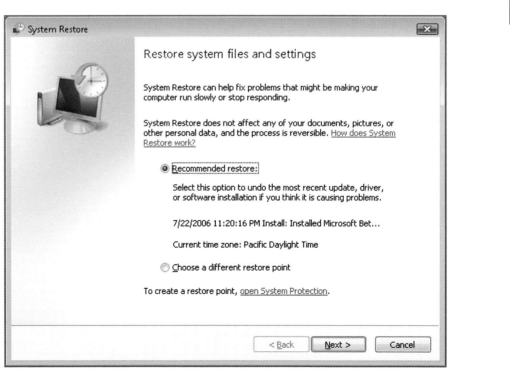

Figure 5-14: You can do a system restore at any of the restore points on the computer and return all of the Windows Vista settings and registry to that point in time.

RUN SYSTEM RESTORE FROM SAFE MODE

Safe Mode means running Windows Vista with the fewest possible drivers and accessories. The reason for this is to allow you to fix whatever is preventing Windows Vista from running normally. You can start System Restore in Safe Mode.

1. If your computer is turned on, turn it off (use Shut Down and make sure the power is off) and let it sit for at least two full minutes. This allows all of the components to fully discharge and will give you a clean restart.

2. After your computer has sat for at least two minutes without power, remove any disks in the floppy, CD, or DVD drives, and turn the computer on. As soon as the memory check is complete, hold down the **F8** key. After a moment, the Advanced Boot Options menu will appear.

3. If necessary, use the **UP ARROW** key to go to the top choice, **Safe Mode**, and then press **ENTER**. If the Operating System menu appears, make sure that Microsoft Windows Vista is chosen, and press **ENTER** again. You will see many lines of information appear about the drivers that are being loaded, and then Windows Vista will begin loading in Safe Mode. Type your user name and password, and press **ENTER** a third time.

4. Press the Windows key on your keyboard, or press **CTRL+ESC**, to open the Start menu. Use the arrow keys to select **All Programs**, press **ENTER**, select **Accessories**, press **ENTER**, select **System Tools**, press **ENTER**, select **System Restore**, and press **ENTER**. The System Restore window will open, as you saw earlier.

5. Follow the instructions in "Run System Restore from Windows" earlier in this chapter, using the arrow keys and pressing **ALT+N** to go to the next page.

6. When you are ready, press **ENTER** to begin the restoration, and press **Y** to answer "Yes," that you want to continue. The restoration process will begin and Windows Vista will restart. The System Restore dialog box will appear, telling you that the restoration was successful. Click **OK**.

Get System Information

When you are working on a computer problem, you, or possibly a technical-support person working with you, will want some information about your computer. The two primary sources are basic computer information and advanced system information.

BASIC COMPUTER INFORMATION

Basic computer information provides general system information, such as the Windows edition, the processor and memory, and the computer name and workgroup (see Figure 5-15). To see the basic computer information:

Click **Start** and click **Control Panel**. In Control Panel Home view, click **System And Maintenance**, and click (double-click in Classic View) **System**. The System window will open. After you have reviewed the information, click **Close**.

ADVANCED SYSTEM INFORMATION

Advanced system information provides detailed system information and lets you look at services that are running, group policy settings, and the error log. To see the advanced system information:

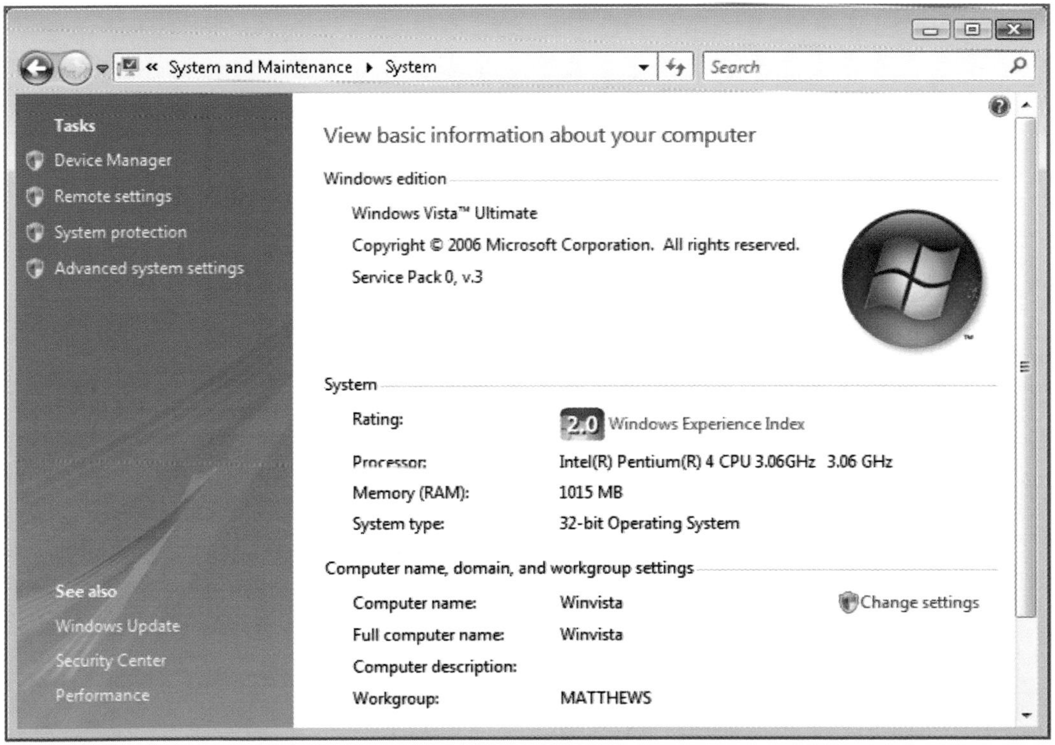

Figure 5-15: Basic computer information provides an overview of the computer and its operating system.

System Information

File Edit View Help

System Summary	
⊟ Hardware Resources	
Conflicts/Sharing	
DMA	
Forced Hardware	
I/O	
IRQs	
Memory	
⊟ Components	
⊞ Multimedia	
CD-ROM	
Sound Device	
Display	
Infrared	
⊞ Input	
Modem	
⊞ Network	
⊞ Ports	
⊞ Storage	
Printing	
Problem Devices	
USB	

Item	Value
OS Name	Microsoft® Windows Vista™ Ultimate
Version	6.0.5728 Service Pack 0, v.3 Build 5728
Other OS Description	Not Available
OS Manufacturer	Microsoft Corporation
System Name	WINVISTA
System Manufacturer	HP Pavilion 061
System Model	EL479AA-ABA a1221n
System Type	X86-based PC
Processor	Intel(R) Pentium(R) 4 CPU 3.06GHz, 3063
BIOS Version/Date	American Megatrends Inc. 3.26, 9/30/200
SMBIOS Version	2.4
Windows Directory	C:\Windows
System Directory	C:\Windows\system32
Boot Device	\Device\HarddiskVolume2
Locale	United States
Hardware Abstraction ...	Version = "6.0.5728.16387"
User Name	Winvista\Marty
Time Zone	Pacific Daylight Time
Total Physical Memory	1,014.75 MB
Available Physical Me...	595.26 MB

Find what: _____ [Find] [Close Find]

☐ Search selected category only ☐ Search category names only

*Figure 5-16: **Advanced system information provides a great depth of information useful in troubleshooting.***

📌 **NOTE**

See Chapter 1 for a discussion of the differences between shutting down a computer, putting it to sleep, and putting it in hibernation. The power settings put it to sleep.

Click **Start** and click **All Programs**. Click **Accessories**, click **System Tools**, and click **System Information**. The System Properties dialog box will appear. Click any of the topics in the left pane to display that information in the right pane. Figure 5-16 shows the summary-level information that is available. Click **Close** when you are done.

Set Power Options

Setting power options is important on laptop and notebook computers that run at least some of the time on batteries. It can also be useful on desktop computers to conserve power. The Windows Vista Power Options feature provides a number of settings that allow you to manage your computer's use of power.

1. Click **Start** and click **Control Panel**. In Control Panel Home view, click **System And Maintenance**, and click (double-click in Classic View) **Power Options**.

2. Choose one of the power plans, depending on whether you want to emphasize battery life (energy savings on desktops) or performance (see Figure 5-17).

3. To see a more detailed setting, click **Choose When To Turn Off The Display**. If you are using a laptop or notebook computer, your power options will look like those in Figure 5-18. (A desktop computer won't have the battery settings.)

4. Click each of the drop-down lists, and select the setting that is correct for you. If you would like to control individual pieces of hardware (disk drives, USB ports, and so on), click **Change Advanced Power Settings**, click the plus signs to open the lists, and click the spinners to adjust the values. Click **OK** when you are finished.

5. When you are ready, click **Save Changes** to accept the changes you have made to your power options settings.

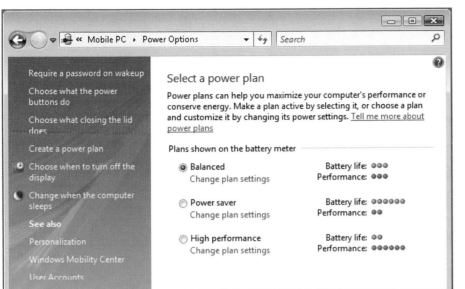

Figure 5-17: Windows Vista has three power plans that let you emphasize either battery life or performance.

Add and Remove Software

Today, almost all application and utility software comes in one of two ways: on a CD or DVD, or downloaded over the Internet.

INSTALL SOFTWARE FROM A CD

If you get software on a CD and your computer is less than seven years old, all you need to do is put the CD in the drive, wait for the install program to automatically load, and follow the displayed instructions, of which there are usually only a few. When the installation is complete, you may need to acknowledge that by clicking **OK** or **Finish**. Then remove the CD from its drive. That is all there is to it.

NOTE

In medium to larger organizations, application software might be available over the LAN (local area network) on a server. Generally, it is better to download the software and then do the installation from your computer than to do the installation over the network in case the network connection is lost during installation.

Change settings for the plan: Balanced

Choose the sleep and display settings that you want your computer to use.

	On battery	Plugged in
Turn off the display:	5 minutes	20 minutes
Put the computer to sleep:	15 minutes	1 hour

Change advanced power settings

Restore default settings for this plan

Save changes   Cancel

Figure 5-18: You can set the amount of idle time before the display and/or the computer are turned off or put to sleep, respectively.

5

TIP

If you are having trouble installing a program for no discernable reason, make sure you are logged on with administrative permissions. Some programs or installation situations require these permissions, and without them, the program refuses to install. See Chapter 8 to see how to establish and work with administrative permissions.

File Download - Security Warning

Do you want to run or save this file?

Name: Firefox Setup 1.5.0.7.exe
Type: Application, 4.88MB
From: ftp-mozilla.netscape.com

[Run]   [Save]   [Cancel]

While files from the Internet can be useful, this file type can potentially harm your computer. If you do not trust the source, do not run or save this software. What's the risk?

Figure 5-19: The File Download dialog box enables you to choose between saving and opening the downloaded file

TIP

Unless you are specifically told otherwise, always save a downloaded file to your hard disk and then, if a program-specific dialog box doesn't auromatically appear, allowing you to start the program, start it by double-clicking the file on your hard disk. That way, if there is a problem, you can restart it without having to download it a second time.

INSTALL SOFTWARE FROM THE INTERNET

To download and install a program from the Internet:

1. Click **Start** and click **Internet**. In the address bar, type the URL (uniform resource locator, also called the address) for the source of the download, and press **ENTER**.

2. Locate the link for the download, and click it. You may need to approve the downloading in Internet Explorer by clicking the bar at the top of the window and clicking **Download File**.

3. A dialog box, shown in Figure 5-19, will appear, asking if you want to run or save the program. Click **Save**. The Save As dialog box will appear and let you choose where you want to save the file. The desktop is a good place, at least initially, because you can easily double-click the program to start it. With the desktop or a folder you choose opened in the Save As dialog box, click **Save**.

4. When you are told the download is complete, click **Run**. If the program does not have a valid digital signature (many do not), decide if you want to continue and, if so, again click **Run**; otherwise, click **Don't Run**. User Account Control will also ask you if you are sure you want to go ahead. Click **Allow** if you do, or click **Cancel** if you don't.

5. When the installation is complete, you may be notified, the program may be started, Windows Explorer may be opened to show where the program is installed, and/or one or more shortcuts may be left on the desktop.

6. Close the Windows Explorer window and any other dialog boxes that are open.

REMOVE SOFTWARE

There are at least two ways to get rid of a program you have installed and one way not to do it. You do not want to just delete the program files in Windows Explorer. That leaves files in other locations and all the settings in the registry. To correctly remove a program, you need to use either the uninstall program that comes with many programs or Windows Vista's Add Or Remove Programs feature. To do the latter:

![Uninstall or change a program window]

Control Panel ▸ Programs and Features ▸ Search

Tasks

View installed updates

Get new programs online at Windows Marketplace

View purchased software (digital locker)

Turn Windows features on or off

Uninstall or change a program

To uninstall a program, select it from the list and then click "Uninstall", "Change", or "Repair".

Organize ∨ | Views ∨ | Uninstall/Change

Name	Publisher	Installed On	Size
Adobe Acrobat 8.0 Professional	Adobe Systems		954 MB
KPLU Broadband Player		6/29/2006	200 KB
Macromedia Flash Player 8	Macromedia	1/12/2006	
Microsoft Office Professional Plus 2007 ...		5/2/2006	469 MB
Quicken 2007	Intuit	6/26/2006	72.2 MB
Realtek High Definition Audio Driver		7/18/2006	
SnagIt 8	TechSmith Corp...	6/25/2006	20.2 MB

Macromedia Flash Player 8   Publisher: Macromedia
                                Product version: 8

Figure 5-20: Programs are removed through the Uninstall Or Change A Program feature.

NOTE

The "change" part of the Uninstall Or Change A Program window is used to install updates and patches to programs. It requires that you have either a CD with the changes or have downloaded them.

1. Click **Start** and click **Control Panel**. In Control Panel Home view, click **Programs** and click (double-click in Classic View) **Programs And Features**. The Uninstall Or Change A Program window will open, as you can see in Figure 5-20.

2. Click the program you want to uninstall, and click **Uninstall** on the toolbar. Follow the instructions as they are presented.

3. When the uninstall has successfully completed, close the Uninstall Or Change A Program window.

Add Hardware

Most hardware today is *Plug and Play*. That means that when you plug it in, Windows recognizes it and installs the necessary driver software automatically, and you can immediately begin using it. Often, when you first turn on the computer after installing the hardware, you see a message telling you that you have new hardware or that Windows is installing the device driver. Frequently, you need do nothing more; the installation will complete by itself. With other equipment, you must click the message for the installation to proceed. In either case, you are told when it has successfully completed.

Installing device driver software ✕
Click here for status.

Problems may occur when you have older hardware and the programs that run it, called *drivers*, are not included with Windows Vista. In that case, you will

Figure 5-21: For older hardware, you may need to locate driver software that will work with Windows Vista.

see a dialog box similar to Figure 5-21 saying you must locate the drivers. Here are some options for locating drivers:

- Let **Windows Vista** see what it can do by itself by clicking **Locate And Install Driver Software** in the Found New Hardware dialog box. It will scan your computer and see what it can find. The original dialog box appears only because a driver wasn't in the standard Windows Vista driver folder. It may well be in other locations.

- **Microsoft** has drivers for the most popular and recent devices and, as a part of Windows Update (discussed earlier in this chapter), the ability to scan your system and see if it has any drivers to help you. The first step is to look at Windows Update by clicking **Start**, clicking **All Programs**, and clicking **Windows Update**. Click **Check For Updates** in the upper-left area, and see if a driver for your device is found.

- The **manufacturer** of the device is generally a good source, but as hardware gets older, manufacturers stop writing new drivers for more recent operating systems. The easiest way to look for manufacturer support is on the Internet. If you know the manufacturer's Web site, you can enter it; or you may have to search for it. If you must search, start out by typing the manufacturer's name in the Internet Explorer address bar. This uses Windows Live search and gives you a list of sites.

- **Third-party** sources can be found using search engines like Google (http://www .google.com) and searching for "device drivers." You should find a number of sources, as you can see in Figure 5-22. Some of these sources charge you for the driver; others are free. Make sure the driver will work with Windows Vista.

Use Remote Assistance

Remote Assistance allows you to invite someone to remotely look at your computer and control it for purposes of assisting you. The other person must be using Windows Vista, Windows XP, Windows Server 2003, or Windows Server 2007, and it will be helpful if both of you have an email account. To use Remote Assistance, you must set it up, and then you can be either the requester or the helper.

NOTE

If you are using Windows Vista and want to use Remote Assistance with someone using Windows XP or Windows Server 2003, you must be on the receiving end of the assistance and you cannot use Windows Vista's Pause feature. Also, the person using Windows XP/Server 2003 cannot use Start Talk for voice capability.

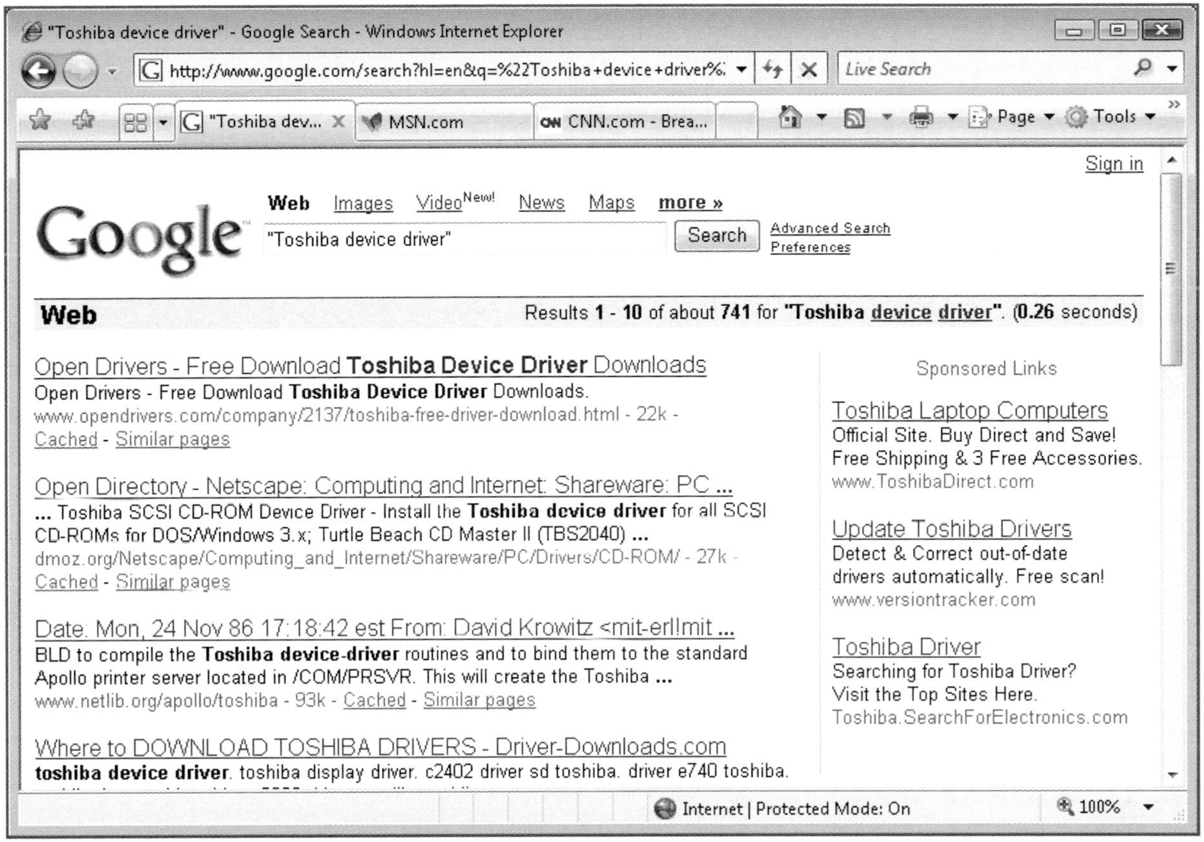

Figure 5-22: *Many device drivers can be found by searching the Internet, although you may have to pay for them.*

SET UP REMOTE ASSISTANCE

Although Remote Assistance is installed with Windows Vista, you must turn it on and set your firewall so that Windows Vista will allow it through. Both of these tasks are done in Control Panel.

1. Click **Start** and click **Control Panel**. In Control Panel Home view, click **System And Maintenance**, click (double-click in Classic View) **System**, and click **Remote Settings** in the left pane. The System Properties dialog box will appear with the Remote tab displayed (see Figure 5-23).

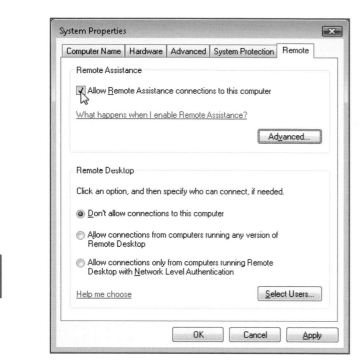

Figure 5-23: *Before using Remote Assistance, it must be turned on.*

NOTE

Remote Desktop, which is discussed in Chapter 10, is different from Remote Assistance, even though it is on the same Remote tab of the System Properties dialog box. Remote Desktop lets you sit at home and log on and use your computer at work as though you were sitting in front of it.

2. Click **Allow Remote Assistance Connections To This Computer** so it is checked, and click **Advanced**.

3. Determine if you want a person to control your computer, and click the **Remote Control** check box accordingly. Set the time an invitation for Remote Assistance is to remain open.

4. Click **OK** twice to close the two open dialog boxes. In Control Panel, click **Control Panel** in the address bar, click **Security**, and click **Windows Firewall**.

5. Click **Change Settings**. The Windows Firewall Settings dialog box will appear and should show that you have your firewall turned on (see Chapter 8).

6. Click the **Exceptions** tab, scroll through the Program Or Port list until you see Remote Assistance, and click it, if it isn't already checked (see Figure 5-24).

7. Click **OK** to close the dialog box, close the Windows Firewall window, and then close Control Panel.

REQUEST REMOTE ASSISTANCE

To use Remote Assistance, first find someone willing to provide it and request the assistance through e-mail. Besides the obvious invitation text, the request for assistance message will include a password to access your computer and the

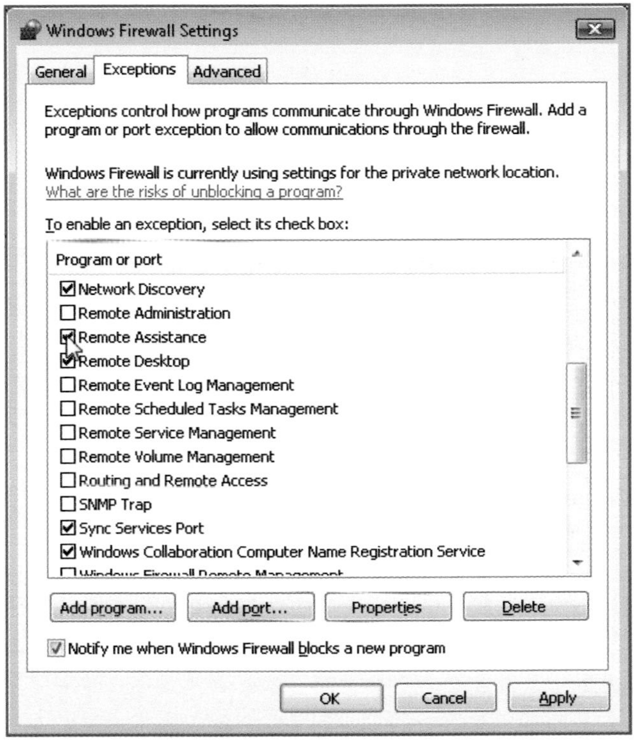

Figure 5-24: *Before you can use Remote Assistance, you must make sure that your firewall will let it through.*

TIP

There is also an e-mail option of using Web-based e-mail, where you save an invitation as a file, open a Web-based e-mail program (such as Google's gmail), and send the invitation as an attachment.

---

code to allow the encryption of information to be sent back and forth. To begin a Remote Assistance session:

1. Click **Start**, click **All Programs**, click **Maintenance**, and click **Windows Remote Assistance** to open the Windows Remote Assistance dialog box.

2. Click **Invite Someone You Trust To Help You** using an e-mail program. If you don't have an e-mail connection you can save the invitation as a file and transfer it via a CD or USB flash drive. Click your choice.

3. Type and retype a password at least six characters long that will be used by the person assisting you, and click **Next**. Your e-mail program will open and display a message to be sent to the person from whom you want assistance, as shown in Figure 5-25.

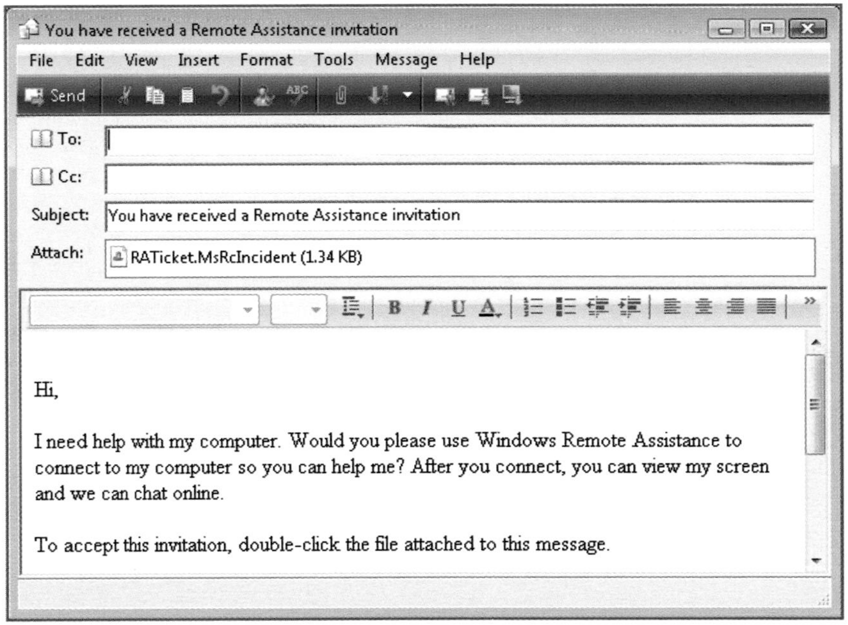

Figure 5-25: *You need to send an invitation that asks a person for assistance and gives him or her the means to communicate in an encrypted manner.*

In addition to sending a person an invitation to give you remote assistance, you must separately give him or her a password to access your computer.

4. Fill in the address of the person to whom you want to send the invitation, add any personal message you want, and click **Send**.

5. Upon sending your invitation, the Remote Assistance window opens. In a separate e-mail or on the phone, tell the other person the password. You might even be a little cryptic, for example, say, "The password is your golf score last week followed by my golf score."

Windows Remote Assistance

Waiting for incoming connection...

Cancel   Stop sharing   Pause   Settings   Chat   Send file   Help

6. When the other person accepts your invitation, you will see a message asking if you would like that person to connect to your computer. If you do, click **Yes**.

7. Click **Chat**, click in the text box at the bottom, and type a message to the other person, who can see anything on your computer (see "Provide Remote Assistance," next). Click **Send**.

Windows Remote Assistance

Would you like to allow Marty to connect to your computer?

After connecting, Marty will be able to see whatever is on your desktop.

Yes   No

What are the privacy and security concerns?

8. If the other person requests control of your computer, you'll see a message asking if that is what you want. If you do, click the check box, and then click **Yes**. If you become uncomfortable, you can click **Stop Sharing** or press ESC at any time.

Windows Remote Assistance

Would you like to allow Marty to share control of your desktop?

To stop sharing control, in the Remote Assistance dialog box, click Stop sharing or press ESC.

☐ Allow Marty to respond to User Account Control prompts

Yes   No

What are the privacy and security concerns?

9. To end the session, send a message to that effect, click **Disconnect**, click **Yes** to confirm that you want to disconnect, and close the Remote Assistance window.

PROVIDE REMOTE ASSISTANCE

If you want to provide remote assistance:

1. Upon receiving a request-for-assistance e-mail (see Figure 5-26), drag the attached invitation to the desktop.

Invitation

2. Double-click your invitation. Enter the password you have been given, and, if the other person approves, you are shown his or her screen and can request control of the other person's computer. You can view the screen in its actual size or scale it to fit on your screen, as shown in Figure 5-27.

3. To request control of the other computer, click **Request Control**. Click **Stop Sharing** to give up control.

4. Click **Disconnect** to end the session, and click **Close** to close the Remote Assistance window.

NOTE

You are protected from misuse of Remote Assistance in five ways: Without an invitation, the person giving assistance cannot access your computer; you can limit both the time the invitation remains open and the time the person can be on your computer; you can determine whether the person can control your computer or just look at it; you can click **Stop Sharing**, press **ESC**, or press any key sequence that includes **ESC** at any time to immediately terminate the other person's control; and you can click the **Disconnect** button to instantly disconnect the other person.

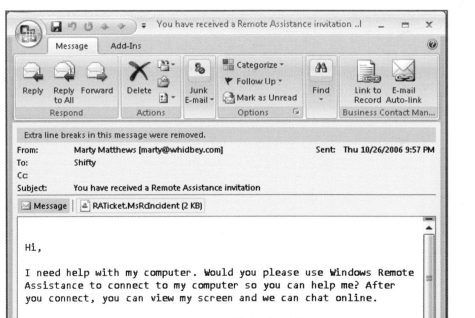

Figure 5-26: The invitation explains
to the helper how they can connect to
and help you.

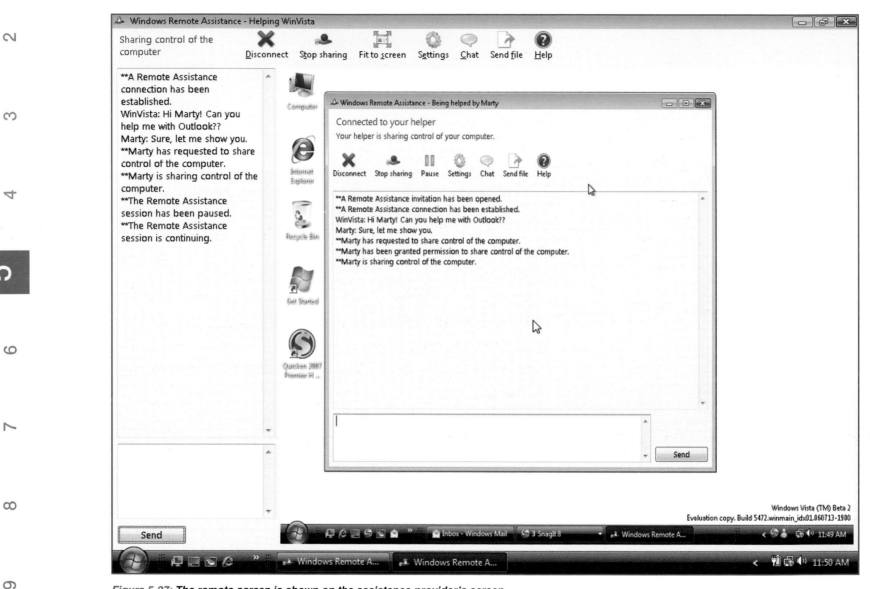

Figure 5-27: The remote screen is shown on the assistance provider's screen.

How to...

- Acquiring a Document
- Create a Picture
- Install Cameras and Scanners
- Scan Pictures
- Import Camera Images
- Work with Photo Gallery Pictures
- Viewing Other Pictures
- Install a Printer
- Printing
- Print Pictures
- Print to a File
- Print Web Pages
- Configure a Printer
- Control Printing
- Handling Fonts
- Set Up Faxing
- Send and Receive Faxes
- Create a Fax Cover Page

Chapter 6
Working with Documents and Pictures

In this chapter you will discover many aspects of creating documents and pictures, as well as how to install and use printers with documents and pictures. You will also learn how to set up and use the Windows fax capability with documents and pictures.

Create Documents and Pictures

Creating documents and pictures is primarily done with programs outside of Windows Vista, although Windows has simple programs to do it. Windows Vista also has facilities to bring documents and pictures in from other computers, from the Internet, and from scanners and cameras.

NOTE

As in other chapters, in the steps here you may be interrupted and asked by User Account Control (UAC) for permission to continue. So long as it is something you started, then you want to click **Continue** or enter a password. To simplify the instructions in this chapter, the UAC instructions have been left out. Chapter 8 discusses UAC in more detail.

UICKSTEPS

ACQUIRING A DOCUMENT

The documents in your computer got there because they were created with a program on your computer, or they were brought to the computer on a disk, transferred over a local area network (LAN), or downloaded from the Internet.

CREATE A DOCUMENT WITH A PROGRAM

To create a document with a program:

1. Start the program. For example, start Microsoft Word by clicking **Start**, clicking **All Programs**, clicking **Microsoft Office**, and clicking **Microsoft Office Word**.

2. Create the document using the facilities in the program. In Word, for example, type the document and format it using Word's formatting tools.

3. Save the document by (again, in Word), clicking the **Office Button**. Then click **Save As**, if needed, click **Browse Folders** and select the disk drive and folder in which to store the document, enter a file name, and click **Save**, as shown in Figure 6-1.

4. Close the program used to create the file.

Continued . . .

Figure 6-1: *Most document-creation programs let you choose where you want to save the files you create.*

Create a Picture

Pictures are really just documents that contain an image. They can be created or brought into your computer in the same way as any other document (see the "Acquiring a Document" QuickSteps). For example, to create and save a picture in Microsoft Paint:

1. Click **Start**, click **All Programs**, click **Accessories**, and click **Paint**.

2. Create the picture using the tools in Paint. For example, click the **Pencil** tool, choose a color, and create the drawing.

3. Save the document by clicking the **File** menu. Then click **Save As**, select the disk drive and folder in which to store the document, enter a file name, select a graphic file format, and click **Save**. Close Paint.

(Save As dialog box shown in figure:)

Save As

Marty ▸ Documents ▸   Search

Organize ▾   Views ▾   New Folder

Favorite Links

Name	Date modif...	Type	Size	Tags
Templates	2007 Budget			
Desktop	Fax			
Computer	Proposals			
Documents	Scanned Documents			
More ≫	SnagIt Catalog			
	Trips			

Folders

File name: Johnston Study Proposal

Save as type: Word Document

Authors: Marty   Tags: Add a tag

☐ Save Thumbnail

Hide Folders   Tools ▾   Open   Cancel

ACQUIRING A DOCUMENT (Continued)

BRING IN A DOCUMENT FROM A DISK

Use Windows Explorer to bring in a document from a disk or other removable storage device.

1. Click **Start** and click **Computer**.

2. Double-click the drive from which you want to retrieve a document (this could be another hard drive, floppy disk, CD, DVD, flash drive, or other device), and double-click to open any necessary folders to locate the document file and display it in the subject (or middle) pane (assuming your Windows Explorer window displays a three-pane view: navigation, subject, and preview).

3. Drag **Folders** to the top of the navigation pane. In the Folders list, display (but do not select or open) the drive and folder(s) in which you want to store the file by clicking their respective triangles on the left.

4. Drag the document file to the displayed folder, as illustrated in Figure 6-2. When you are done, close Windows Explorer.

DOWNLOAD A DOCUMENT ACROSS A NETWORK

Use Windows Explorer to bring in a document from another computer on your network.

1. Click **Start** and click **Network**.

2. Double-click the other computer from which you want the document, and double-click to open any necessary drives, folders, and subfolders to locate the document file.

Continued . . .

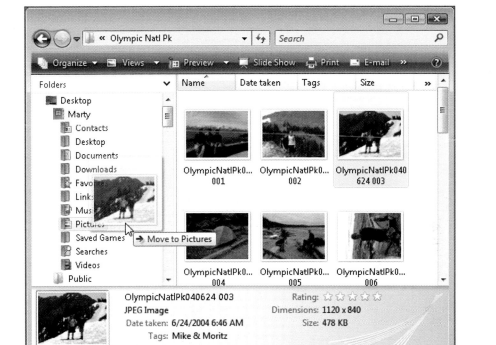

Figure 6-2: **You can drag a document file from either a disk on your computer or from another computer on your network.**

Install Cameras and Scanners

Installing cameras and scanners depends a lot on the device—whether it is Plug and Play (you plug it in and it starts to function), what type of connection it has, and so on. Most recent cameras and scanners are Plug and Play devices. To use them:

1. Plug the device into the computer, and turn it on. If it is Plug and Play, the first time you plug it in, you will see a message that a device driver is being installed and then that it is ready to use. Finally an AutoPlay dialog box may appear and allow you to choose what you want to do. If this happens for you and you plugged in a scanner, skip to "Scan Pictures" later in this chapter. If you plugged in a camera, skip to "Import Camera Images," also later in this chapter. Otherwise, continue to step 2.

⏰ QUICKSTEPS

ACQUIRING A DOCUMENT (Continued)

3. Drag **Folders** to the top of the navigation pane. In the Folders list, display (but do not select or open) the drive and folder(s) in which you want to store the file by clicking their respective triangles on the left.

4. Drag the document file to the displayed folder. When you are done, close Windows Explorer.

DOWNLOAD A DOCUMENT FROM THE INTERNET

Use your Internet browser to bring in a document from a site on the Internet.

1. Click **Start** and click **Internet**.

2. Type an address, search, or browse to a site and page from which you can download the document file.

3. Use the links and tools on the Web site to select and begin the file download. For example, right-click a picture and click **Save Picture As**.

4. In the Save As dialog box, use Folders in the navigation pane to select the disk and open the folder(s) in which you want to store the file on your computer.

5. Complete the download. When you are done, close your browser.

2. Click **Start** and click **Control Panel**. In Control Panel Home, click **Hardware And Sound**, and click (double-click in Classic view) **Scanners And Cameras**. If you see your device, installation is complete, as shown in Figure 6-3, and you can skip the remainder of these steps.

3. Click **Add Device**. The Scanner And Camera Installation Wizard opens. Click **Next**. Scroll through the manufacturer and model lists, and see if your device is there. If so, select it and click **Next**. Confirm the name you want to use, click **Next**, and then click **Finish** to complete the installation.

4. If you don't see your device on the lists and you have a disk that came with it, place the disk in its drive, and click **Have Disk**. If a driver appears, complete the installation and close the Scanner And Camera Installation Wizard. If you cannot find the driver, close the Scanner And Camera Installation Wizard, and use the manufacturer's installation program on the disk.

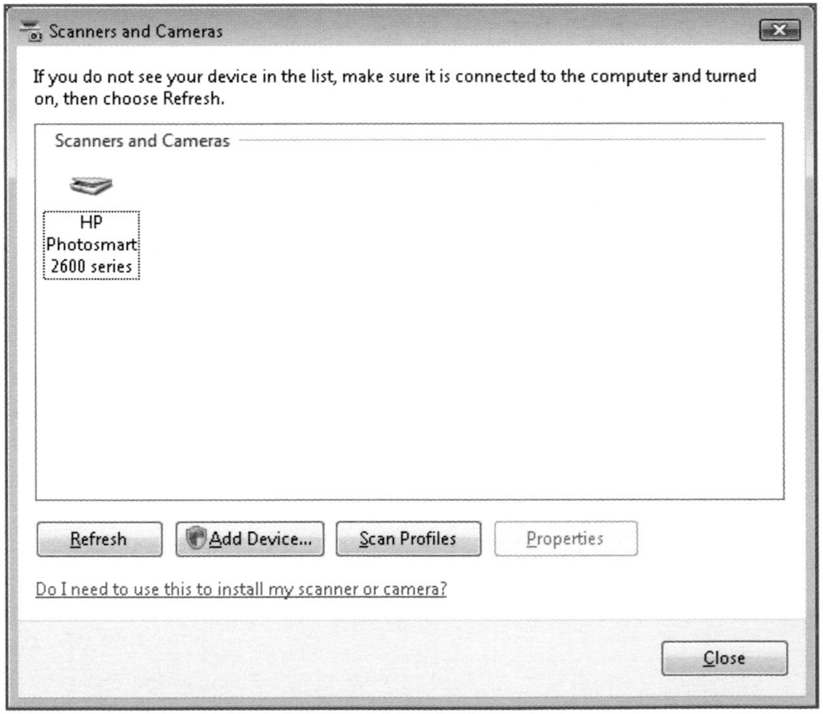

Figure 6-3: **Most recent Plug and Play cameras and scanners are automatically found and installed.**

NOTE

Windows Fax And Scan, used in Windows to operate a scanner or a fax, is only available with the Business, Enterprise, and Ultimate editions of Windows Vista. In other editions, you can still do scanning and faxing with the software that came with your scanners and faxes.

TIP

The scanning software in Windows may or may not be superior to the software that comes with your scanner.

Scan Pictures

Scanners allow you to take printed images and convert them to digital images on your computer. The scanner must first be installed, as described in "Install Cameras and Scanners" earlier in this chapter. If you ended up using the manufacturer's software to install the scanner, then you also need to use it to scan images. If you used Windows to install the scanner, then use the following steps to scan an image.

1. Turn on your scanner, and place what you want to scan onto the scanning surface.
2. Click **Start**, click **All Programs**, and click **Windows Fax And Scan**. The Windows Fax And Scan window opens.
3. Click **New Scan** on the toolbar. The New Scan dialog box appears. The scanner you installed should be displayed in the upper-left area. Change the scanner if you wish.
4. Choose the color, file type, and resolution you want to use, and click **Preview**. The image in the scanner will appear in the dialog box.
5. Adjust the margins around the page by dragging the dashed lines on the four sides, as shown in Figure 6-4. When you are ready, click **Scan**.
6. The scanned image will appear in the Windows Fax And Scan window (see Figure 6-5). Select the image in the list at the top of the window and, using the toolbar, choose to:
   - **Forward As Fax** using the Windows fax capability described later in this chapter
   - **Forward As E-mail** using your default e-mail application
   - **Save As** using Windows Explorer to save the image as a file on one of the storages devices available to you

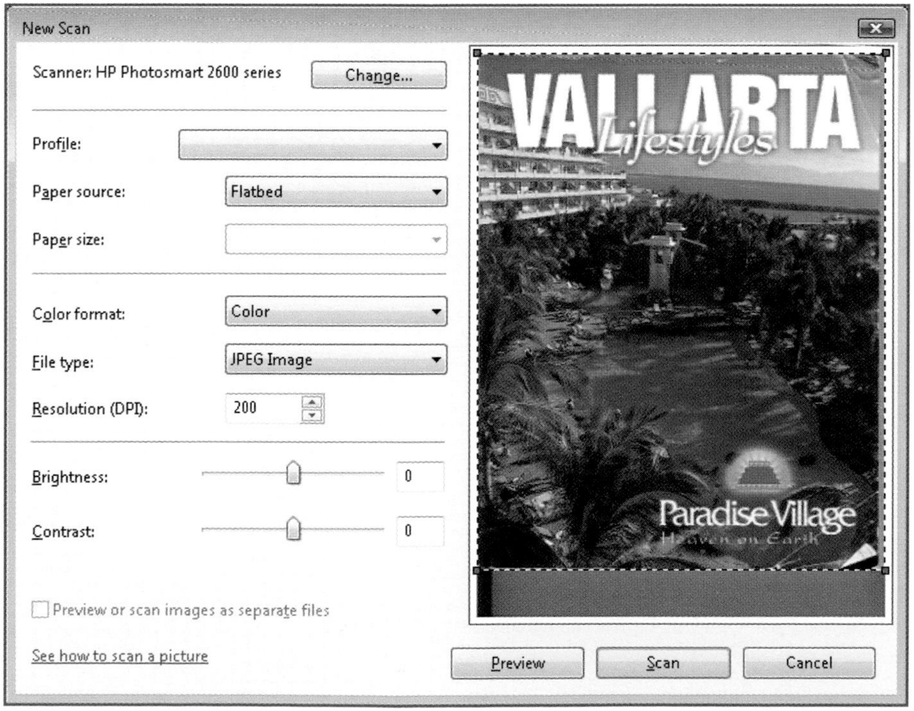

Figure 6-4: ***In the Windows Vista scanning software you can change a number of the parameters including the margins of what to include, and see the results in the preview pane.***

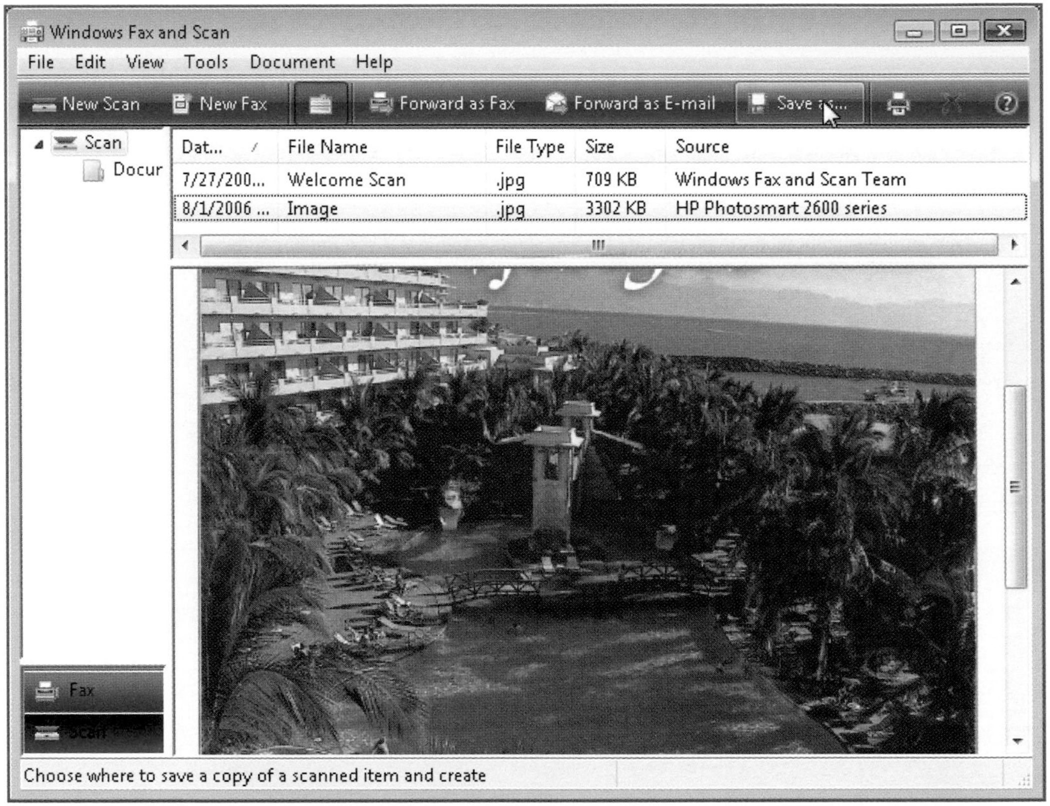
Windows Fax and Scan
File Edit View Tools Document Help
New Scan
New Fax
Forward as Fax
Forward as E-mail
Save as...
Scan
Docur
Dat...
File Name
File Type
Size
Source
7/27/200...
Welcome Scan
.jpg
709 KB
Windows Fax and Scan Team
8/1/2006 ...
Image
.jpg
3302 KB
HP Photosmart 2600 series
Fax
Scan
Choose where to save a copy of a scanned item and create

Figure 6-5: ***Images that you scan can be faxed, e-mailed, saved, and printed.***

- **Print** using a printer available to you
- **Delete** the image

7. Work through the related dialog box(es) that appear to complete the scanning process. When you are ready, close the Windows Fax And Scan window.

TIP

Documents that you scan into your computer are automatically saved in Documents\Scanned Documents.

Import Camera Images

When most digital cameras are plugged into the computer, turned on, and installed (see "Install Cameras and Scanners" earlier in this chapter), the

AutoPlay dialog box should automatically appear, calling the camera a removable disk and asking if you want to:

- **Import Pictures**, in essence, copying them to your hard disk
- **View Pictures** in your camera using Windows Photo Gallery Viewer
- **View Pictures** in your camera using Windows Media Center
- **Open Folder To View Files** to look at your camera as if it were a disk and the pictures as files using Windows Explorer

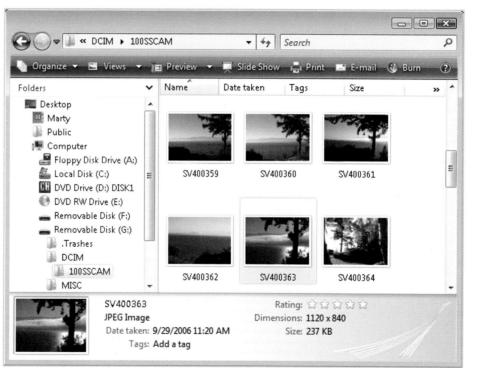

NOTE

If the AutoPlay dialog box didn't appear, click **Start**, click **Computer**, click **Removable Disk** (if you have more than one of them, it would be the most recent one), and open the necessary folders to see images of your pictures in your camera.

Click **Import Pictures**. The Importing Pictures And Videos dialog box should appear. Type a tag to add to the file name of all the pictures (the date is already a part of the name), and click **Import**. You will see each of the pictures as they are imported. When the process is completed, the Windows Photo Gallery will open and show thumbnails of the pictures, as you can see in Figure 6-6.

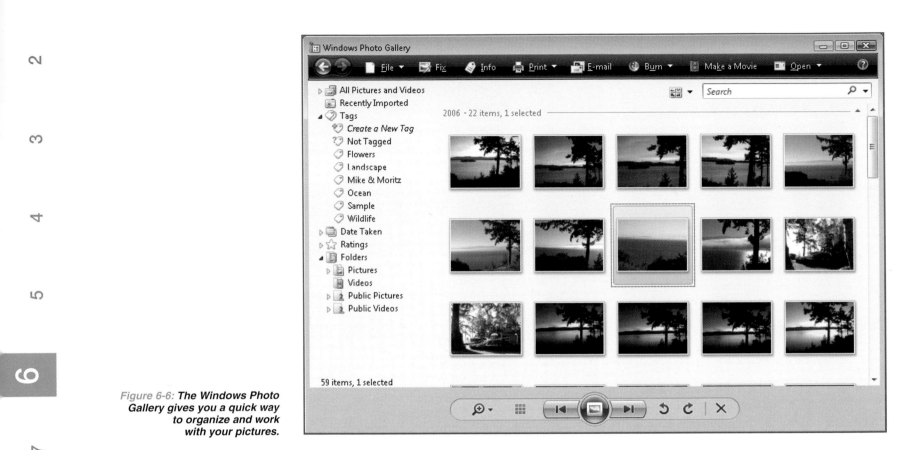

Figure 6-6: *The Windows Photo Gallery gives you a quick way to organize and work with your pictures.*

Work with Photo Gallery Pictures

Once you have brought pictures into your computer from a camera, a scanner, an Internet download, or a removable disk, you can look at them on your computer screen. Assuming that you brought your pictures into Photo Gallery as discussed in "Import Camera Images" or "Scan Pictures" earlier in this chapter:

1. Click **Start**, click **All Programs**, and click **Windows Photo Gallery**. The Windows Photo Gallery should open.

2. Select the tag you assigned or date your pictures were taken to open the category that contains them, as was shown in Figure 6-6.

SV400351.JPG   9/25/2006 1:44 PM
Not Rated   239 KB (1120 × 840)

3. Hover your mouse over a picture to see an enlarged image.

4. To see an even larger image, double-click its thumbnail. The image will take over the Photo Gallery window, similar to what is shown in Figure 6-7. The controls at the bottom of the window allow you to cycle through a number of pictures and work with them, as shown in Figure 6-7.

5. If you have several pictures you want to view, click the right and left arrows on the bottom of the window to go through them sequentially. You can also use the other controls at the bottom of the window or in the menus at the top to perform their stated functions.

6. When you are done, close the Windows Photo Gallery.

*Figure 6-7: **The Photo Gallery single-image window offers a great way to see a set of pictures on your computer.***

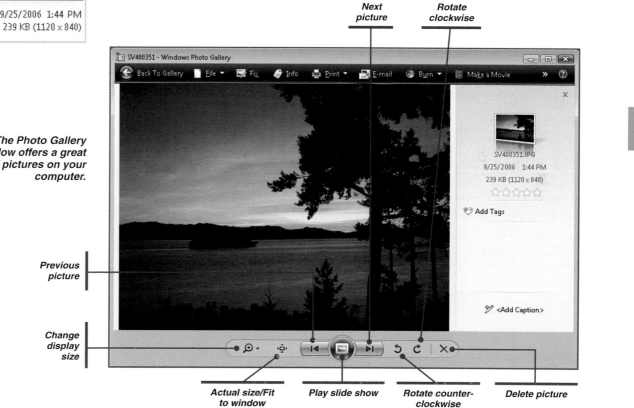

If your pictures are not in the Photo Gallery, to locate and view them:

1. Click **Start**, click **Computer**, and open the drive and folders necessary to locate your pictures.

2. Click the **Views** menu down arrow, and click **Large Icons**; or adjust the slider so that you can adequately see the thumbnail images.

3. Double-click the picture you want to view in a larger size. The Photo Gallery Viewer will open and display the picture. From here, you can work with the picture, including adding it to the gallery, as described in "Work with Photo Gallery Pictures" elsewhere in this chapter.

NOTE

Some versions of Windows XP and earlier versions of Windows have a Printers And Faxes option on the Start menu. In Windows Vista, it isn't there by default, but printers can be added through the Customize Start Menu dialog box, as discussed in Chapter 2.

NOTE

Some laptop computer and printer combinations are connected through an infrared beam or other wireless connections. In this case, "plugging the printer into the computer" means to establish that wireless connection.

Print Documents and Pictures

It is important to be able to install and fully use printers so that you can transfer your digital documents to paper.

Install a Printer

All printers are either automatically installed or done so using the Printers window. Because there are differences in how the installation is done, look at the sections in this chapter on installing local Plug and Play printers, installing other local printers, installing network printers, and selecting a default printer. Also, if you are installing a local printer, first consider the following checklist.

CHECKLIST TO USE PRIOR TO INSTALLING A PRINTER

A local printer is one that is attached to your computer with a cable or wireless connection. Make sure that your printer meets the following conditions *before* you begin to install:

- It is plugged into the correct port on your computer (see manufacturer's instructions).
- It is plugged into an electrical outlet.
- It has fresh ink, toner, or ribbon, which, along with the print heads, is properly installed.
- It has adequate paper.

INSTALL A LOCAL PLUG AND PLAY PRINTER

Installing Plug and Play printers is supposed to be fairly automatic, and, for the most part, it is.

1. With your computer and printer turned off, connect the devices to each other. Then make sure the other points in the above checklist are satisfied.

2. Turn on your computer, let it fully boot, and then turn on your printer. Your computer should find and automatically install the new printer and give you messages to that effect.

3. Click **Start**, click **Control Panel**, and, in Control Panel Home, click **Printer** under Hardware And Sound; or, in Classic view, double-click **Printers**. The Printers window should open, and you should see your new printer. Select that printer and leave the

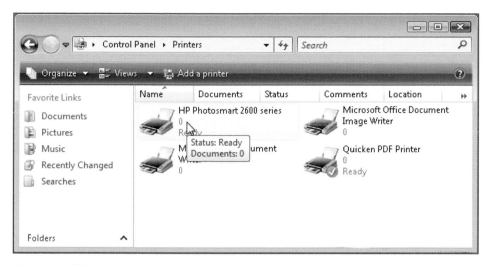

mouse pointer there. You should see "Status: Ready," as shown in Figure 6-8. (If you don't see your printer, it was not installed. Go to the next section.)

4. Right-click the new printer, click **Properties**, and click **Print Test Page**. If the test page prints satisfactorily, click **Close**. Otherwise, click **Troubleshoot Printer Problems**, follow the suggestions, and close the Help window when you are done. When you are ready, click **OK** to close the printer properties dialog box.

5. If you want the new printer to be the default printer used by all applications on the computer, right-click the printer and click **Set As Default Printer**.

6. Close the Printers and Control Panel windows.

Figure 6-8: **When you connect a Plug and Play printer, it should be recognized by the computer and automatically installed.**

INSTALL MANUALLY LOCAL PRINTER

If a printer isn't automatically installed in the process of using steps 1 through 3 above, you must install it manually.

1. If a CD came with your printer, providing it says that it is for Windows Vista, place that CD in the drive, and follow the on-screen instructions to install the printer. When this is complete, go up to step 3 in "Install a Local Plug and Play Printer," and determine if the printer will print a test page. If so, skip to step 7.

2. If you don't have a manufacturer's CD, click **Start**, click **Control Panel**, and, in Control Panel Home, click **Printer** under Hardware And Sound; or, in Classic view, double-click **Printers**. The Printers window should open.

3. Click **Add A Printer** on the toolbar, and click **Add A Local Printer**.

4. Click **Use An Existing Port:**, open the drop-down list, and select the correct port (on newer printers, it is probably USB 1; on the majority of other printers, it is LPT1), and click **Next**.

Choose a printer port

A printer port is a type of connection that allows your computer to exchange information with a printer.

◉ Use an existing port: LPT1: (Printer Port)

◯ Create a new port:
    Type of port: Local Port

TIP

If your printer was automatically installed, but a CD came with your printer and you wonder if you should install using the CD, the general answer is no. Most printer drivers in Windows Vista originally came from the manufacturers and have been tested by Microsoft, so they should work well. Unless the printer came out after the release of Windows Vista (November 2006), the driver in Vista should be newer.

5. Select the manufacturer and model of the printer you want to install (see Figure 6-9). If you can't find your printer, click **Windows Update** to download the latest printer drivers. Then, once more, search for the manufacturer and model. When you find the correct printer, click **Next**.

6. Confirm or change the printer name, and choose whether you want this printer to be your default printer. Click **Next**.

7. Click **Print A Test Page**. If the test page prints satisfactorily, click **Close**. Otherwise, click **Troubleshoot Printer Problems**, follow the suggestions, and close the Help window when you are done. When you are ready, click **Finish** to close the Add Printer dialog box and close the Printers window.

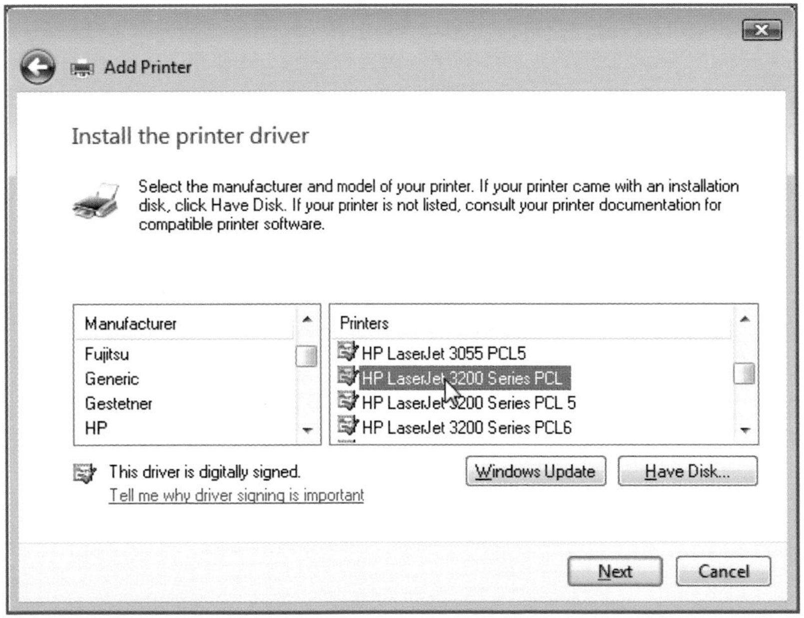

INSTALL A NETWORK PRINTER

Network printers are not directly connected to your computer, but are available to you as a result of your computer's connection to a network and the fact that the printers have been shared. There are three types of network printers:

- Printers connected to someone else's computer, which are shared
- Printers connected to a dedicated printer server, which are shared
- Printers directly connected to a network (which, in effect, have a built-in computer)

The first two types of network printers are installed with the Network Printer option in the Add Printer dialog box and will be described here. The third option is installed with the Local Printer option, often automatically.

1. Click **Start**, click **Control Panel**, and, in Control Panel Home, click **Printer** under Hardware And Sound; in Classic view, double-click **Printers**. The Printers window should open.

2. Click **Add A Printer** on the toolbar, and click **Add A Network, Wireless Or Bluetooth Printer**. Windows will search for network printers.

3. Scroll through the printers to locate the one you want. Click that printer and click **Next**.

Figure 6-9: *Manually installing a printer requires that you know some facts about the printer.*

4. If the search did not find the network printer you were looking for, click **The Printer That I Want Isn't Listed**. Click **Browse For A Printer**, and click **Next**. Click the triangle on the computer to which the printer is attached, click the printer (as shown in Figure 6-10), and click **OK**.

5. You are warned that you are about to be connected to a printer on another computer and that its driver will be installed on your computer and might contain a virus. Decide if you want to take this probably small risk, and click **Yes** or **No**.

6. Adjust the name of the printer if you want, select if you want to make this your default printer, and click **Next**. Click **Print A Test Page**. If the test page prints satisfactorily, click **Close**. Otherwise, click **Troubleshoot Printer Problems**, follow the suggestions, and close the Help window when you are done. When you are ready, click **Finish** to close the Add Printer dialog box and close the Printers window.

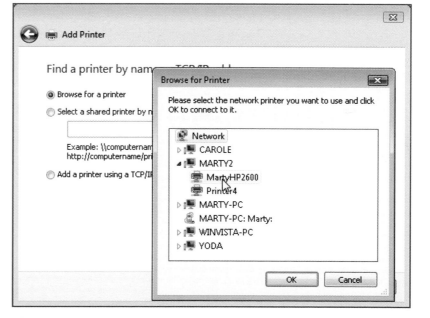

*Figure 6-10: **Printers on another computer must be shared by that computer before you can use it.***

PRINTING

Most printing is done from a program. Using Microsoft Office Word 2007, whose Print dialog box is shown in Figure 6-11, as an example:

PRINT DOCUMENTS

To print the document currently open in Word:

Click **Quick Print** on Word's Quick Access toolbar to immediately print using the default settings.

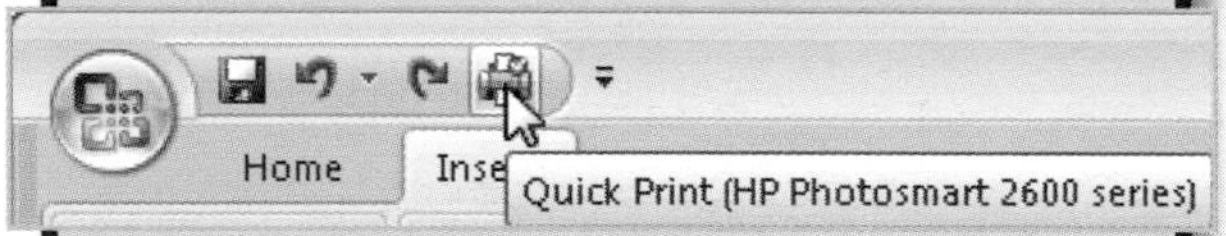

Home   Inse   Quick Print (HP Photosmart 2600 series)

CHOOSE A PRINTER

To choose which printer you want to use:

Click the **Office Button**, and click **Print** to open Word's Print dialog box shown in Figure 6-11. Open the printer **Name** drop-down list, and choose the printer you want.

DETERMINE SPECIFIC PAGES TO PRINT

In the Page Range section of the Print dialog box, you can select:

- **All** to print all pages
- **Current Page** to print only the currently selected page
- **Selection** to print the text that has been selected
- **Pages** to print a series of individual pages and/or a range of pages by specifying the individual pages separated by commas and specifying the range with a hyphen. For example: typing 4,6,8-10,12 will cause pages 4, 6, 8, 9, 10, and 12 to be printed.

IDENTIFY A DEFAULT PRINTER

If you have several printers available to you, one must be identified as your default printer—the one that will be used for printing whenever you don't select another one. To change your default printer:

1. Click **Start**, click **Control Panel**, and, in Control Panel Home, click **Printer** under Hardware And Sound; in Classic view, double-click **Printers**. The Printers window should open.

2. Right-click the printer you want to be the default, and click **Set As Default Printer**.

3. Close the Printers window when finished.

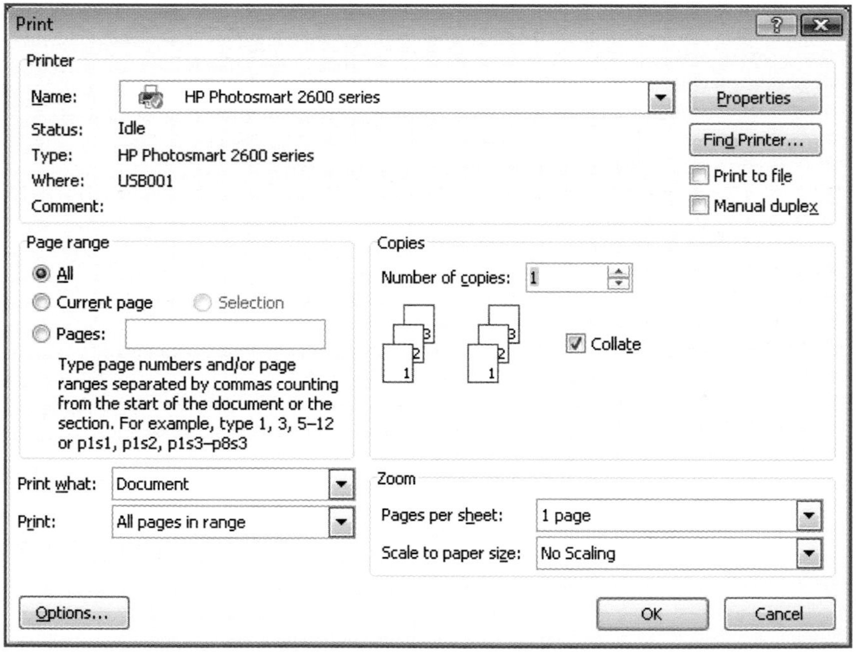

Figure 6-11: **The Microsoft Office Word 2007 Print dialog box is similar to those in other programs.**

TIP

If Quick Print isn't on your Quick Access toolbar, click the **Customize** down arrow to the right of the Quick Access toolbar and click **Quick Print**.

NOTE

You can print just the even or odd pages in a document by opening the **Print** drop-down list in the bottom-left of the Print dialog box and making the relevant selection.

SHARE A PRINTER

If you have a printer attached to your computer and you want to let others use that printer, you can share it.

1. In the Printers window, right-click the printer you want to share, and click **Sharing**. The printer's Properties dialog box will appear.

2. Click **Change Sharing Options**, click **Share This Printer**, enter a share name, and click **OK**.

3. Close the Printers window.

Print Pictures

Printing pictures from a program is exactly the same as described in the "Printing" QuickSteps. In addition, Windows has a Print Pictures dialog box used to print pictures from either Windows Explorer or the Picture Gallery.

1. Click **Start** and click **Pictures** to use Windows Explorer; or click **Start**, click **All Programs**, and click **Windows Photo Gallery** to use that program.

2. In either program, select the picture(s) you want to print. To select a contiguous set of pictures, click the first one, hold down **SHIFT**, and click the last picture. To select noncontiguous pictures, hold down **CTRL** while clicking the pictures you want.

3. Click **Print** on the toolbar. The Print Pictures dialog box will appear, as shown in Figure 6-12.

4. Select the printer, paper size, quality, paper type, number to print on a page, number of copies, and whether to fit the picture to a frame. You can also click **Options** above the Cancel button to look at and possibly change several print settings. Click **OK** after looking at the options.

5. When you are ready, click **Print**. The pictures will be printed. When you are done, close Windows Explorer or Windows Photo Gallery, whichever you have open.

Print to a File

There are two primary reasons to print to a file: to have a file you can take to a remote printer, and to get information out of one program and into another. The first requires formatting the information for a printer and then sending it

1 2 3 4 5 6 7 8 9 10

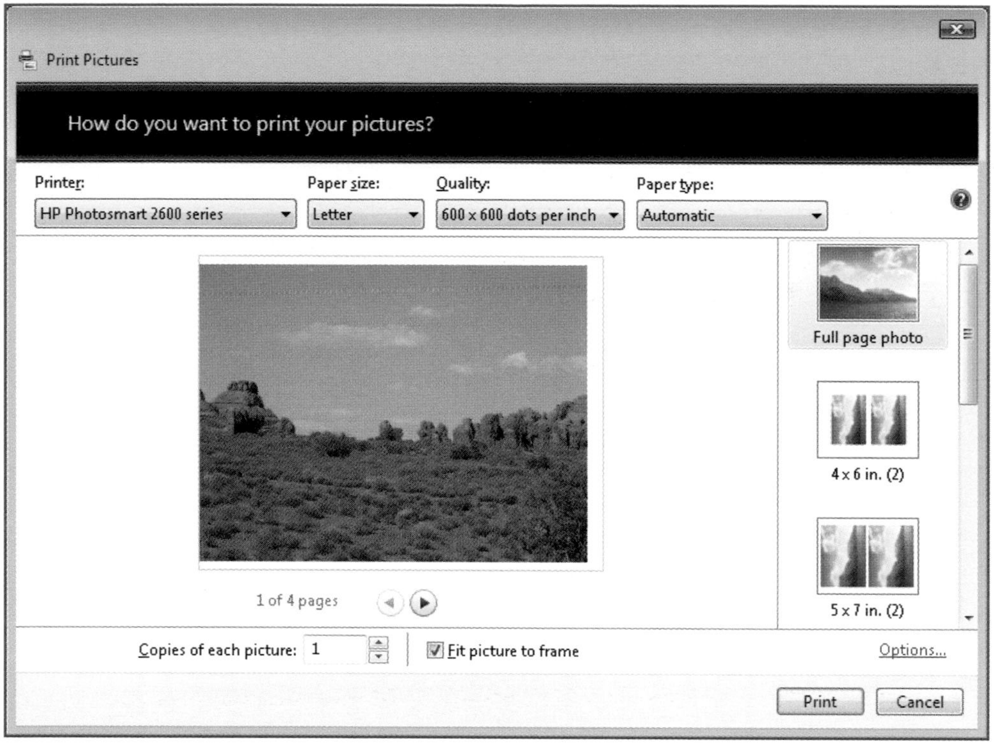

Print Pictures

How do you want to print your pictures?

Printer:	Paper size:	Quality:	Paper type:
HP Photosmart 2600 series	Letter	600 x 600 dots per inch	Automatic

Full page photo

4 x 6 in. (2)

5 x 7 in. (2)

1 of 4 pages

Copies of each picture: 1   ☑ Fit picture to frame   Options...

Print   Cancel

*Figure 6-12: **If you use high-quality photo paper and a newer color printer, you can get almost professional-grade pictures.***

to a file. The actual printer must be installed on your computer even though it is not physically connected to your computer. In the second case, you must create a "printer" to produce unformatted generic text. The following sections explain first how to create a text file printer and then how to print to a file.

CREATE A TEXT FILE PRINTER

1. Click **Start**, click **Control Panel**, and, in Control Panel Home, click **Printer** under Hardware And Sound; in Classic view, double-click **Printers**. The Printers window should open.

2. Click **Add A Printer** on the toolbar, and click **Add A Local Printer**. Click the **Use An Existing Port** down arrow, and click **File (Print To File)**.

3. Click **Next**. In the Install The Printer Driver dialog box, scroll down and click **Generic** as the manufacturer and **Generic/Text Only** as the printer.

Generic / Text Only
0
Ready

4. Click **Next**. Enter a name for the printer, and, if needed, click to uncheck **Set As The Default Printer** (assuming you, in fact, do not want to use print-to-file as your default). Click **Next**.

5. Skip printing a test page, and click **Finish**. A new icon will appear in your Printers window. Close the Printers window when you are done.

SELECT PRINT TO FILE

Whether you want to print to a file so that you can print on a remote printer or so that you can create a text file, the steps are same once you have created a text file printer.

1. In the program in which you are printing, click the **File** menu (or the **Office Button** in Microsoft Office 2007 programs), and click **Print**.

2. Select the ultimate printer or the generic text file printer, and click **Print To File**. Select the print range, number of copies, and other settings; and click **OK**. Select the folder, type the file name to use, and click **OK**.

Print Web Pages

Printing Web pages is little different from printing any other document.

1. Click **Start** and click **Internet** to open your browser (assumed to be Internet Explorer).

2. Browse to the page you want to print, and click the **Print** icon. Or, if you have turned on the menu bar, click the **File** menu, click **Print**, select the printer and other options, and again click **Print**.

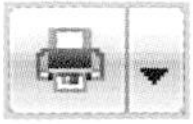

3. Close your Internet browser.

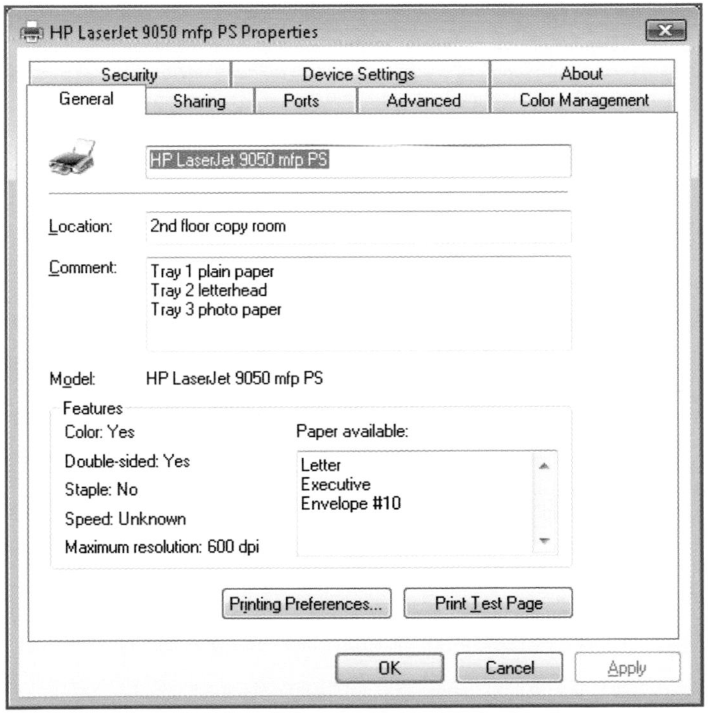

Configure a Printer

Configuration of a printer is usually done for special purposes and often isn't required. Nevertheless, all configuration is done from the printer's Properties dialog box.

1. Click **Start**, click **Control Panel**, and, in Control Panel Home, click **Printer** under Hardware And Sound; in Classic view, double-click **Printers**. The Printers window should open.

2. Right-click the printer you want to configure, and click **Properties**. The printer's Properties dialog box will appear.

On the General tab (shown in Figure 6-13), you can change the printer name, its location, and enter a comment. In the Ports tab, you can specify the port used by the printer, configure ports, and set up printer pooling. In the Device Settings tab, you can set what is loaded in each paper tray, how to handle font substitution, and what printer options are available (your printer may be different). Though most printer configurations are self-explanatory, several items are worthy of further discussion and are explained in the following sections.

Figure 6-13: **Printers, while having many settings, are often run without ever changing the default settings.**

ENABLE PRINTER POOLING

Printer pooling allows you to have two or more physical printing devices with the same print driver assigned to one printer. When print jobs are sent to the printer, Windows determines which of the physical devices is available and routes the job to that device.

1. In the Properties dialog box for the printer to which all work will be directed, click the **Ports** tab, and click **Enable Printer Pooling**.

2. Click each of the ports with a printing device that is to be in the pool. When all the ports are selected, click **OK** to close the Properties dialog box.

3. If the printer that contains the pool isn't already selected as the default printer, right-click the printer and click **Set As Default Printer**.

SET PRINTER PRIORITY

Assigning several printers to one printing device allows you to have two or more settings used with one device. If you want to have two or more priorities automatically assigned to jobs going to a printer, create two or more printers that all point to the same printer port but that have different priorities. Then have high-priority print jobs printed to a printer with a priority of 99 and low-priority jobs printed to a printer with a priority of 1.

1. Install all printers as previously described in "Install a Printer," all with the same port. Name each printer to indicate its priority, such as "High-Priority Printer" and "Low-Priority Printer."

2. In the Printers window, right-click the high-priority printer, and click **Properties**.

3. Click the **Advanced** tab, type a priority of 99, and click **OK**.

4. Similarly, right-click the other printers, open their Properties dialog boxes, click the **Advanced** tab, and set the priority, from 1 for the lowest priority to 98 for the second highest priority.

Jobs with the highest priority will print before jobs with a lower priority if they are in the *queue* (waiting to be printed) at the same time.

ASSIGN PAPER TRAYS

Some printers have more than one paper tray, and each tray can have different types or sizes of paper. If you assign types and sizes of paper to trays in the

TIP

If you have a program that automatically prints certain tasks, such as incoming orders, you might want to assign it a lower priority than a word-processing task, such as a new proposal.

HP LaserJet 9050 mfp PS Properties

General	Sharing	Ports	Advanced	Color Management
Security		Device Settings		About

HP LaserJet 9050 mfp PS Device Settings
- Form To Tray Assignment
  - Printer Auto Select: Letter
  - Manual Feed in Tray 1: Letter
  - Tray 1: Letter
  - Tray 2: Executive
  - Tray 3: Envelope #10
  - Tray 4: Letter
  - Tray 5: Letter
  - Tray 6: Letter
  - Tray 7: Letter
  - Tray 8: Letter
  - Tray 9: Letter
  - Ex Tray (MP5): Letter
  - Ex Tray (MP6): Letter
  - Ex Tray (MP7): Letter
  - Ex Tray (MP8): Letter

[OK] [Cancel] [Apply]

Figure 6-14: **You can set the paper type and size in each paper tray.**

NOTE

The Print Spooled Documents First check box, located below the spool options, is selected by default. Normally, you want to keep it that way.

printer's Properties dialog box and a user requests a type and size of paper when printing, Windows Vista automatically designates the correct paper tray for the print job.

1. In the Properties dialog box for the printer whose trays you want to assign, click the **Device Settings** tab.

2. Open each tray and select the type and size of paper in that tray, similar to what you see in Figure 6-14.

3. When you have set the paper type and size in each tray, click **OK**.

CONFIGURE SPOOL SETTINGS

The time it takes to print a document is normally longer than the time it takes to transfer the information to the printer. *Printer spooling* temporarily stores information on disk, allowing Windows to feed it to the printer as it can be handled. Under most circumstances, you want to use printer spooling and not tie up the program waiting for the printer. The printer's Properties Advanced tab lets you choose to spool or not and gives you two options if you spool.

- Spool print documents so program finishes printing faster
  - Start printing after last page is spooled
  - Start printing immediately
- Print directly to the printer

- **Start Printing After Last Page Is Spooled** waits to print until the last page is spooled, allowing the program to finish faster and the user to get back to the program faster, but it takes longer to finish printing.

- **Start Printing Immediately** allows printing to be done sooner, but the program will be tied up a little longer.

The default, Start Printing Immediately, provides a middle ground between getting the printing done and getting back to the program.

USE SEPARATOR PAGES

If you have several jobs on a printer, it might be helpful to have a separator page between them. A separator page can also be used to switch a printer between PostScript (a printer language) and PCL (Printer Control Language) on Hewlett-Packard (HP) and compatible printers. Four sample SEP separation files come with Windows Vista and are installed in the \Windows\System32\ folder:

- **Pcl.sep** prints a separation page before the start of each print job on PCL-compatible printers. If the printer handles both PostScript and PCL, it will be switched to PCL.
- **Pscript.sep** does *not* print a separation page, but printers with both PostScript and PCL will be switched to PostScript.
- **Sysprint.sep** prints a separation page before the start of each print job on PostScript-compatible printers.
- **Sysprtj.sep** is the same as Sysprint.sep, but in the Japanese language.

You can choose to have a separator page added at the beginning of each print job by clicking **Separator Page** on the Advanced tab of the Properties dialog box, browsing for and selecting the page you want, clicking **Open**, and clicking **OK** twice.

Separator Page dialog box:

Separator pages are used at the beginning of each document to make it easy to find a document among others at the printer.

Separator page: C:\Windows\System32\pcl.sep   Browse...

OK   Cancel

Control Printing

To control printing means to control the process as it is taking place, whether with one print job or with several in line. If several print jobs are spooled at close to the same time, they form a *print queue*, waiting for earlier jobs to finish. You may control printing in several ways, as described below. These tasks are handled in the printer's window, which is similar to that shown in Figure 6-15, and is opened by double-clicking the appropriate printer in the Printers window or by clicking the printer icon in the notification area of the taskbar.

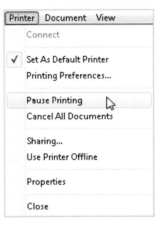

*Figure 6-15: **Controlling printing takes place in the printer's window and allows you to pause, resume, restart, and cancel printing.***

NOTE

You cannot change the order in which documents are being printed by pausing the current document that is printing. You must either complete printing the current document or cancel it. You can, however, use Pause to get around intermediate documents that are not currently printing. For example, suppose you want to immediately print the third document in the queue, but the first document is currently printing. You must either let the first document finish printing or cancel it. You can then pause the second document before it starts printing, and the third document will begin printing when the first document is out of the way.

PAUSE, RESUME, AND RESTART PRINTING

While printing, a situation may occur (such as needing to add toner) where you want to pause and then resume printing, either for one or for all documents:

- **Pause all documents:** In the printer's window, click the **Printer** menu and click **Pause Printing**. "Paused" will appear in the title bar, and, if you look in the Printer menu, you will see a check mark in front of Pause Printing.

- **Resume printing all documents:** In the printer's window, click **Printer** and click **Pause Printing**. "Paused" disappears from the title bar and the check mark disappears from the Pause Printing option in the Printer menu.

- **Pause a document:** In the printer's window, select the document or documents to pause, click **Document**, and click **Pause**. "Paused" will appear in the Status column of the document(s) you selected.

- **Resume printing a paused document where it left off:** In the printer's window, select the document, click **Document**, and click **Resume**. "Printing" will appear in the Status column of the document selected.

- **Restart printing at the beginning of a document:** In the printer's window, select the document, click **Document**, and click **Restart**. "Restarting" and then "Printing" will appear in the Status column.

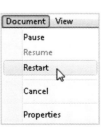

CANCEL PRINTING

Canceling printing can be done either at the printer level for all the jobs in the printer queue or at the document level for selected documents. A canceled job is deleted from the print queue and must be restarted by the original program:

- **Cancel a job:** In the printer's window, select the job or jobs that you want canceled. Click **Document** and click **Cancel**. Click **Cancel** a second time to confirm the cancellation. The job or jobs will disappear from the window and the queue.

- **Cancel all the jobs in the queue:** In the printer's window, click **Printer** and click **Cancel All Documents**. You are asked whether you are sure you want to cancel all documents. Click **Yes**. All jobs will disappear from the queue and the printer window.

REDIRECT DOCUMENTS

If you have two printers with the same print driver, you can redirect all the print jobs that are in the queue for one printer to the other, where they will be printed without having to be resubmitted. You do this by changing the port to which the queue is directed.

1. In the printer's window, click **Printer**, click **Properties**, and click the **Ports** tab.
2. If the second printer is in the list of ports, select it. Otherwise, click **Add Port** to open the Printer Ports dialog box. Click **Local Port** and click **New Port**, which opens the Port Name dialog box.
3. Enter the UNC (Uniform Naming Convention) name for the printer (for example, \\Server3\HPLJ9050), and click **OK**.
4. Click **Close** and then click **OK**. The print queue will be redirected to the other printer.

CHANGE A DOCUMENT'S PROPERTIES

A document in a print queue has a Properties dialog box, shown in Figure 6-16, which is opened by right-clicking the document and selecting **Properties**. The General tab allows you to change a number of things:

- **Priority:** To change a document's default priority of 1, the lowest priority, so that the document can be printed before another that hasn't started printing yet, set the document's priority in the document's Properties dialog box to anything higher than the other document by dragging the **Priority** slider to the right.

- **Who to notify:** To change who is optionally notified of any special situations occurring during printing, as well as when a document has finished printing, put the name of

NOTE

To notify the owner or other person specified when a document has completed printing on a printer connected to this computer, click **Start**, click **Control Panel**, and, in Control Panel Home, click **Printer** under Hardware And Sound; or, in Classic view, double-click **Printers**. On the toolbar, click **Organize**, click **Layout**, and click **Menu Bar**. In the menu bar, click the **File** menu, click **Server Properties**, click the **Advanced** tab, and click **Show Informational Notifications For Local Printers**. This notification is turned off by default.

1
2
3
4
5
6
7
8
9
10

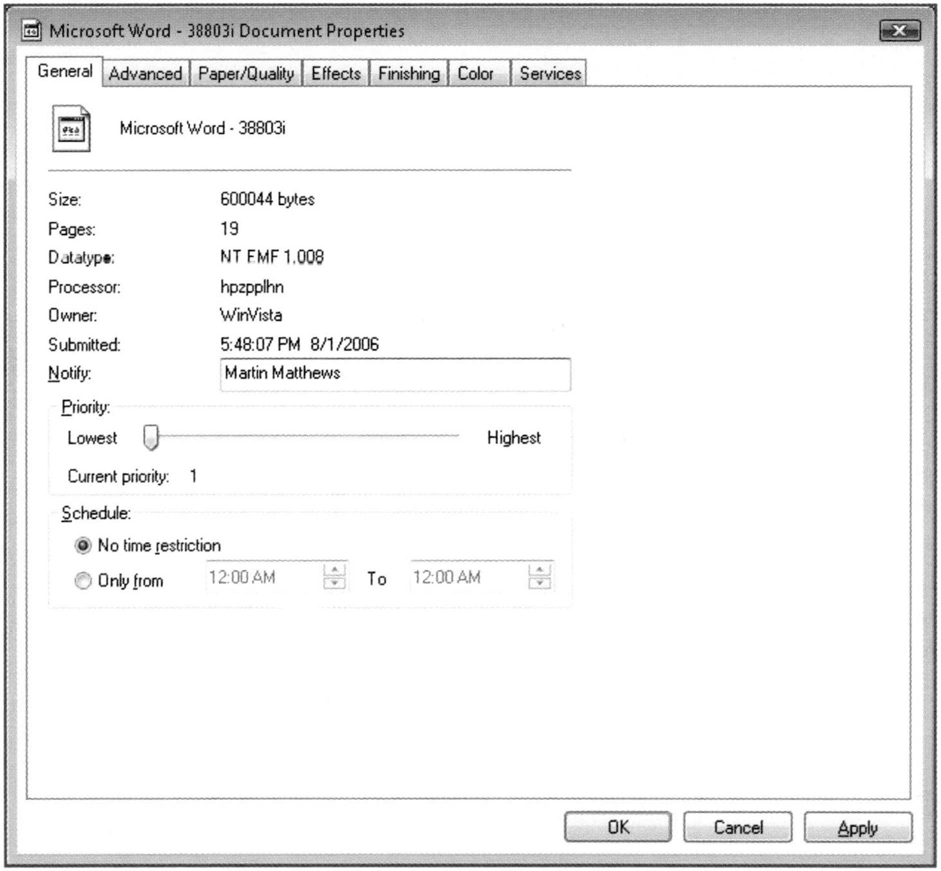

Microsoft Word - 38803i Document Properties
General
Advanced
Paper/Quality
Effects
Finishing
Color
Services
Microsoft Word - 38803i
Size: 600044 bytes
Pages: 19
Datatype: NT EMF 1.008
Processor: hpzpplhn
Owner: WinVista
Submitted: 5:48:07 PM 8/1/2006
Notify: Martin Matthews
Priority:
Lowest
Highest
Current priority: 1
Schedule:
No time restriction
Only from
12:00 AM
To
12:00 AM
OK
Cancel
Apply

Figure 6-16: ***Setting the properties of a document in the print queue can change its priority and when it prints.***

another person (the individual's user name on a shared computer or network) in the Notify text box of the document's Properties dialog box.

- **Set print time:** To change when a job is printed, open a document's Properties dialog box, click **Only From** at the bottom under Schedule, and then enter the time range within which you want the job printed. This allows you to print large jobs, which might otherwise clog the print queue, at a time when there is little or no load.

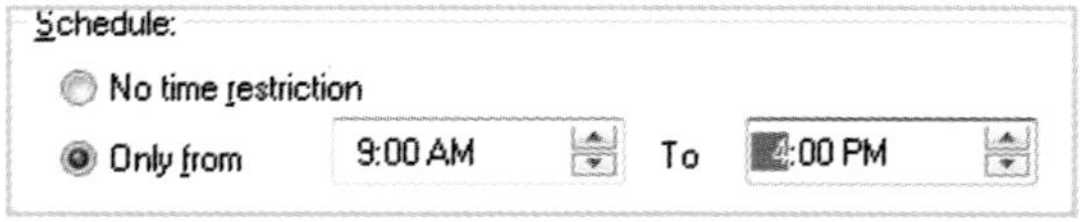

Schedule:
No time restriction
Only from
9:00 AM
To
4:00 PM

TIP

To select several fonts in the Add Fonts dialog box, hold down **SHIFT** and click the first and last font (to select several contiguous fonts), or hold down **CTRL** and click each font (to select several fonts that are not contiguous).

QUICKSTEPS

HANDLING FONTS

A *font* is a set of characters with the same design, size, weight, and style. A font is a member of a *typeface* family, all with the same design. The font 12-point Arial bold italic is a member of the Arial typeface with a 12-point size, bold weight, and italic style. Windows Vista comes with a large number of fonts, a few of which are shown in Figure 6-17.

ADD FONTS

To add fonts to those that are installed by Windows Vista:

1. Click **Start**, click **Control Panel**, click **Appearance And Personalization** in Control Panel Home, and click (double-click in Classic view) **Fonts**. The Fonts window opens.

2. Right-click a blank area of the subject pane, and click **Install New Font**. The Add Fonts dialog box appears, like the one shown in Figure 6-18.

3. Open a drive and folder that contains the fonts you want (this can be a flash drive, a CD/DVD, or a network drive).

4. Select the fonts you want to install from the List Of Fonts, click the **Copy Fonts To Fonts Folder** check box, and then click **Install**.

5. When you are done, close the Add Fonts dialog box. The new fonts appear in the Fonts window.

DELETE FONTS

Remove fonts simply by selecting them in the Fonts window and pressing **DELETE** or by right-clicking the font(s) and clicking **Delete**. In either case, you are asked whether you are sure. Click **Yes** if you are. The fonts will

Continued . . .

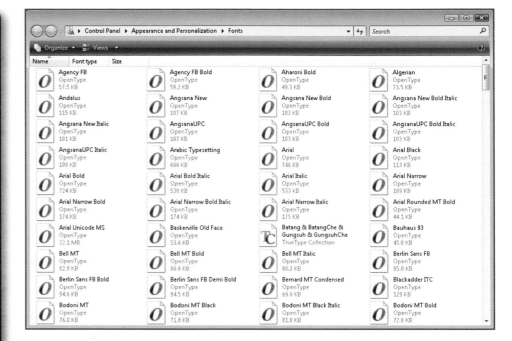

Figure 6-17: *Windows Vista comes with a large number of fonts, but you can add others.*

Figure 6-18: *Fonts can be added from another computer on the network.*

HANDLING FONTS *(Continued)*

be placed in the Recycle Bin, from where they can be retrieved if you've made a mistake.

USE FONTS

Fonts are used or specified from within a program. In Microsoft Word, for example, you can select a line of text and then open the Font drop-down list on the Formatting toolbar (in versions prior to Office 2007) or in the Font group (in Office 2007). Every program is a little different. One nice feature in recent versions of Word is that the list shows what the fonts look like.

Calibri	11	A˅ A˄	
𝕋 *Brush Script MT*			
𝕋 Calibri			
𝕋 Californian FB			
𝕋 Calisto MT			
𝕋 Cambria			
𝕋 **Cambria Math**			
𝕋 Candara			
𝕋 CASTELLAR			
𝕋 Centaur			
𝕋 Century			
𝕋 Century Gothic			
𝕋 Century Schoolbook			
𝕋 *Chiller*			
𝕋 Colonna MT			
𝕋 Comic Sans MS			

NOTE

Faxing capability is not available in Windows Vista Home Basic and Home Premium editions.

NOTE

If you are in a larger organization and want or need to use a fax server, you will have to get information about how to do that from your IT support staff.

Fax Documents and Pictures

Windows Vista has realigned its faxing capability to pair it with scanning, which allows you to scan a document to be faxed, as well as print to a fax. The fax capability requires that you have a fax modem in your computer or a fax connected to it and a phone line plugged into the modem (see Chapter 5 on setting up and working with modems).

Set Up Faxing

The faxing capability must be set up before you can use it.

1. Click **Start**, click **All Programs**, and click **Windows Fax And Scan**. The Windows Fax and Scan window will open, as you saw in Figure 6-5 earlier in this chapter.

2. Click **New Fax**. The first time you do that, you are led through a series of steps to set up faxing. Click **Connect To A Fax Modem**, type a name for the fax, and click **Next**.

3. Choose whether the fax modem should answer incoming calls automatically or notify you and have you choose whether to answer.

4. If you get a message that the Windows Firewall has blocked some features of this program, click **Unblock**.

5. When Setup is done, the New Fax window will open. Continue with "Send a Fax Message" in this chapter.

Send and Receive Faxes

Windows Vista lets you directly send and receive faxes as you would e-mail messages; fax from a program, such as Microsoft Word, by specifying "fax" as a printer; and scan documents that are then faxed.

SEND A FAX MESSAGE

To send an e-mail-type message as a fax:

1. Click **Start**, click **All Programs**, click **Windows Fax And Scan**, and click **New Fax**. After you have set up faxing (see "Set Up Faxing"), when you click **New Fax**, the New Fax windows opens directly, as you can see in Figure 6-19.

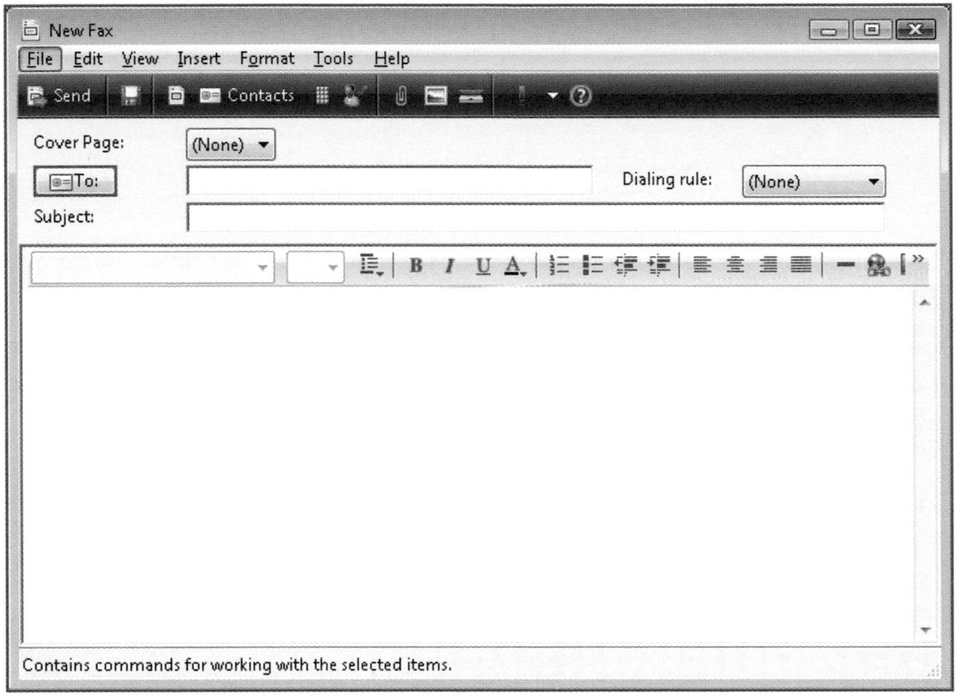

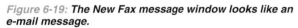

Figure 6-19: **The New Fax message window looks like an e-mail message.**

2. Select a cover page, if you want one (see "Create a Fax Cover Page" later in this chapter), type a phone number to be used for faxing (or click **To** and select one from your contacts list), type a subject, any cover page notes, and then the message.

3. Click **Preview** on the toolbar to look at the cover page before and/or after adding fax text. Also, you can attach documents and pictures by clicking their respective buttons on the toolbar.

4. When you are ready, click **Send**. The New Fax window will close, and the Review Fax Status dialog box will appear, where, if you click **View Details**, you can see the status of the fax being sent, as shown in Figure 6-20.

5. When the fax has been sent, you will see a message to that effect, as well as see it in the status dialog box. When you are done, close the status dialog box and the Windows Fax And Scan window.

ⓘ The fax was sent successfully
The fax was successfully sent to < >.

SEND A FAX BY "PRINTING"

Printing to a fax is as easy as any other printing method.

1. Open a document in a program such as Microsoft Word. Click the **File** menu or **Office Button**, and click **Print**. Open the printer **Name** drop-down list, click **Fax**, and click **OK**. The New Fax dialog box will appear with your Word document listed in the Attach box.

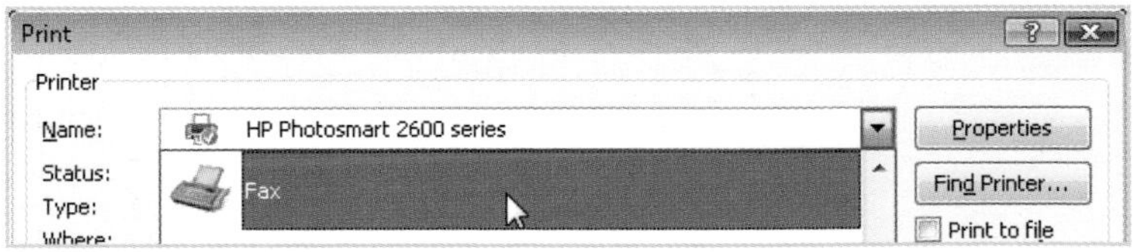

Print

Printer

Name: HP Photosmart 2600 series   Properties

Status: Find Printer...
Type: Fax
Where: ☐ Print to file

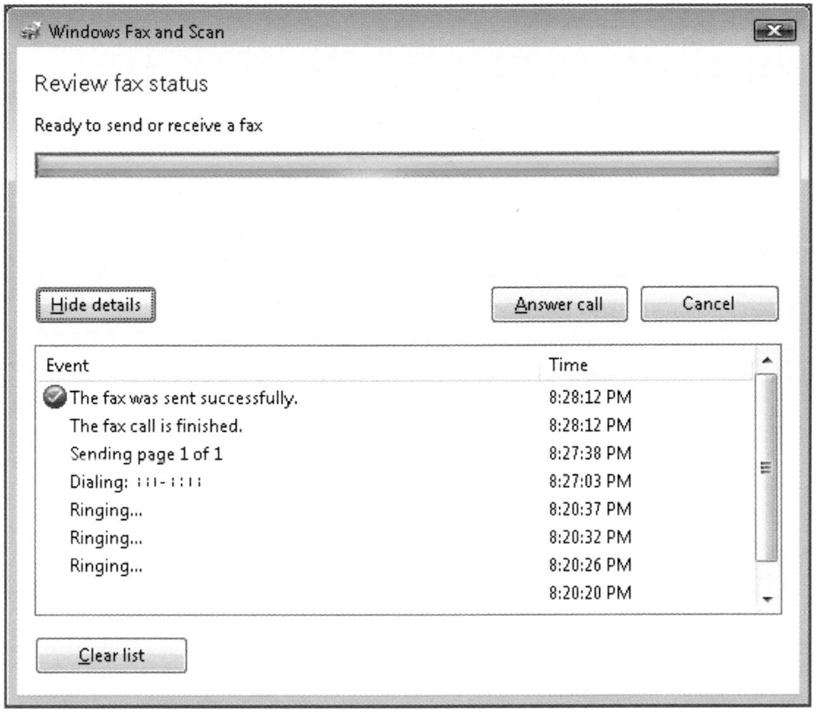

Figure 6-20: *The Review Fax Status dialog box shows you everything that is happening on the phone line connected to the computer.*

2. Follow the instructions starting at step 2 of "Send a Fax Message." If this is the first time you have used the fax, you will first see the setup questions described in "Set Up Faxing" earlier in the chapter.

SCAN AND FAX A DOCUMENT

To scan and fax a document:

1. Follow the first five steps in "Scan Pictures" earlier in this chapter.

2. When scanning is complete, click **Forward As Fax**. The New Fax message window will open with the image you scanned attached.

3. Follow the instructions starting at step 2 of "Send a Fax Message" earlier in this chapter. If this is the first time you have used the fax, you will first see the setup questions described in "Set Up Faxing," also earlier in the chapter.

RECEIVE A FAX

You receive faxes using the Windows Fax And Scan window. In order to receive a fax, you must have set up the fax as described in "Set Up Faxing" earlier in the chapter.

1. With the computer's fax/modem plugged into a phone line and the fax set up, when you get any phone call, you will see a message on your screen that the phone is ringing and that you can click the message to answer the call as a fax. You can pick up the phone receiver and see if you hear the fax tone and then click the message.

If you chose to not be notified upon receipt of a fax (automatic receipt) in setting up the fax (see "Set Up Faxing" earlier in this chapter), you can change from automatic to manual receipt in the Windows Fax And Scan window. Click the **Tools** menu, click **Fax Settings**, in the General tab click **Manually Answer**, and click **OK**.

2. If you click the **Ringing** message, the Review Fax Status dialog box will appear. If you click **View Details**, you will see the fax events as they happen. When the fax has been received, you will receive a message to that effect and the Review Fax Status dialog box will also display that, as shown in Figure 6-21.

3. To see and possibly print the fax, click **Start**, click **All Programs**, click **Windows Fax And Scan**, and click **Fax** in the lower-left corner.

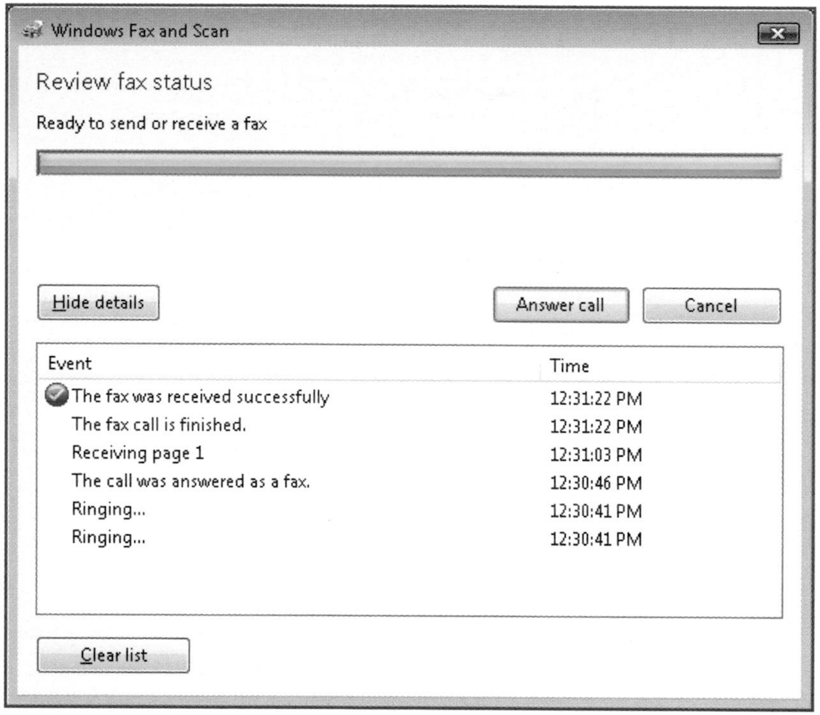

Figure 6-21: *In the Review Fax Status dialog box, click View Details to see what is happening with the fax.*

CAUTION

The four standard cover pages have coded fields that automatically add data. If you change them, you'll lose the auto-fill capability.

4. If you open the Windows Fax And Scan window while the fax is still being received, click **Incoming** in the navigation pane, and watch as the fax is received.

5. When the fax has been received, click **Inbox** in the navigation pane, scroll through the list of faxes at the top of the subject pane, and click the fax you want to view. It will be displayed in the lower part of the subject pane.

6. With a fax selected and displayed, you can use the toolbar to reply to the fax by sending a new fax to the sender, forward the fax to one or more recipients, forward the fax as e-mail, or delete the fax. Also, you can right-click the fax image in the subject pane and, from the context menu, view, zoom, save, and print the fax, as shown in Figure 6-22.

7. When you are done, close the Windows Fax And Scan window.

Create a Fax Cover Page

Windows Vista includes four fax cover pages you can use, as well as a Fax Cover Page Editor that you can use to modify one of the included covers or create a cover page of your own. To modify an existing one:

1. Click **Start**, click **All Programs**, click **Windows Fax And Scan**, and click **Fax** in the lower-left corner.

2. Click the **Tools** menu, and click **Cover Pages**. Click **Copy**, select one of the four standard cover pages, and click **Open** (Generic was selected for this illustration). Select the cover page, and click **Open**. The cover page will open in the Fax Cover Page Editor, as shown in Figure 6-23.

3. Use the following tools on the Drawing toolbar to modify an existing cover page, thereby creating a new one of your own:

- Use the **Select** tool to select parts of a cover page.
- Use the **Text** tool to enter text.
- Use the **Line** tool to draw straight lines.

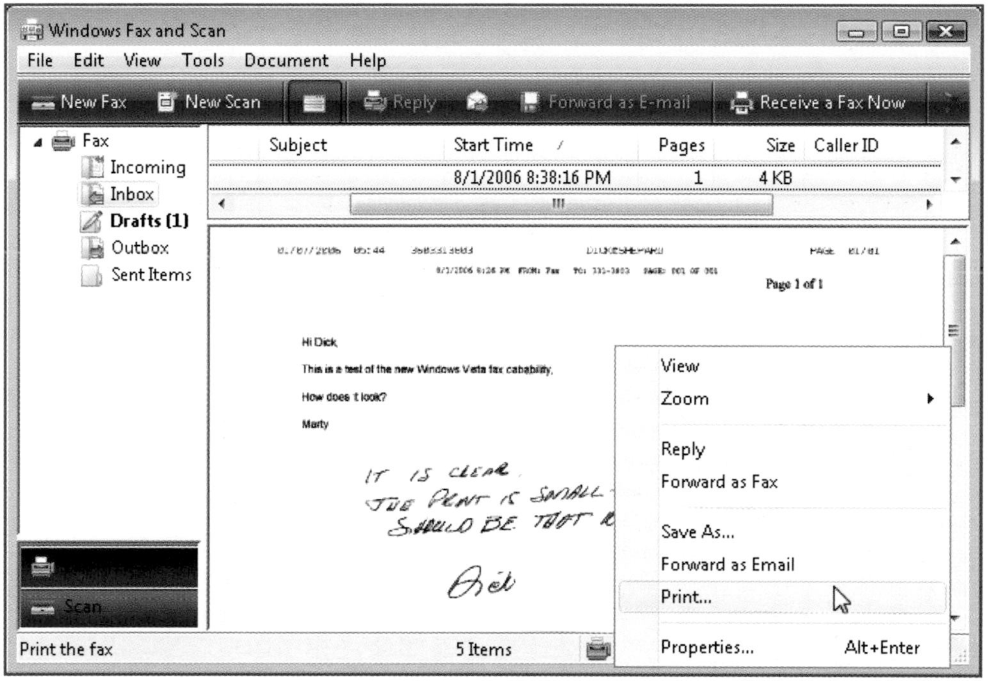

Figure 6-22: *Faxes you receive can be forwarded both as a fax and as an e-mail, as well as saved and printed.*

- Use the **Rectangle** tool to draw rectangles.

- Use the **Rounded Rectangle** tool to draw rounded rectangles.

- Use the **Polygon** tool to draw multisided polygons.

- Use the **Ellipse** tool to draw ovals and circles.

- Click **Bring To Front** to move a selected item to the front of a stack of items.

- Click **Send To Back** to move a selected item to the back of a stack of items.

- Click **Space Across** to equally space items horizontally.

- Click **Space Down** to equally space items vertically.

- Click **Align Left** to align text and objects on the left margin.

- Click **Align Right** to align text and objects on the right margin.

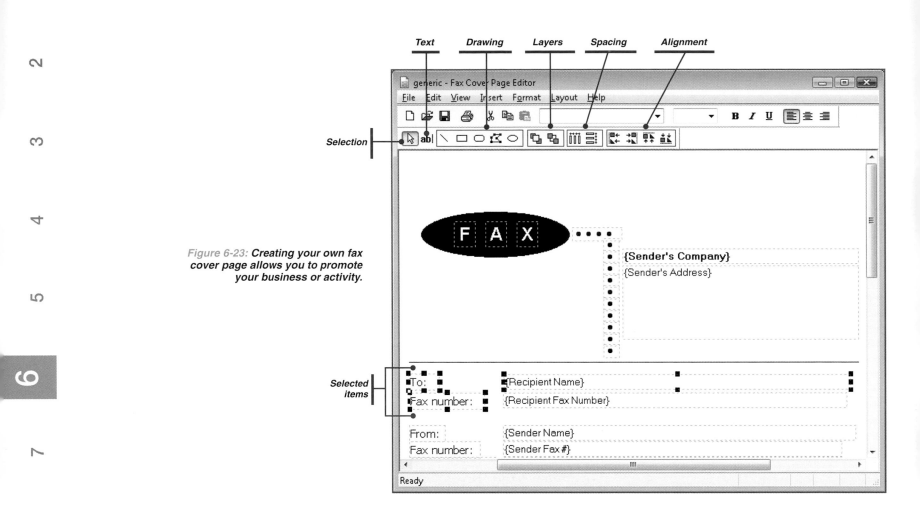

Figure 6-23: *Creating your own fax cover page allows you to promote your business or activity.*

- Click **Align Top** to align text and objects on the top margin.

- Click **Align Bottom** to align text and objects on the bottom margin.

4. When you have your cover page the way you want it, click **Save** to save it with its existing name; or click the **File** menu, and click **Save As** to give your cover page a new name. Close both the Fax Cover Page Editor and the Fax Cover Pages dialog box, as well as the Windows Fax And Scan window.

How to...

- *Play CDs*
- *Control the Volume*
- *Listen to Radio Stations*
- *Locate Music on the Internet*
- *Copy (Rip) CDs to Your Computer*
- *Organize Music*
- *Make (Burn) a Music CD*
- *Changing the Visualizations in Windows Media Player*
- *Copy to (Sync with) Music Players*
- *Play DVDs*
- *Preparing to Make a Movie*
- *Import Video from a Camcorder*
- *Make a Movie*
- *Select Video Clips*
- *Edit Video Clips*
- *Import Other Files*
- *Add Titles to a Movie*
- *Employing Effects and Transitions*
- *Add Sound to a Movie*
- *Publish a Movie*
- *Exploring Windows Media Center*

Chapter 7
Working with Multimedia

Multimedia is the combination of audio and video. Windows Vista, as an operating system, has to be able to handle audio and video files and accept their input from a number of different devices. It has four major programs—Windows Media Player, Windows Movie Maker, Windows DVD Maker, and Windows Media Center—that enable you to work with these files and read and write them onto CDs, DVDs, flash drives, and music players. We'll look first at sound by itself, then at video with sound.

7

Work with Audio

Audio is sound. Windows Vista works with and uses sound in several ways, the simplest being to alert you of various events, like an incoming e-mail message or closing down the system. Chapter 2 shows you how to customize the use of sounds for these purposes.

The other use of sound is to entertain or inform you—be it listening to music or lectures from CDs, Internet radio, or another Internet site. It is this use of sound that is the subject of this section.

Play CDs

Playing a CD is as easy as inserting a disk in the drive. When you do that, you will be asked if you want Windows Media Player to play the disk. If you click **Play Audio CD Using Windows Media Player**, Media Player will open and begin playing the disk, as shown in Figure 7-1. The Media Player window has a variety of controls that enable you to determine how it functions and looks. These controls are located either in the functional controls and option menus at the top of the window or in the playback controls at the bottom:

- **Functional controls** allow selection of the primary Media Player functions:
  - **Now Playing** shows visualizations of audio or the display of video.
  - **Library** creates playlists and organizes, manages, and shares media.
  - **Rip** copies audio CDs to the Media Library.
  - **Burn** copies playlists from the Library to writable CDs and DVDs.
  - **Sync** synchronizes content between portable music devices and your PC.
  - **Media Guide** opens the currently selected online media store and the Windows Media Guide, where you can connect to Internet radio.
- **Options menus** provide options for the functional area they are under.
- **View pane** displays video presentations as well as visualizations of audio-only music.

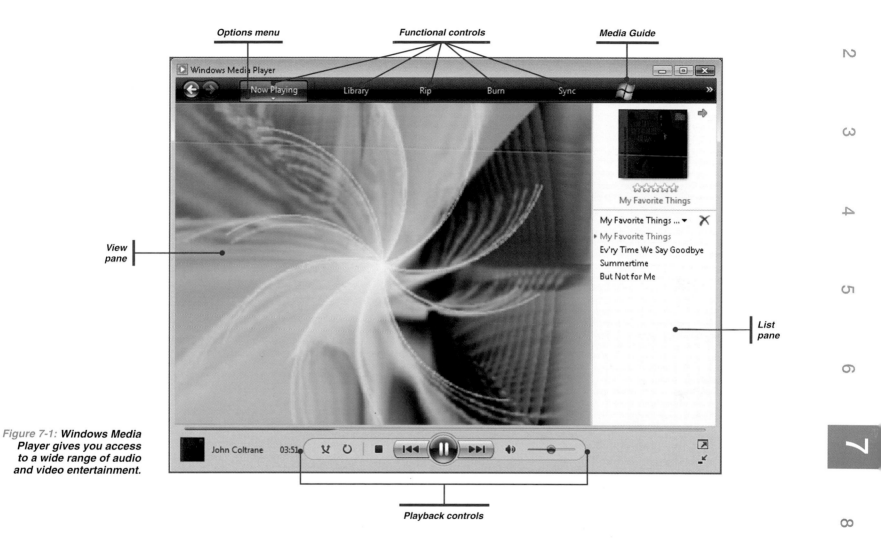

Options menu   **Functional controls**   **Media Guide**

View
pane

List
pane

*Figure 7-1: Windows Media
Player gives you access
to a wide range of audio
and video entertainment.*

Playback controls

- **List pane** lists what is currently being played.

  - **Close List pane** closes the List pane.

  - **Buy CD/DVD** enables you to buy the item you are listening to or watching.

  - **Clear List pane** stops what is being played.

  - **View full screen** expands the view pane to fill the screen.

Close List pane

Buy CD/DVD

Last Rose of Summer (Intro)/Walking in ...

Clear list pane

Celtic Woman [Manhattan] ▾	
▸ Last Rose of Summer (Intro)/...	4:22
May It Be - Celtic Woman; Lisa	3:48
Isle of Inisfree - Celtic Woma...	3:28
Danny Boy - Celtic Woman; ...	3:26
One World - Celtic Woman	3:50
Ave Maria - Celtic Woman; C...	2:56
Send Me a Song - Celtic Wom...	4:23
Siúil a Rún (Walk My Love)	3:17
Orinoco Flow - Celtic Woman	3:32
Someday - Celtic Woman; Chl...	4:22
She Moved Thru' the Fair	3:31
Nella Fantasia - Celtic Woman;...	3:42
The Butterfly - Celtic Woman;...	3:02
Harry's Game - Celtic Woman...	2:32
The Soft Goodbye - Celtic Wo...	3:59
You Raise Me Up - Celtic Wo...	4:34
The Ashoken Farewell/The Co...	4:10
Sí Do Mhaimeo Í (The Wealth...	2:13

View full screen

Switch to mini mode

- **Switch to mini mode** collapses the window to just the playback controls.

- **Playback controls** provides CD player-like controls to play/pause, stop, go to previous, go to next, and adjust volume.

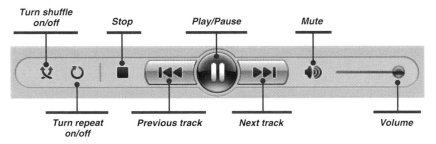

Turn shuffle on/off   Stop   Play/Pause   Mute

Turn repeat on/off   Previous track   Next track   Volume

The options menus provide several different sets of controls, including the ability to turn on a graphic equalizer by clicking the **Now Playing** menu, clicking **Enhancements**, and clicking **Show Enhancements**.

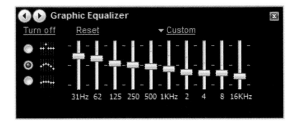

Control the Volume

You can control your computer's audio volume from several places, including the physical volume control on your speakers or on your laptop computer, the volume control on the bottom-right of the playback controls of the Media Player, and the volume icon in the notification area on the right of the taskbar.

Clicking the **Volume** icon in the notification area opens a small Volume slider that you can drag for louder or softer sound, or you can click **Mute** (the blue speaker at the bottom of the slider) to do just that. Click anywhere on the desktop to close the Volume slider.

Listen to Radio Stations

If you have a broadband Internet connection (as described in Chapter 4) of at least 128 Kbps and sound capability, you can listen to Internet radio stations around the world. Windows Media Player gives you access to these stations through the Media Guide Radio option, which you can see in Figure 7-2. The Radio Tuner gives you several ways of finding and playing a particular station:

- Choosing from a featured set of stations or an editor's picks of the day

- Selecting a type of music or genre for which to search, or using keywords to search for a station's call letters, for instance, or the ZIP code where it is located

- Choosing a station that you have recently played or that you have added to a list of your favorite stations

To display the Radio Tuner, locate a station and add it to My Stations.

1. Click **Start**, click **All Programs**, click **Windows Media Player**, and then click the **Online Store/ Media Guide** icon, which may be different from the one shown in Figures 7-1 and 7-2.

*Figure 7-2: **Media Player's Radio Tuner allows you to listen to Internet radio stations.***

2. In the options menu that appears, click **Media Guide**. In the Web page that displays, click **Radio** on the menu bar, and click the **Internet Radio** link on the right.

3. In the Search text box, highlight **Search Keyword**, type the call letters of a radio station, and either press **ENTER** or click the **Search** arrow. The Search Results list will appear.

⟨ **Return to My Stations**
Browse by Genre:
Any Genre: ▼

Search:
KPLU   →

Zip Code (US Only):
Zip Code   →

⌄ **Use Advanced Search**

Search Results: KPLU

Station Name ▲	Speed	Location
▷ KPLU 88.5 FM Pacific Lutheran University (20k)	28K	Tacoma, WA
KPLU 88.5 FM Pacific Lutheran University (48k)	56K	Tacoma, WA

KPLU 88.5 FM Pacific Lutheran University
(48k)
🖑
       z : Tacoma, WA
Play station
      er Internet Jazz Source

4. Select your choice within the Search Results list, and click **Add To My Stations**. Then click the green arrow to the left of the station name in the Search Results list to listen to or "play" the station.

Locate Music on the Internet

There are many other sources of music on the Internet in addition to radio stations. The Media Guide in the Media Player provides links to many of these sites. Like the Radio Tuner, the Media Guide offers links that you can follow to featured sites and categories of sites. You can also search for a site—the site of a particular artist, for example.

1. Click **Start**, click **All Programs**, click **Windows Media Player**, click the **Online Store/ Media Guide** icon, and then click **Media Guide** on the menu. The Media Guide home page will open, as shown in Figure 7-3.

2. Type in the **Search** text box (the cursor should be there by default) the name of an artist, song, or movie about whom you would like to locate sites. Click **Search**. The search results will appear.

3. Click the link you want.

TIP

The next time you want to listen to the station you saved in My Stations, after opening the Radio Tuner, click **My Stations** and click the green arrow to the left of the station name.

NOTE

In the All Media Results page, the little pair of notes designates music, and the little strip of film designates a music video.

*Figure 7-3: **Media Player allows you to search the Internet for music that you like.***

Copy (Rip) CDs to Your Computer

Media Player gives you the ability to copy (or "rip") CD tracks that you like to your hard disk so that you can build and manage a library of your favorite music and copy this material to a recordable CD. To copy from a CD (see Figure 7-4):

1. Insert the CD from which you want to copy tracks. Click **Play Audio CD Using Windows Media Player** to open Windows Media Player, and then click **Rip** in the Windows Media functional controls.

2. Select the tracks you want to copy to your hard disk by clicking the check boxes to the left of each track. Click **Play** in the playback controls to listen to the tracks and to make sure your choices are correct.

3. When you are satisfied that you have selected the correct tracks, click **Start Rip**. The selected tracks will be copied to your hard disk. When you are done, close Media Player.

Figure 7-4: Media Player can be used to build a music library from your CDs.

NOTE

Copying a music track from a CD to a digital file on your hard disk is time-consuming, even on a relatively fast computer. It also produces large files. To see the copying progress, look at the Rip Status column on the right of the Rip window, as you can see on the right of Figure 7-4.

NOTE

The material on most CDs and DVDs is owned and copyrighted by some combination of the composer, the artist, the producer, and/or the publisher. Copyright law prohibits using the copyrighted material in ways that are not beneficial to the owners, including giving or selling the content without giving or selling the original CD or DVD itself. To enforce this, most CDs and DVDs are protected to make copying difficult. Media Player provides the ability to copy copyrighted material to your hard disk and then to a recordable CD or a USB Flash drive with the understanding that the copy is solely for your own personal use and you will not sell or give away copies. This is both a great gift and a responsibility. As one who makes his living on copyrighted material, I urge you not to abuse it.

Figure 7-5: *Media Player's Library provides a way to manage the media you store on your computer.*

TIP

When listening to a playlist, you can randomize the order in which the pieces will play by clicking **Turn Shuffle On** in the playback controls, which is the first button on the left.

Organize Music

Once you have copied several CDs and have downloaded other music to your hard disk, you will likely want them organized. This is the function of Media Player's Library, shown in Figure 7-5. When music and videos are copied to the Library, the contents are automatically indexed alphabetically by album, artist, and genre. You can also combine them into a playlist that allows you to play pieces from several albums. To build a new playlist:

1. Click **Library** in the Windows Media Player functional controls, and then click **Create Playlist** in the navigation pane on the left. Enter the name you want for the new playlist, and press **ENTER**.

2. Open an album, artist, or genre, and select a piece you want in the new playlist. Drag the piece to the playlist. The contents of the playlist are shown as you build it in the list pane on the right of the window.

3. When you have added all the pieces that you initially want (you can always add more later), click **Save Playlist.**

4. Listen to the playlist by selecting it and clicking **Play** in the playback controls. When you are done, click **Clear List Pane** in the List pane.

Make (Burn) a Music CD

Once you have created a playlist (see "Organize Music" earlier in this chapter), you can write (or "burn") it to a writable or rewritable CD or DVD using Media Player's Burn feature.

7

1. Put a blank recordable disk in the CD or DVD recording drive. The AutoPlay dialog box will appear and ask what you want to do. Click **Burn An Audio CD** to open the Windows Media Player with the Burn functional area displayed.

2. Open your playlists in the navigation pane, and drag a playlist (or individual songs from an open playlist) that you want on the CD or DVD to the Burn List on the right. You can see how much of the CD is being used and the amount of time remaining just above the Burn List, as shown in Figure 7-6.

3. You can make corrections to the Burn List by dragging additional songs there until you use up the remaining time, or by right-clicking a song on the Burn List and clicking **Remove From List** in the context menu that opens. You can also clear the Burn List and start over.

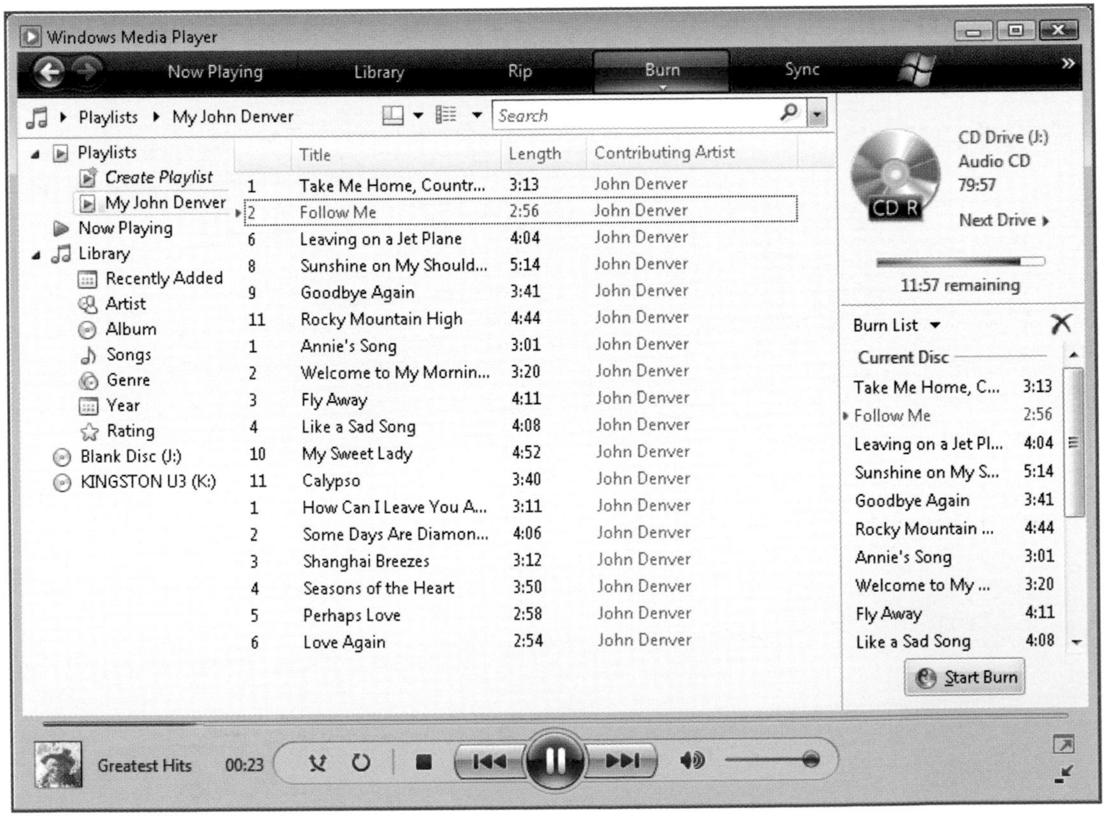

Figure 7-6: Burning a playlist to a writable CD or DVD allows you to create a disc that has just your favorite songs.

CHANGING THE VISUALIZATIONS IN WINDOWS MEDIA PLAYER

In Media Player's Now Playing pane, there is, by default, a graphic visualization of the music that is playing, as shown earlier in Figure 7-1. There are over 25 visualizations that come with Media Player, and you can download more. To select a different visualization:

1. Click the **Now Playing** options menu, click **Visualizations**, select one of the three types of visualizations (Album Art is a static display), and then click the visualization you want to use.

Now Playing	Library
✓ Show List Pane	
Enhancements ▶	
Visualizations ▶	No Visualization
Plug-ins ▶	● Album Art
	Alchemy ▶
More Options...	Bars and Waves ▶ Bars
Help with Playback	Battery ▶ Ocean Mist
	Fire Stor
	Download Visualizations Scope
	Options...

2. If you want to download additional visualizations, click the **Now Playing** options menu, click **Visualizations**, and click **Download Visualizations**. Then follow the instructions on the Web sites you will visit.

4. When you are sure you have the list of pieces you want to burn, click **Start Burn**. The digital files will first be converted to analog music files and then written to a CD or DVD. The Status column will show you the progress (it is not very fast!). When the burn is complete and if no one has changed the default settings, the disc will be ejected from the drive. Write the title on the disc with a soft felt-tip marker, or use a LightScribe drive to burn a label on the special discs you use for this purpose.

The resulting CD should be playable in most CD players.

Copy to (Sync with) Music Players

Windows Media Player allows you to plug in a digital music device, such as an iPod, and transfer music to and from (sync with) the device.

1. Click **Start**, click **All Programs**, and click **Windows Media Player**.

2. Click **Sync** in the Windows Media Player functional controls. You will be told to connect your device.

3. Start your device and then plug it into your computer. The first time you do that, Windows will install a driver for it, and then the Device Setup dialog box will appear.

Windows Media Player - Device Setup

Device Setup

ERIC'S IPOD (18.5 GB)   Configure Sync

Name your device:

ERIC'S IPOD

When you click Finish, your device will be updated to mirror your Windows Media Player library. In the future, the device will be updated whenever you connect it to your computer.

What are my options with sync?

< Back   Finish   Cancel

7

If you have more than 4 gigabytes (GB) in your device and your entire music library will fit on it, if you click **Finish**, your entire library will automatically be copied. Each time you plug your device into your computer, it will be synchronized with any changes in your library (songs you removed from your library will be removed from your device; songs you added to your library will be added to your device).

If you don't have at least 4 GB in your device, or if your library won't fit in it, or if you click **Cancel** in the Device Setup dialog box, you can manually select playlists and songs that you want copied to the device, as shown in Figure 7-7.

Figure 7-7: *A digital music device can mirror your Media Player library if it has enough room and that is what you want.*

4. In the Devices Setup dialog box, click **Finish** or **Cancel**, depending on your situation. If you click **Cancel**, drag the playlists and/or songs you want on the device to the Sync Lists on the right. If you wish, you can play the Sync List by double-clicking the first playlist or song.

5. When you are certain that you have all the music in the Sync List that you want on your device, click **Start Sync**. The music will be copied to the device.

Work with Video

Windows Vista lets you play videos from a DVD using either Windows Media Player or Windows Media Center. It also allows you to capture and edit videos or slide shows from a camcorder or imported material using Windows Movie Maker.

Play DVDs

Playing DVDs is as easy as playing CDs: simply insert a DVD into its drive. When you do that, the AutoPlay dialog box will appear, and you will be asked if you want to play the DVD using Windows Media Player or the Windows Media Center. We'll discuss Media Center later in this chapter, but if you click **Play DVD Movie** using Windows Media Player, the player will open and play the disk. The Media Player controls are virtually the same for DVDs as they are for CDs, except the View Full Screen option enlarges the movie or video you are watching to fit the full screen.

UICKSTEPS

PREPARING TO MAKE A MOVIE

Making a movie with a computer takes more hardware than any other task. The faster your CPU, the more memory it has, the better your video display adapter, and the larger your disk, the more smoothly the task will go. The beauty is that today's new computers have most of what you need by default.

DETERMINE REQUIREMENTS

The recommended hardware requirements for making movies are:

COMPONENT	RECOMMENDED HARDWARE
CPU	1 GHz Intel Pentium 4, AMD Athlon 64, or better
RAM memory	1 GB
Hard drive free space	60 GB
Optical drive	DVD±R
Video display card	Supports DirectX 9, WDDM driver, Windows Aero, pixel and vertex shaders 2.0, 32 bits/pixel, 128 MB dedicated video memory or more
Video recording from DV camcorders	IEEE 1394 FireWire card, OHCI-compliant
Video capture from analog VCR/ camera /TV	Windows Vista–compatible video capture card
Audio capture from microphone, tape	Windows Vista–compatible audio card and microphone

NOTES ON REQUIREMENTS

- Memory is most important. The more, the better.
- CPU capability is a close second in importance. To work with full-motion video, you need a lot of it. 1 MHz is really the bare-bones minimum.
- The video display card has become quite important to Movie Maker. It will not work without the minimum shown in the table.

Continued . . .

Import Video from a Camcorder

Importing video directly from your camcorder to your hard disk is simple using the Import Video option in Windows Vista.

1. Plug your camera into an OHCI-compliant FireWire port on your computer, and turn on your camcorder. Windows Vista will detect it, install the necessary driver software, and ask you if you want to import the video.

2. Click **Import Video**. Import Video will start. Type a name for the video, select where you want the video file stored, and the format you want it stored in. Click **Next**.

3. Click whether you want to import the entire videotape to your computer, immediately burn that file to a DVD, or import only parts of the videotape, and click **Next**.

   If you choose to import the entire videotape, Windows will start your camcorder, rewind the tape, and begin playing and importing the video, as shown in Figure 7-8.

4. If you choose to import only parts of a videotape, you are given the standard playback controls of play, pause, stop, fast rewind, fast forward, previous frame, and next frame, as shown in Figure 7-9. You can use these controls to position the tape at the location you want start importing it on to your disk. When you reach that point, back up just a bit, click **Start Video Import**, import as much as you want, and then click **Stop Video Import**. Repeat this process as needed until you are finished.

5. When the importation is complete, you will see a message to that effect. Click **OK**. Windows Photo Gallery will open and show you where your video is stored.

QUICKSTEPS

PREPARING TO MAKE A MOVIE

(Continued)

- With a digital video (DV) camcorder and an IEEE 1394 FireWire interface, get an OHCI-compliant FireWire interface card for your computer, if one isn't built in.
- A video capture card can bring in an analog video signal from a TV, a VCR, an analog camcorder, and (in most cases) a DV camcorder; however, the result is not as good as a digital recording.

TIP

You have a choice between the Audio Video Interleaved (AVI) format and the Windows Media Video (WMV) format. The AVI format creates much larger formats (as much as six times the size), but can be used on computers other than those running Windows. If you are going to just use the video on Windows–based computers, choose WMV.

TIP

When recording several segments of a tape, you may want to back up the tape in the camcorder just a bit each time you stop to position the tape before restarting the recording.

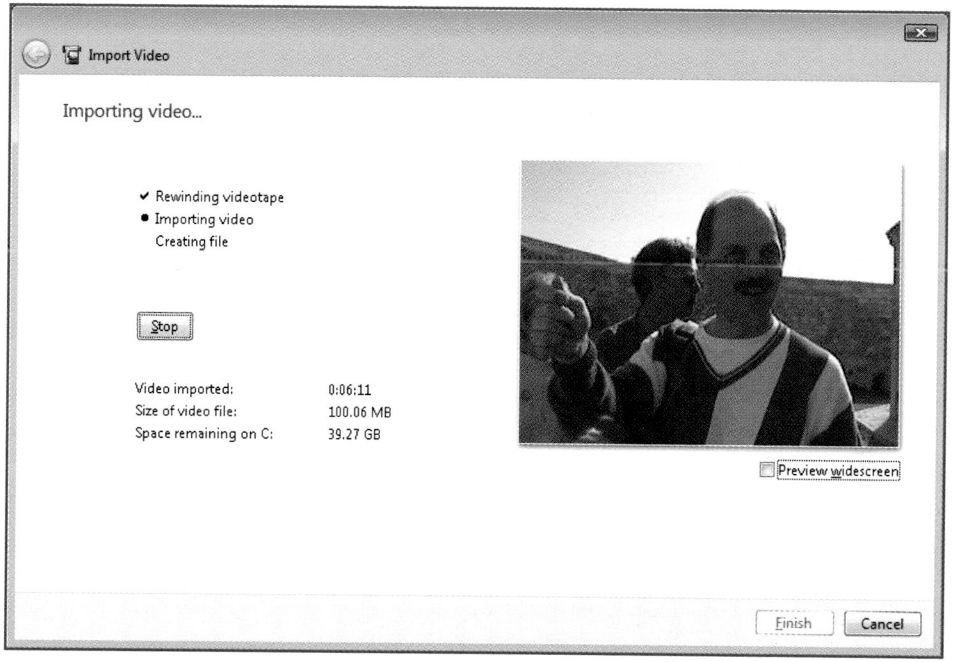

Figure 7-8: ***With a digital video (DV) camcorder, you can directly record the contents of a tape onto your hard disk.***

Make a Movie

Making a movie out of the imported camcorder video and other material involves selecting and editing the available material, assembling it into the order in which you want it, adding narration, titles, and special effects, and finally publishing the finished product. Windows Movie Maker provides the means to do that. While working in Movie Maker, you are working on what Movie Maker calls a "project," which is a fluid collection of video clips, still pictures, titles, audio clips, narration, and special effects laid out along a timeline. So long as you are in the project and have not published the movie, you can change almost anything. Projects can be saved and reopened for as long as you like.

1 2 3 4 5 6 7 8 9 10

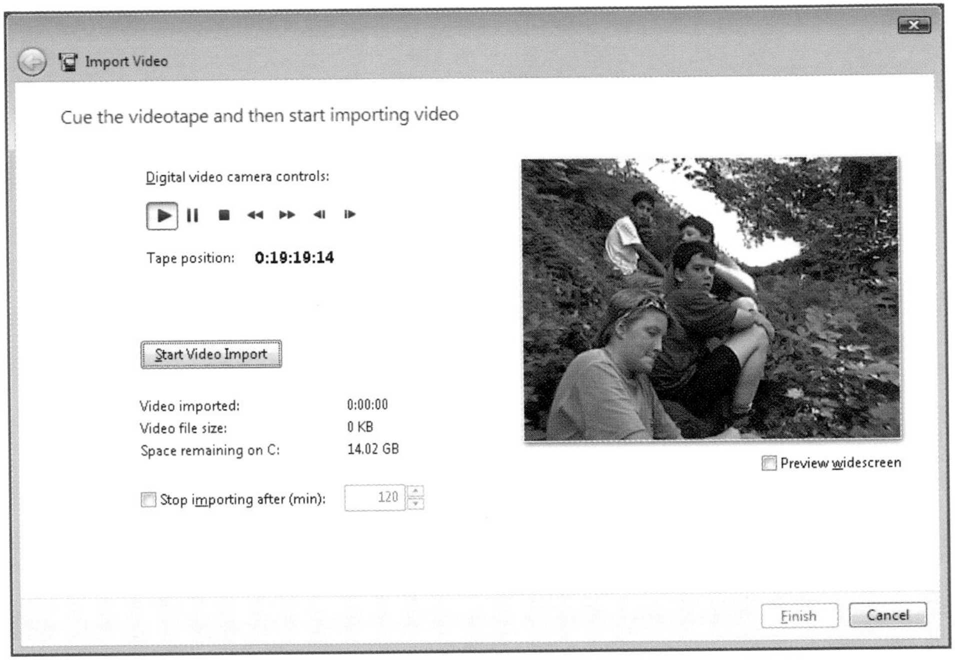

*Figure 7-9: **You can choose
whether you want to import
the entire video from the camcorder
or just selected parts.***

To make a movie using the imported camcorder video:

1. If you are not already in Windows Photo Gallery, click **Start**, click **All Programs**, and click **Windows Photo Gallery**. Click **All Pictures And Videos**, and then click **Videos**.

2. Click the particular video footage you want to work with, and click **Make A Movie**. Windows Movie Maker will open, as shown in Figure 7-10. This window has four panes, two of which have two views:

   - The **Navigation** pane has two views:
     - **Tasks** view lists the movie-making tasks that you can perform.
     - **Collections** view displays folders of effects, transitions, and your imported and stored videos.
   - The **Contents** pane, in the center of the window, displays segments ("clips") of the video you are editing. If you want more room for the clips in the Contents pane,

Project toolbar **Panes toolbar** **Contents pane**

Tasks view, Navigation pane

Preview monitor

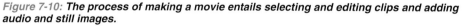

Storyboard view, Workspace pane

*Figure 7-10: **The process of making a movie entails selecting and editing clips and adding audio and still images.***

you can drag the border between the Collections view and the Contents pane, or turn off either the Tasks or Collections views by clicking the view icon above the Contents pane.

- The **Preview Monitor**, on the right of the window, displays or plays the current clip or the entire movie and displays still images.

- The **Workspace** pane, on the bottom of the window, has two views:
  - **Storyboard** view (shown in Figure 7-10) is the default view, and allows you to easily sequence your clips and rearrange them by dragging, as well as add transitions and effects.
  - **Timeline** view gives you a precise time measurement of your clips, and allows you to trim them, adjust the transitions between clips, and add music and narration.

The Movie Maker window holds a number of tools to help you convert video clips, sound, and still images into a movie. In addition to a complete set of menus, two toolbars can be displayed:

- The **Project** toolbar has five icons: Import Media opens the Import Media Items dialog box that allows you to select items stored on your computer and network. The Undo button undoes the last action you took; the down arrow opens a list of recent actions that you can select to undo a number of actions at once. The Redo button reinstates actions you have undone. AutoMovie automatically creates a movie out of your clips without editing. Publish Movie finishes what you have created and writes it to your hard disk, a DVD, or to the video tape in your computer.

- The **Panes** toolbar lets you choose whether to display the Tasks view, the Collections view, or neither; which collection to see; and whether to display thumbnails or file details and how to arrange the icons.

In the workspace, especially in Timeline view, there are additional tools that are discussed in "Edit Video Clips."

Select Video Clips

The selecting and organizing of clips is a laborious phase, but it provides the foundation for your project and determines what you have to work with in the editing phase, so it is time well spent. The process of selecting which parts of which video clips to use has four steps:

1. Double-click the first clip to play it. Decide if you want to use it, if it needs to be trimmed and where, and make appropriate notes as to the timing of where you want to trim.

2. If you want to use the clip, drag it to the workspace, dropping it where you want it in the string of existing clips.

1 2 3 4 5 6 7 8 9 10

3. Periodically right-click the workspace, and click **Play Storyboard** or click the blue right-pointing arrow to see how the selection and organization is coming along in the series of clips.

4. If desired, rearrange the clips by dragging them to a different location in the string and/or by deleting a clip you no longer want in the project/movie.

While working in this phase, the Storyboard view of the workspace is probably the best view to use, offering the easiest means to see the progression of clips and to drag the clips around the storyboard.

NOTE

Deleting a clip in the workspace does not delete it from the collection; you can reinsert it at a later time, if desired.

Edit Video Clips

Editing consists of combining, splitting, and trimming clips to get what you want and then adjusting the transitions between clips to produce the effects you want. When editing clips, the Timeline view is probably the best (except for combining clips). In the Timeline view, shown in Figure 7-11, clips are shown in proportion to the amount of time they take, and there are a number of tools for project editing.

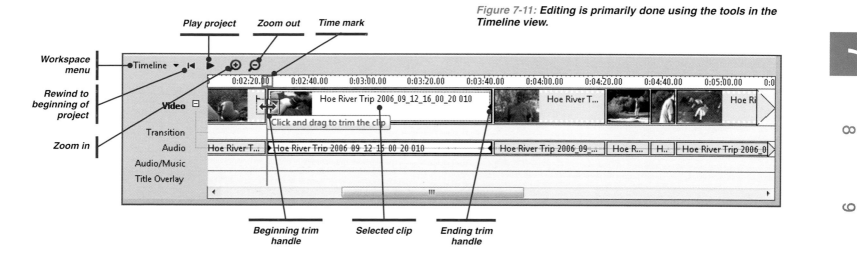

Figure 7-11: *Editing is primarily done using the tools in the Timeline view.*

COMBINE CLIPS

Movie Maker creates clips on a "best guess" basis, breaking a clip where the camera was paused. To combine two or more clips:

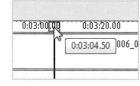

1. In either the Contents pane or the Workspace Storyboard view, click a short clip that you want to combine with its adjacent clip.

2. Hold down **CTRL**, click the adjacent clip, and click as many more adjacent clips as you want to combine.

3. When the clips you want to combine have been selected, right-click them and click **Combine** from the context menu. The selected clips will become one clip. Press **SPACEBAR** to play the combined clip.

SPLIT A CLIP

To remove frames from the middle of a clip, you need to split them clip. You can then remove frames on either side of the split.

1. In Timeline view, click a clip that you want to split. Press **SPACEBAR** to start playing the clip. When it reaches the point where you want to split it, press **SPACEBAR** to pause playing.

2. Drag the green square, the time mark, at the top of the Timeline forward or backward until you have found the precise spot in the clip where you want it split. If you have zoomed in enough (click the magnifier ⊘) and if you drag slowly, you will be able to move what you see in the preview monitor (see Figure 7-12) one frame at a time. The frame you see just before clicking Split will be the first frame of the new clip.

3. Click **Split** on the right of the playback controls.

Figure 7-12: Use the play controls to move back and forth and to select a split point in a clip.

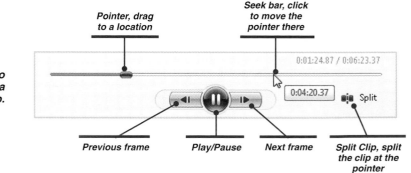

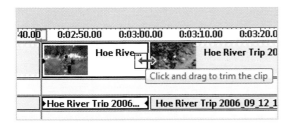

TRIM CLIPS

You can remove unwanted frames by *trimming,* or deleting, frames from the beginning or end of a clip.

1. Select Timeline view, if it isn't already selected, and click the clip you want to trim. It will appear with *trimming handles,* which are the small triangles on either end at the beginning and end of the clip and its soundtrack (in the Audio bar). When you put the mouse pointer on a trimming handle, it turns into a red double-headed arrow.

2. Click **Zoom In** (the plus sign) to increase the level of detail displayed and to give you greater accuracy in trimming.

3. If you want to trim the beginning of the clip, position the green square time mark at the beginning of the clip, press **SPACEBAR**, and play the clip to the point you want to trim.

4. Press **SPACEBAR** again and then drag the green square time mark back and forth until it is exactly placed. Then:

   - Click the **Clip** menu, and click **Trim Beginning**.

     –Or–

   - Note the exact time under the time mark, and drag the left trimming handle to the right until you reach that time. After an initial trim, play the clip and see the result. If you don't like it, you can adjust the trim in either direction, including recovering the material you trimmed.

5. To trim the right end of the clip, move the mouse pointer in the numbers at the top of the timeline until a black vertical line appears. Click when you get to the approximate point where you want to trim off the rest of the clip.

6. Press **SPACEBAR** to begin playing the clip. If you are, in fact, in the area you want to trim, press **SPACEBAR** again and then drag the green square time mark back and forth until it is exactly placed at the trim point. Then:

   - Click the **Clip** menu, and click **Trim End**.

     –Or–

   - Note the exact time under the time mark, and drag the left trimming handle to the left until you reach that time. Again, play the clip and adjust the trim as needed.

ADJUST TRANSITIONS

When you drag a clip to the workspace, it simply abuts the preceding clip. The last frame of the preceding clip plays, and then the first frame of the new clip plays. Movie Maker allows you to partially overlap one clip with another,

TIP

While you are still working with a project and have not published the movie, you can think of trimming as simply "hiding" the ends of the clips. You can recover what you have trimmed until you publish the movie.

TIP

The zoom in and zoom out features in the Timeline view of the workspace are time-oriented, not visually oriented. In other words, when you zoom in, each timeline division uses a smaller increment of time and each clip takes up more space. This is useful for trimming a clip.

NOTE

Because there is no way to delete individual frames from the middle of a clip, you need to split a clip if you want to delete frames from its middle.

simultaneously creating a fade out/fade in transition between the two clips. You do this in Timeline view.

1. Click the rightmost clip of a pair you want to overlap. Move the mouse pointer inside the green time mark at the beginning of the clip, and note the time.

2. Move the mouse pointer to the lower middle of the clip, and hold down the left mouse button while dragging the clip to the left, over the other clip. You can do this for as much of the clip as you want, but the recommended time is about half a second. Release the mouse button when you are done.

Import Other Files

In addition to bringing video in from a camcorder, Windows Movie Maker can import a number of file formats, including video, audio, and still pictures (as shown in Table 7-1). These files can be used alone or in combination with camcorder clips.

TYPE OF FILE	FILE FORMATS
Audio	AIF, AIFC, AIFF, ASF, AU, MP2, MP3, MPA. SND, WAV, WMA
Still Images	BMP, DIB, EMF, GIF, JFIF, JPE, JPEG, JPG, PNG, TIF, TIFF, WDP, WMF
Video	ASF, AVI, DVR, M1V, MP2, MP2V, MPE, MPEG, MPG, MPV2, WM, WMV

Table 7-1: *File Formats That Can Be Imported into Movie Maker*

1. If it isn't already open, start Windows Movie Maker by clicking **Start**, clicking **All Programs**, and clicking **Windows Movie Maker**.

2. In Movie Maker's Tasks view (if it isn't open, click 🖽), click **Videos, Pictures**, or **Audio Or Music**, whichever you want to bring in. The Import Media Items dialog box will appear.

3. Select the files you want to import, and click **Import**. If you are importing a video file, Movie Maker will divide it into clips if the file came with the necessary information. If you are importing either a still image or an audio file, it will simply go into Movie Maker.

In all cases, the material you imported will appear in the Contents pane of Movie Maker for use in editing and assembling a movie.

PLACE STILL PICTURES

To place still pictures you have imported to a Movie Maker project:

1. Click the **Workspace** menu, and click **Storyboard** if it isn't already open.

2. Drag the picture in the Contents pane to the storyboard at the point where you want it.

By default, still pictures are played for five seconds, but you can drag the right trimming handle to the right to lengthen its play time as long as you wish.

Add Titles to a Movie

Windows Movie Maker provides the means to add titles and text to movies you create. These can play alone or overlay video footage, and can run for any amount of time.

1. If it isn't already open, start Windows Movie Maker by clicking **Start**, clicking **All Programs**, and clicking **Windows Movie Maker**.

2. Click the **Workspace** menu, and click **Timeline** to switch to that view. Then click **Titles And Credits** in the Tasks view; or click the **Tools** menu, and click **Titles And Credits**. You are given a choice of adding a title or credits in four ways.

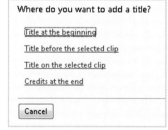

3. Click **Title At The Beginning**, type the primary title in the top text box, and type the subtitle—if you want one—in the bottom text box. You will see the title appear in the preview monitor, as shown in Figure 7-13. When you are done, replay the title by clicking the play button in the playback controls.

4. Click **Change The Title Animation** to add effects to the title. Double-click each of the animations to see if you want it. If you do, leave it selected as you proceed.

NOTE

Only Fade In And Out can be used with titles on two lines.

*Figure 7-13: **The ability to add titles is a major addition to Movie Maker in Windows Vista.***

Select title font and color

Font:

| Segoe Print ▼ | **B** *I* <u>U</u> |

Color: Transparency: 0%   Size: Position:

⟂ 🔲 [slider]   A⁺ A⁻   ≣ ≣ ≣

Change the background color

More options:

Edit the title text

Change the title animation

[Add Title] [Cancel]

5. Click **Change The Text Font And Color**. The font and color panes are displayed. Click the **Font** down arrow to change the font; click to apply bold, italic, or underline; click to open the color palette and change the color for the text and/or the background; and use the remaining tools to change the transparency, size, and position of the text.

6. At any time you can click **Edit The Title Text** to return to the title text boxes and edit what's there.

7. When you are satisfied with the title, click **Add Title**, and the title will be added at the beginning of the timeline. By default, the title slide is played for five seconds, but you can drag the right trimming handle to the right to lengthen its play time or to the left to shorten it.

TIP

To edit a title once it has been placed, right-click the title block and click **Edit Title**.

UICKSTEPS

EMPLOYING EFFECTS AND TRANSITIONS

Windows Movie Maker includes a number of special effects and transitions that you can add to the movies that you create.

ADD EFFECTS

Effects are added to an entire clip and specify how that clip, be it a title, a video, or still image, performs when it is played. Examples of effects are blurs, fades, pans, and zooms. A clip may have more than one effect. To add effects to an ongoing project:

1. Click **Effects** in Tasks view. A number of effects will appear in the Contents pane. Double-click any of the effects you may be interested in to see how they work.

2. When you find an effect you want to use, drag it to the clip where you want to use it in either Storyboard or Timeline view. A small star icon will appear in the clip, as you can see in Figure 7-14.

3. To change, add, or remove effects, right-click the clip and click **Effects**. The Add Or Remove Effects dialog box appears. Select effects on either side, and click **Add** or **Remove**. When you are done, click **OK**.

Continued . . .

Figure 7-14: *Your viewers might find the overuse of effects in your movies annoying.*

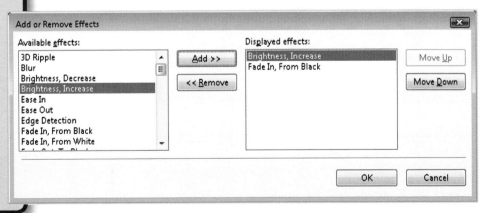

| | | |

UICKSTEPS

EMPLOYING EFFECTS AND TRANSITIONS *(Continued)*

USE TRANSITIONS

Transitions are added in between clips and specify how any two contiguous clips transition from one clip to the next. Examples of transitions are bars, dissolve, flip, and iris. A clip may have more than one transition. To add transitions to an ongoing project:

1. Click **Transitions** in Tasks view. A number of transitions will appear in the Contents pane. Double-click any of the transitions you may be interested in to see how they work.

2. When you find a transition you want to use, drag it to the space between clips where you want to use it (in Storyboard view), or drag it to the Transition layer (in Timeline view). In Storyboard view, the transition will appear between the clips. In Timeline view, the transition will appear as a block in the transition layer.

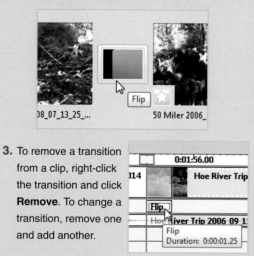

3. To remove a transition from a clip, right-click the transition and click **Remove**. To change a transition, remove one and add another.

The other types of titling are similar to the title at the beginning, except that you have to select where in the timeline they belong. Titles before a selected clip and credits at the end place a block in the video timeline. Titles that overlay selected clips put a block in the Title Overlay layer of the timeline, where you can drag it any place you want it.

Add Sound to a Movie

If you have imported video from a camcorder, you probably have sound that was recorded with the video. In addition, you can add sound to a project by either inserting an audio clip or recording narration.

PLACE AN AUDIO CLIP

An audio clip is an audio file that has been imported into Movie Maker (see "Import Other Files" earlier in this chapter). It can be of any length and in any of the identified formats. Once it has been imported into the Contents pane:

1. Drag a selected audio clip from the Contents pane to where you want it in the Timeline view's Audio/Music layer.

2. Shorten the audio clip by dragging the right end to the left. You can also drag the entire audio clip to move it left or right in the project.

3. Adjust the volume of the clip by right-clicking it and clicking **Volume**. The Audio Clip Volume control is displayed. Drag the slider to where you want it, and click **OK**.

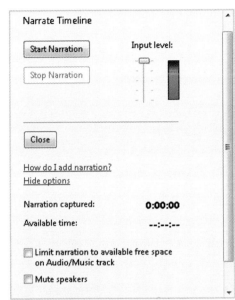

Narrate Timeline

| Start Narration | Input level: |

| Stop Narration |

| Close |

How do I add narration?
Hide options

Narration captured: **0:00:00**

Available time: --:--:--

☐ Limit narration to available free space
   on Audio/Music track

☐ Mute speakers

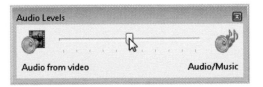

RECORD NARRATION

Narration occupies the same Timeline layer as the audio clips that you placed there. To record narration:

1. Make sure your microphone is connected to your computer and working properly. Then click the **Workspace** menu, and click **Narrate Timeline**. The Narrate Timeline pane will open.

2. Click **Show Options**, drag the bottom border of the workspace down, if needed, and then click **Mute Speakers** so that they won't send feedback into your microphone. Also, if you want to limit your narration to the time between the green time mark and the start of any audio clip you placed, click **Limit Narration To Available Free Space On Audio/Music Track**.

3. Drag the green time mark to the point in the timeline where you want the narration to begin. If you clicked **Limit Narration**, the available time will appear in the Narrate Timeline pane.

4. Click **Start Narration**, record the narration you want to add, and click **Stop Narration** when you are finished. Type the name of the audio file that will be saved, and click **Save**. Click **Close** to close the Narrate Timeline pane. The recorded sound clip will appear on the timeline.

5. Adjust the volume of the clip by right-clicking it and clicking **Volume**. The Audio Clip Volume control is displayed. Drag the slider to where you want it, and click **OK**.

MIX SOUND TRACKS

After adding a sound clip, either an imported file or a narrated one, you have two sound tracks—one that was on the original camcorder importation (assuming you imported video from a camcorder) and one that you have added. By default, the volume level of both tracks is the same. You can adjust the relative level between the two soundtracks by clicking the **Workspace** menu and clicking **Audio Levels**. The Audio Levels dialog box will appear, as you can see in the illustration. Dragging the slider one way or the other sets the relative level between the two tracks for the entire project. Close the Audio Levels dialog box when you are done.

Publish a Movie

The final step in making a movie is to publish it as movie file that can be played by Windows Media Player. When you are happy with your project:

1. Click **Publish Movie** on the project toolbar. The Publish Movie dialog box will appear, as shown in Figure 7-15.

2. Click how you want to replay this movie. (The most versatile way is to save it for replay on either your computer or a DVD player.) Click **Next**.

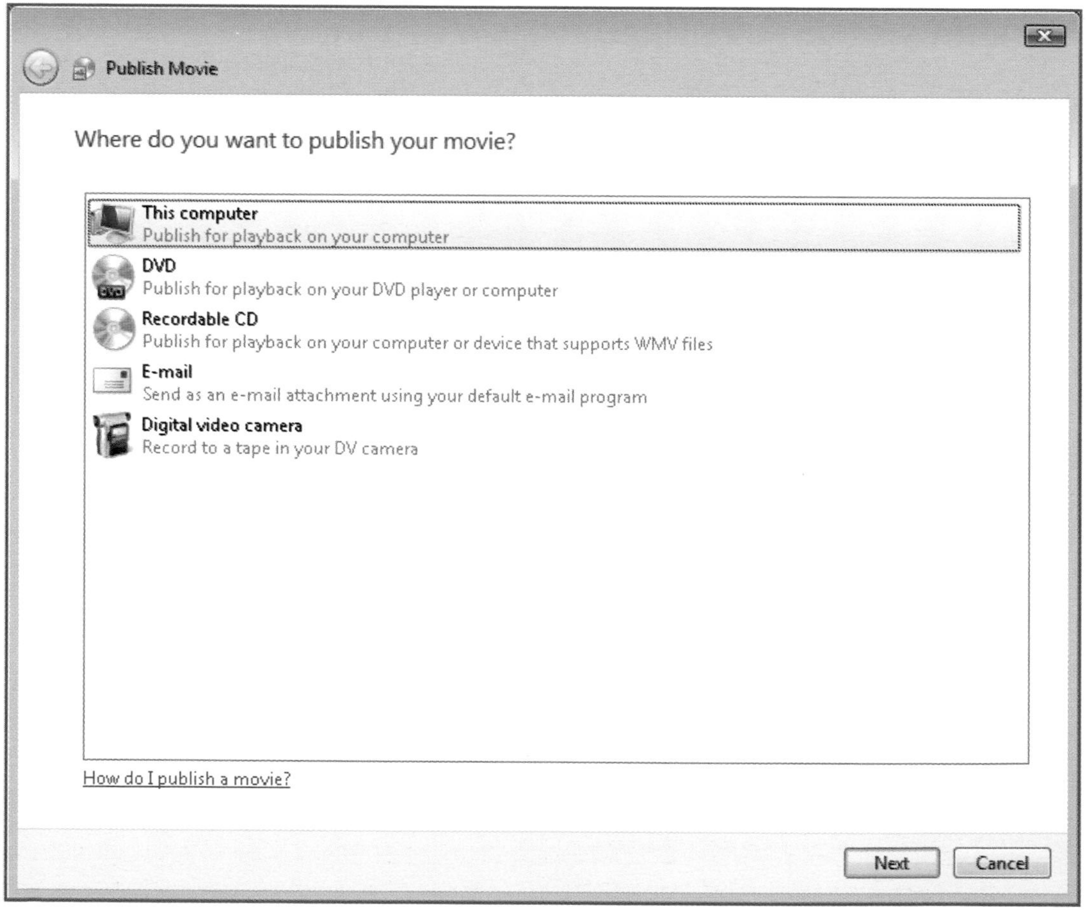

Publish Movie

Publish Movie

Where do you want to publish your movie?

This computer
Publish for playback on your computer

DVD
Publish for playback on your DVD player or computer

Recordable CD
Publish for playback on your computer or device that supports WMV files

E-mail
Send as an e-mail attachment using your default e-mail program

Digital video camera
Record to a tape in your DV camera

How do I publish a movie?

Next   Cancel

*Figure 7-15: **Saving a movie is equivalent to printing a document: You still have the original content to rebuild the movie, but the movie itself can't be edited.***

QUICKSTEPS

EXPLORING WINDOWS MEDIA CENTER

Windows Media Center, with the right equipment, allows you to view, record, and play back live TV. It also provides an enhanced playback and viewing experience with DVDs, CDs, and the music and photographic libraries you have on your computer. It connects you to many Web services—some from Microsoft, and many from other vendors. Windows Media Center is available in Windows Vista Home Premium and Windows Vista Ultimate editions.

To effectively use and get full benefit from Windows Media Center, you need all the recommended computer components discussed in the "Preparing to Make a Movie" QuickSteps, as well as a TV tuner card in your computer. These cards are available for approximately $100 from several companies. Look for compatibility with Windows Media Center.

To use Media Center, click **Start**, click **All Programs**, and click **Windows Media Center**. The first time you do that, you will go through an initial setup (see Figure 7-16) that looks at the hardware that is available on your computer. You will then need to click **Set Up TV**, and Media Center will be configured for the type of TV signal you have (antenna, cable, or satellite). Then you will be asked questions about your ZIP code so that you can receive

Continued . . .

3. With the DVD choice, Movie Maker will save the project, and Windows DVD Maker will open. Type a new name if the default project name is not satisfactory, and then click **Options**.

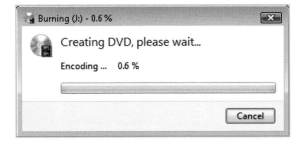

4. The DVD Options dialog box will appear. Select the choices you want, click **OK**, and then click **Next.**

5. Choose the style of menu, which provides links to play the movie or view scenes, and click **Burn**. If you have a blank DVD in your drive, the process will begin It will take a bit of time, depending on the speed of your computer and DVD drive.

QUICKSTEPS

EXPLORING WINDOWS MEDIA CENTER (Continued)

an online TV guide tailored to your local area. When you are done with the setup, you will see the main Media Center screen with none of the standard Windows components, as you can see in Figure 7-17. At this point, you can use your mouse, the keyboard, or the TV remote control that came with your TV tuner card to navigate. The possibilities of what you can do are significant.

Figure 7-16: *Setting up Windows Media Center can be practically automatic, requiring that you answer only a couple of questions.*

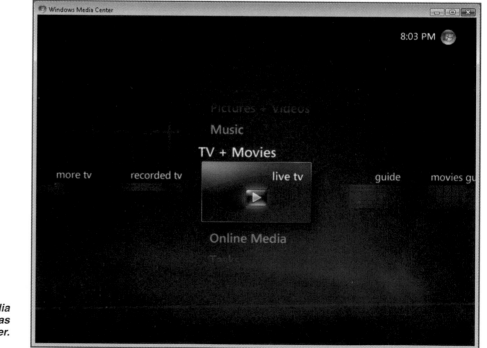

Figure 7-17: *The Windows Media Center brings live as well as recorded TV to your computer.*

How to...

- *Set Up Users*
- *Understanding User Account Control*
- *Setting Passwords*
- *Reset a Password*
- *Replace Passwords*
- *Customize a User Account*
- *Switch Among Users*
- *Set Parental Controls*
- *Control What Parts of Windows Can Be Used*
- *Set File and Folder Sharing*
- *Testing an Internet Firewall*
- *Use and Add Groups*
- *Understanding Permissions*
- *Protect Files and Folders*
- *Locking a Computer*
- *Use Encrypted Files and Folders*

Chapter 8
Controlling Security

Controlling computer security is a complex subject because of the many different aspects of computing that need protection. In this chapter you'll see how to control who uses a computer, control what users do, and protect data stored in the computer.

Control Who Is a User

Controlling who uses a computer means identifying the users to the computer, giving them a secure way of signing on to the computer, and preventing everyone else from using it. This is achieved through the process of adding and managing users and passwords.

With Windows Vista, like previous versions of Windows, the first user of a computer is, by default, an administrator; however, unlike previous versions of Windows, the Vista administrator operates like a standard user until there is a need to be an administrator. Then a new Vista feature called *User Account Control* (UAC) pops up and asks if the administrator started the process. If so,

NOTE

This book talks about setting up *local* user accounts, which are those that are set up on and use a local computer, as well as a workgroup local area network (LAN). If your computer is part of a domain (generally found in larger organizations—see Chapter 9 for a discussion of domains), it is important to use domain user accounts that are set up on a domain controller rather than local user accounts, since local user accounts are not recognized by the domain.

TIP

If your personal account on your computer is currently set up as an Administrator account, it is strongly recommended that you create a new Standard User account and use that for your everyday computer use. Only use the Administrator account for installing software, changing and adding user information, and performing other tasks requiring an administrator.

click **Continue** to proceed. A non-administrative user in the same circumstance would have to enter an administrator's password to continue.

Even though you may initially, as the first user, be an administrator, *it is strongly recommend that your normal everyday account be as a standard user*. The reason for this is that if you are signed on as an administrator and a hacker or malevolent software (called "malware") enters your system at the same time, the hacker or software might gain administrator privileges through you. The best solution is to use a separate administrator account with a strong password just for installing software, working with users, and performing other tasks requiring extensive administrator work.

Set Up Users

To add users to your computer, or even to change your user characteristics (as well as to perform most other tasks in this chapter), you must be logged on as an administrator, so you first need to accomplish that. Then you may want to change the characteristics of your account and add a Standard User account for yourself. Finally, if you have multiple people using your computer, you may want to set up separate user accounts and have each user sign in to his or her account.

LOG ON AS AN ADMINISTRATOR

The procedure for logging on as an administrator depends on what was done when Windows Vista was installed on your computer:

- If you are in an organization with people responsible for supporting the computers in the organization, you will most likely need to contact them to determine the procedure for logging on as an administrator.

- If you installed Windows Vista on your computer, or you bought a computer with it already installed, and did nothing special to the default installation regarding administrator privileges, you should be the administrator and know the administrator's password (if you established one).

- If you did not do the installation or you got the computer with Vista already installed and you are unsure about your administrator status or password, the instructions here will help you log on as an administrator. The first step is to determine the administrator status on your computer.

1. Click **Start** and click **Control Panel**. In Control Panel Home, click **User Accounts And Family Safety**, and then click (or double-click in Classic view) **User Accounts**. The User Accounts window opens, as shown in Figure 8-1.

   If your User Accounts window opens and shows you are a standard user, as does Figure 8-1, you need to proceed with these steps. If the window shows you are an administrator, then you can skip these steps and go on to "Change Your Account" later in this chapter.

2. Click **Change Your Account Type**:

   - If you are not an administrator, the User Account Control dialog box will appear and ask you to type the administrator's password. If you can, do that and skip to "Change Your Account" later in the chapter.

   - If you are an administrator, the dialog box will ask if you started this action. If so, click **Continue** and skip to "Change Your Account" later in the chapter.

   - If you are not an administrator and you don't know an administrator's password, try leaving the Password field blank and clicking **OK**, which would be the password if someone didn't fill one in. If that doesn't work, you will need outside support to log on as an administrator.

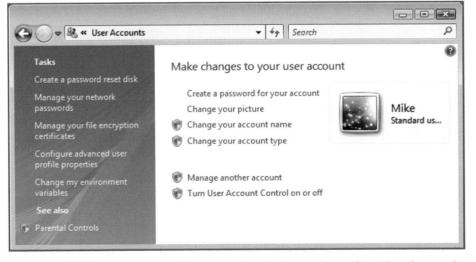

Figure 8-1: *Setting up users provides a way of protecting each user from the others and from unauthorized use.*

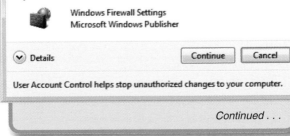

QUICKFACTS

UNDERSTANDING USER ACCOUNT CONTROL *(Continued)*

If you have both Administrator and Standard User accounts, then, while you are using the Standard User account, you can simply enter the administrator's password when needed—you don't need to switch users. In addition, if a program requires you to be an administrator in order to run it, you can right-click the program and click **Run As Administrator**. If you are logged on as an administrator, that's all you have to do. If you are not logged on as an administrator, then you will have to enter a password and click **OK**.

All operations that require administrative privileges have a little shield icon beside them, as shown here:

> **Open**
> Open file location
> 🛡 Run as administrator
> Pin to Start Menu
> Add to Quick Launch

For a while, especially if you are installing several programs, the UAC dialog boxes can be irritating. You can turn it off in the User Accounts control panel, but this is strongly discouraged. If you do turn it off while you are installing several programs, it is strongly recommended that you turn it back on when you are finished.

TIP

For a password to be *strong,* it must be eight or more characters long; use both upper- and lowercase letters; and use a mixture of letters, numbers, and symbols, including spaces. It also should not be a recognizable word, name, or date.

CHANGE YOUR ACCOUNT

You can change an account name, the display picture, add or change a password, and possibly change the account type.

1. Click **Start** and click **Control Panel**. In Control Panel Home, click **User Accounts And Family Safety**, and then click (or double-click in Classic view) **User Accounts**.

2. Click **Change Your Account Name**. The User Account Control dialog box will appear and, if you are not already logged on as an administrator, ask you to type an administrator's password. If you are signed on as an administrator, the dialog box will ask if you started this action. Type the password or click **Continue**.

3. Type a new name, and click **Change Name**.

In a similar manner, you can change your display picture. If you are the only administrator, you will not be allowed to change your account type or delete your account. Changing and setting passwords are discussed in the "Setting Passwords" QuickSteps in this chapter.

SET UP ANOTHER USER

To set up another user account, possibly a Standard User account for your use:

1. Click **Start** and click **Control Panel**. In Control Panel Home, click **User Accounts And Family Safety**, and then click (or double-click in Classic view) **User Accounts**. The User Accounts window opens.

2. Click **Manage Another Account**, and click **Continue**; or type a password, and click **OK** to open the Manage Accounts window, as shown in Figure 8-2.

3. Click **Create A New Account**. Type a name of up to 20 characters. Note that it cannot contain just periods, spaces, or the @ symbol; it cannot contain " / \ [ ] : ; | = ,+ * ? < >; and leading spaces or periods are dropped.

4. Accept the default account type, **Standard User**, or click **Administrator** as the account type. You can see a summary of the privileges available to each user type.

> ⦿ Standard user
> Standard account users can use most software and change system settings that do not affect other users or the security of the computer.
>
> ○ Administrator
> Administrators have complete access to the computer and can make any desired changes. To help make the computer more secure, administrators are asked to provide their password or confirmation before making changes that affect other users.

5. Click **Create Account**. You are returned to the Manage Accounts window. Changing other aspects of the account is described in later sections of this chapter.

8

UICKSTEPS

SETTING PASSWORDS

Passwords are the primary keys used to allow some people to use a computer and to keep others away. While there are recent alternatives to passwords (see "Replace Passwords" in this chapter), most computer protection depends on them.

CREATE A PASSWORD

After setting up a new user account, you can add a password to it that will then be required to use that account.

1. Click **Start** and click **Control Panel**. In Control Panel Home, click **User Accounts And Family Safety**, and then click (or double-click in Classic view) **User Accounts**. The User Accounts window opens.

2. If it is not your account that you want to add a password to, click **Manage Another Account**, and click **Continue**; or type a password, click **OK**, and click the account you want. In your account or in the other account that opens, click **Create A Password**.

   The Create A Password window will open, as shown in Figure 8-3. Note the warning message. This is true every time you create, change, or delete a password.

3. Type the new password, click in the second text box, type the new password again to confirm it, click in the third text box, type a non-obvious hint to help you remember the password, and click **Create Password**.

4. Close the Change An Account window.

Continued . . .

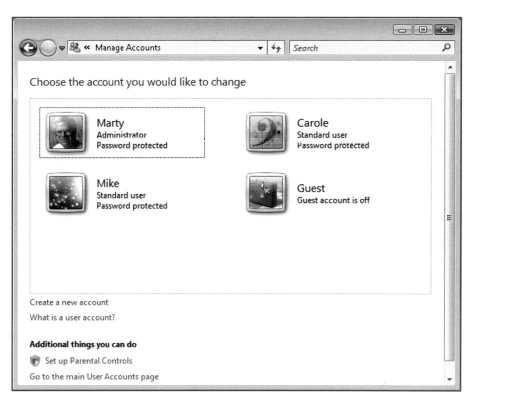

*Figure 8-2: **User Accounts provides password and user account management.***

Reset a Password

Windows Vista allows you to reset a password you have forgotten if you have previously created a password reset disk.

CREATE A RESET DISK

1. Insert a USB flash drive in its socket, or insert a writable CD or a formatted and unused floppy disk into its respective drive. Close the AutoPlay window if it opens.

2. Click **Start** and click **Control Panel**. In Control Panel Home, click **User Accounts And Family Safety**, and then click (or double-click in Classic view) **User Accounts**. The User Accounts window opens.

QUICKSTEPS

SETTING PASSWORDS *(Continued)*

CHANGE A PASSWORD

It is a good idea to periodically change your password in case it has been compromised.

1. Click **Start** and click **Control Panel**. In Control Panel Home, click **User Accounts And Family Safety**, and then click (or double-click in Classic view) **User Accounts**. The User Accounts window opens.

2. If it is not your account that you want to change, click **Manage Another Account**, and click **Continue**; or type a password, click **OK**, and click the account you want to change. In your account or in the other account that opens, click **Change Your/The Password**.

3. Type the current password, click in the second text box, type a new password, click in the third text box, and type the new password again to confirm it. Click in the fourth text box, type a non-obvious hint to help you remember the password, and click **Change Password**.

4. Close the Change An Account window.

REMOVE A PASSWORD

If you move a computer to a location that doesn't need a password, for example, if it is not accessible to anyone else, or if you want to remove a password for some other reason, you can do so.

1. Click **Start** and click **Control Panel**. In Control Panel Home, click **User Accounts And Family Safety**, and then click (or double-click in Classic view) **User Accounts**. The User Accounts window opens.

Continued . . .

*Figure 8-3: **Creating, changing, or deleting a password will lose all items that are based on passwords, such as encrypted files, certificates, and other passwords.***

3. Click **Create A Password Reset Disk** in the list of tasks on the left. If needed, click **Continue**; or type a password, and click **OK**.

4. The Forgotten Password Wizard opens. Click **Next**. Click the drive down arrow, and select the drive on which you want to create the password key. Click **Next**.

5. Type the current user account password, and again click **Next**. The disk will be created. When it is done, click **Next**. Then click **Finish**. Remove and label the disk, and store it in a safe place.

6. Close the User Accounts window.

UICKSTEPS

SETTING PASSWORDS *(Continued)*

2. If it is not your account in which you want to remove the password, click **Manage Another Account**, and click **Continue**; or type a password, click **OK**, and click the account you want. In your account or in the other account that opens, click **Remove Your/The Password**.

3. Type the current password, and click **Remove Password**.

4. Close the Change An Account window.

NOTE

If your password is over 14 characters, you will not be able to log on to a network from a Windows 95/98/Me computer.

CAUTION

With a password reset disk, anyone can reset a password. Therefore, it is important to store the reset disk in a safe place.

CAUTION

If an administrator resets your password all passwords and encrypted files tied to the original password are permanently no longer accessible with the new password. If you use a password reset disk to reset your password you will retain access to all your original information.

USE A RESET DISK

If you have forgotten your password and there isn't another person with administrator permissions on your computer who can reset it, you can use a reset disk you have previously created.

1. Start your computer. When you see the Welcome screen, click your user name. If you have forgotten your password, click the right arrow. You will be told that the user name or password is incorrect.

2. Click **OK** to return to the password entry, and look at your hint.

3. If the hint isn't of any help, click **Reset Password**. The Password Reset Wizard opens.

4. Click **Next**. Insert your reset disk in the drive. Click the drive down arrow, select the drive the reset disk is in, and again click **Next**. Type a new password, confirm it, type a password hint, click **Next**, and click **Finish**.

5. Enter your new password, and press ENTER.

Replace Passwords

The weakest link in the Windows Vista security scheme is the use of passwords. Users give their passwords to others or forget them, and passwords are often stolen or just "found." There is nothing to tie a password to an individual, which is handy for sharing, but also a security risk. Two potential means of replacing passwords are smart cards and biometric devices.

SMART CARDS

Smart cards are credit card-sized pieces of plastic that have a tamper-resistant electronic circuit embedded in them that permanently stores an ID, a password, and other information. Smart cards require a personal identification number (PIN), so they add a second layer (smart card plus PIN in place of a password) that is needed to log on to a system.

Windows Vista detects and supports smart cards, and lets them be used to log on to a computer or network, as well for other authentication needs.

Smart cards require a reader be attached to the computer, either through a USB (universal serial bus) port or a PCMCIA (Personal Computer Memory Card

NOTE

A CD, a floppy disk, or a USB flash drive can hold the password reset for only one user at a time.

NOTE

In case you wondered, the PIN is encrypted and placed on the smart card when it is made. The PIN is not stored on the computer.

International Association) slot. With a smart card reader, users only need to insert their card into the reader at the logon screen, at which point they are prompted for their PIN. With a valid card and PIN, users are authenticated and allowed on the system in the same way as they would by entering a valid user name and password.

Windows Vista lists a number of smart card readers that Microsoft has tested with Windows Vista. The drivers for these devices either are included with or are available for Windows Vista, and installing them is not difficult; you need only follow the instructions that come with them.

With a smart card reader installed, set up new accounts (as described under "Set Up Users") and then, for both new and old accounts, open each user's Create Password page, and click **Smart Card Is Required For Interactive Logon**, which will appear when a smart card is present. You do not have to enter a password.

BIOMETRIC DEVICES

Smart cards do provide an added degree of security over passwords, but if someone obtains both the card and the PIN, he or she's home free. The only way to be totally sure that the computer is actually talking to the authorized person is to require some physical identification of the person.

This is the purpose of *biometric devices,* which identify people by physical traits, such as voice, handprint, fingerprint, face, or eyes. Often, these devices are used with a smart card to replace the PIN. Biometric devices are just beginning to move into the mass production stage, and nothing is built into Windows Vista specifically to handle them. Devices and custom installations are available for under $100, for a fingerprint scanner, to several thousand dollars for a face scanner. More and more laptops have fingerprint scanners built in. Depending on your needs, you may want to keep these devices in mind.

Customize a User Account

Each user account can be unique, with a custom Start menu, desktop, color scheme, and screen saver. When programs are installed, you can choose whether they are for just the current user or for all users. When you set up a new user, it is as though you are setting up a new computer. The previous chapters of this book talk about the steps to set up a computer.

As you may have seen earlier in this chapter, a number of elements of the account itself can be changed, including the name, password, display picture, and account type. You can change the name and password in a manner almost identical to what you used to create them, as described in "Set Up Users" and the "Setting Passwords" QuickSteps earlier in this chapter.

Switch Among Users

When you have multiple users on a computer, one can obviously log off and another log on; however, with the Welcome screen, you can use Fast User Switching. This allows you to keep programs running and files open when you temporarily switch to another user. To use Fast User Switching:

1. Click **Start**, click the shut-down options arrow, and click **Switch User**. The Welcome screen will appear. Let the other person log on.

2. When the other person has finished using the computer and has logged off (by clicking **Start**, clicking the shut-down options arrow, and clicking **Log Off**), you can log on normally. When you do, you will see all your programs exactly as you left them.

Control What a User Does

User accounts identify people and allow them to log on to your computer. What they can do after that depends on the permissions they have. Windows Vista has two features that help you control what other users do on your computer: Parental Controls and the ability to turn Windows features on and off for a given user. In addition, Vista's NT File System (NTFS) allows the sharing of folders and drives as well as the assignment of permissions to use a file, a folder, a disk, a printer, and other devices. The permissions are given to individuals and to groups to which individuals can belong. So far, you've seen two groups: Administrators and Standard Users (also called just "Users,"), but there are others, and you can create more.

You can limit the sharing of files and folders to the *Public folder* within the Users folder on your computer. To do so, you must move the files and folders you want to share into the Public folder. The other option is to directly share the other folders on your computer. This is made easier by the *inheritance* attribute, where subfolders automatically inherit (take on) the permissions of their parent folder. Every object in Windows Vista NTFS, however, has its own set of *security descriptors* that are attached to it when it is created, and with the proper permission, these security descriptors can be individually changed.

When permissions are appropriately set, other users on your computer can access and optionally change your files and folders. Also, with appropriate permissions and other settings (see Chapter 9 for a discussion on sharing across a network), people on other computers or even you on another computer on the local area network (LAN) of which your computer is a member, can access and optionally change your files and folders.

By default, the disks, folders, and files on your computer are not shared and only you can access them. You will see in the following sections how to share everything on your computer except your entire C: drive—the drive on which Vista is installed. Unlike previous versions of Windows, you can no longer share the entire C: drive, although you can share as many folders on it as you wish.

Set Parental Controls

If you have a child as one of the users on your computer and you are an administrator with a password, you can control what your child can do on your computer, including hours of usage, programs he or she can run, and access to the Internet. When your child encounters a blocked program, game, or Web site, a notice is displayed, including a link the child can click to request access. You, as an administrator, can allow one-time access by entering your user ID and password.

1. Click **Start** and click **Control Panel**. In Control Panel Home, click **User Accounts And Family Safety**, and then click (or double-click in Classic view) **Parental Controls**. Click **Continue**; or type a password, and click **OK**. The Parental Controls window opens.

Set up how Mike will use the computer

Parental Controls:
- ● On, enforce current settings
- ○ Off

Activity Reporting:
- ● On, collect information about computer usage
- ○ Off

Windows Settings

🌐 **Windows Vista Web Filter**
Control allowed websites, downloads, and other use

⏱ **Time limits**
Control when Mike uses the computer

🏆 **Games**
Control games by rating, content, or title

🖼 **Allow and block specific programs**
Allow and block any programs on your computer

Current Settings:

Mike
Standard user
No Password

🖼 View activity reports

Web Restrictions:	Medium
Time Limits:	Off
Game Ratings:	Off
Program Limits:	Off

OK

Figure 8-4: ***Parental Controls allow you to determine what a child can do and see on your computer.***

2. If you do not have a password, you will be reminded that you need to create one in order to set Parental Controls. To add a password, click the reminder note. Type the password, click the second password box, and type the password again. Click in the password hint box, and type the hint. Click **OK**.

3. Click the user for whom you want to set Parental Controls to open the individual User Controls window.

4. Click **On** under Parental Controls, and, if you want it, click **On** under Activity Reporting, as shown in Figure 8-4.

5. Click **Windows Vista Web Filter**, and then, in each case if desired, click **Block Some Web Sites Or Content**; click **Edit The Allow And Block List**, type the sites to be blocked or allowed, and click **OK**; click **Only Allow Websites Which Are On The Allow List**; click the Web restriction level you want; click **Block File Downloads**; and click **OK**.

6. Click **Time Limits**, drag the hours to block or allow (you only need to select one or the other, and you can drag across multiple days), and then click **OK**.

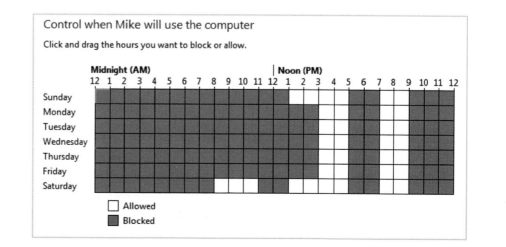

Control when Mike will use the computer

Click and drag the hours you want to block or allow.

☐ Allowed
■ Blocked

7. Click **Games** and choose if any games can be played. Click **Set Game Ratings**, choose if games with no rating can be played, click a rating level, choose type of content you want blocked, and click **OK**. Click **Block Or Allow Specific Games**, click whether to block or allow specific games, and click **OK**. Click **OK** again to leave Game Controls.

8. Click **Allow And Block Specific Programs**, and choose whether to allow the use of all programs or only the ones you choose. If you choose to pick specific programs to allow, a list of all the programs on the computer is presented. Click those for which you want to allow access, and click **OK**.

9. Click **OK** to close the User Controls window.

Control What Parts of Windows Can Be Used

As an administrator, you can control what parts of Windows Vista each user can use.

1. Log on as the user for whom you want to set Windows feature usage.

2. Click **Start** and click **Control Panel**. In Control Panel Home, click **Programs** and then click (or double-click in Classic view) **Programs And Features**.

3. Click **Turn Windows Features On Or Off**. Click **Continue**; or type a password, and click **OK**. The Windows Features dialog box appears.

4. Click an unselected check box to turn a feature on, or click a selected check box to turn a feature off. Click the plus sign (+) where applicable to open the sub-features and turn them on or off.

5. When you have selected the features the user will be allowed, click **OK**.

6. Close the Programs And Features window.

Set File and Folder Sharing

Files are shared by being in a shared folder or drive. Folders and drives are shared by their creator or owner or by an administrator. To share folders and drives, as well as printers and other devices, both locally and over a network, you must

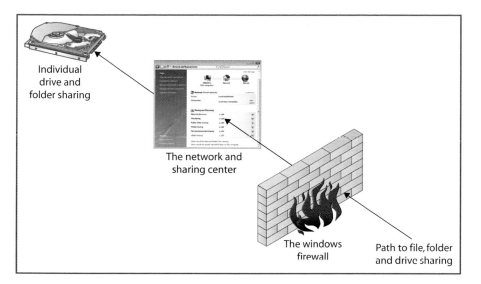

Individual
drive and
folder sharing

The network and
sharing center

The windows
firewall

Path to file, folder
and drive sharing

Figure 8-5: **The sharing of your computer requires that you set up your firewall, the Network And Sharing Center, and the individual drives and folders to accomplish that.**

address three components of Windows Vista that allow you to control access to your computer and its components (see Figure 8-5):

- **The Windows Firewall**, which protects your computer and its contents from network access

- **The Network And Sharing Center**, which is the primary means of controlling sharing in Windows Vista

- **Sharing individual drives and folders**, which lets you determine if a drive, folder, or other device is shared, who has permission to access it, and what they can do with the contents

SET UP THE WINDOWS FIREWALL

Windows Vista includes the Windows Firewall, whose objective is to slow down and hopefully prevent anybody from accessing your computer without your permission, while at the same time, allowing those with whom you want to use your computer to do so. The Windows Firewall is turned on by default. Check to see if it is; if it isn't, turn it on.

1. Click **Start** and click **Control Panel**. In Control Panel Home, click **Network And Internet**, and then click (or double-click in Classic view) **Windows Firewall**. The Windows Firewall window opens and shows your firewall status.

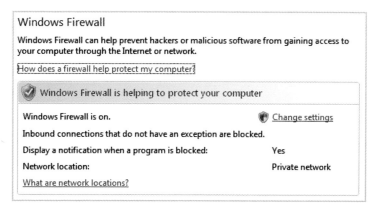

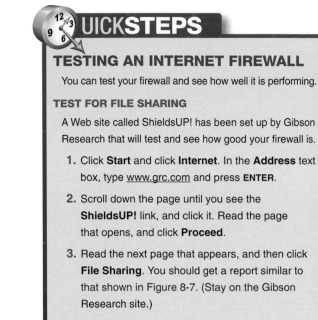

TESTING AN INTERNET FIREWALL

You can test your firewall and see how well it is performing.

TEST FOR FILE SHARING

A Web site called ShieldsUP! has been set up by Gibson Research that will test and see how good your firewall is.

1. Click **Start** and click **Internet**. In the **Address** text box, type www.grc.com and press **ENTER**.

2. Scroll down the page until you see the **ShieldsUP!** link, and click it. Read the page that opens, and click **Proceed**.

3. Read the next page that appears, and then click **File Sharing**. You should get a report similar to that shown in Figure 8-7. (Stay on the Gibson Research site.)

The Windows Vista Firewall generally does pretty well on this test.

TEST FOR PORT VULNERABILITY

Gibson Research has a second test for specific port vulnerability. (In this case, "ports" are pre-assigned addresses that, when combined with your computer's address, allow a specific type of traffic, like e-mail, into your computer).

1. While still on the Gibson Research site's ShieldsUP! page, scroll down and click **Common Ports**. Scroll down and look at the details. It is far better than Gibson would have you believe.

   On the computer in Figure 8-7 the test shows that only the FTP port is open. In my opinion, this is not a serious issue. Anyone who actually tried to exploit this vulnerability would have a hard time doing so with any success.

2. When you are done, close Internet Explorer.

Continued . . .

2. If your firewall is not turned on or if you want to turn it off, click **Turn Windows Firewall On Or Off** in the pane on the left. Click **Continue**; or type a password, and click **OK**. The Windows Firewall Settings dialog box appears. Click the respective option button to turn on your firewall (highly recommended) or to turn it off. Click **OK**.

3. To change the settings for what the firewall will and won't let through, click **Change Settings**. Click **Continue**; or type a password, and click **OK**. The Windows Firewall Settings dialog box appears.

4. Click the **Exceptions** tab. In the Exceptions tab, shown in Figure 8-6, select the services running on your computer that you want to allow people to come in from the

*Figure 8-6: **The Windows Vista Firewall can be configured to allow certain programs and features to come through.***

TESTING AN INTERNET FIREWALL

(Continued)

Windows Vista Firewall is very good and one of the easiest to use. If you are still concerned about Internet security, however, there are both hardware and other software firewalls available. To start, consider the firewalls that come with antivirus software such as Norton Antivirus. You can also look at ZoneAlarm from Zone Labs (both free and paid-for software) at www.zonelabs.com and WatchGuard (various models of hardware) at www.watchguard.com.

TIP

In the Windows Firewall Settings Exceptions tab, you can determine what each option does by highlighting it and clicking **Properties** at the bottom of the dialog box.

NOTE

You will probably have other programs checked such as Internet Explorer and Messenger that allow you to use those programs on the Internet.

TIP

If you have a specific program not on the Windows Firewall Exceptions list, you can include that program by clicking **Add Program** on the Exceptions tab in the Windows Firewall Settings dialog box. Select the program from the list or browse to its location, and click **OK**.

Internet and use your computer. To share information across a local area network (LAN), click at least the following items:

- Core Networking
- File And Printer Sharing
- Network Discovery
- Windows Collaboration Computer Name Registration Service
- Windows Peer To Peer Collaboration Foundation

5. Click to select each exception you want enabled. Click **OK** to close the Windows Firewall Settings dialog box.

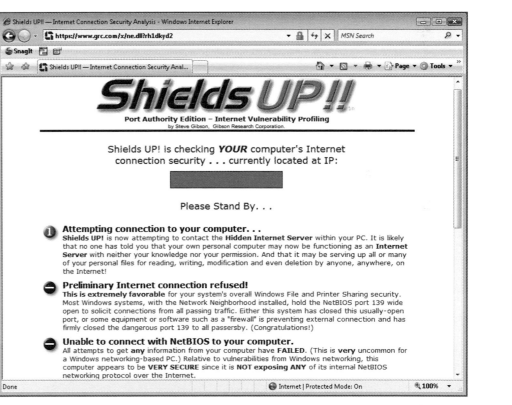

Figure 8-7: *The Windows Vista Firewall does well in the firewall tests.*

Turn off Password Protected Sharing if you want the easiest sharing of resources with other computers on your LAN.

USE THE NETWORK AND SHARING CENTER

The second layer of file-sharing protection in Windows Vista is controlled with the Network And Sharing Center, shown in Figure 8-8, which allows you to turn on or off the primary components of sharing information among users on a computer and across a network.

The first time Windows Vista was run, a choice was made between a public and private network. The Network And Sharing Center allows you to change that. If you are primarily sharing your computer with other computers within an organization or a residence, then you should select Private, where network sharing is relatively simple. If you are primarily using public wireless or cable Internet connections and very little sharing of your computer, select Public, which makes it more difficult for someone to get onto your computer.

Figure 8-8: *The Network And Sharing Center is the primary means of sharing your computer.*

1. Click **Start** and click **Control Panel**. In Control Panel Home, click **Network And Internet**, and then click (or double-click in Classic view) **Network And Sharing Center**. The Network And Sharing Center window opens, as shown in Figure 8-8.

2. If you want to change the type of network (private or public) you are connected to, click **Customize**, click **Public** or **Private**, click **Continue** or type a password and click **OK**, click **Next**, and click **Close**.

3. Click each of the Sharing And Discovery settings you think you might want to turn on, click the down arrow on the right, read the description, click the appropriate sub-options, and click **Apply**. Click **Continue** or type a password and click **OK**, as requested. For sharing within a private network you most likely want to turn on:

    - Network Discovery
    - File Sharing
    - Public Folder Sharing
    - Printer Sharing

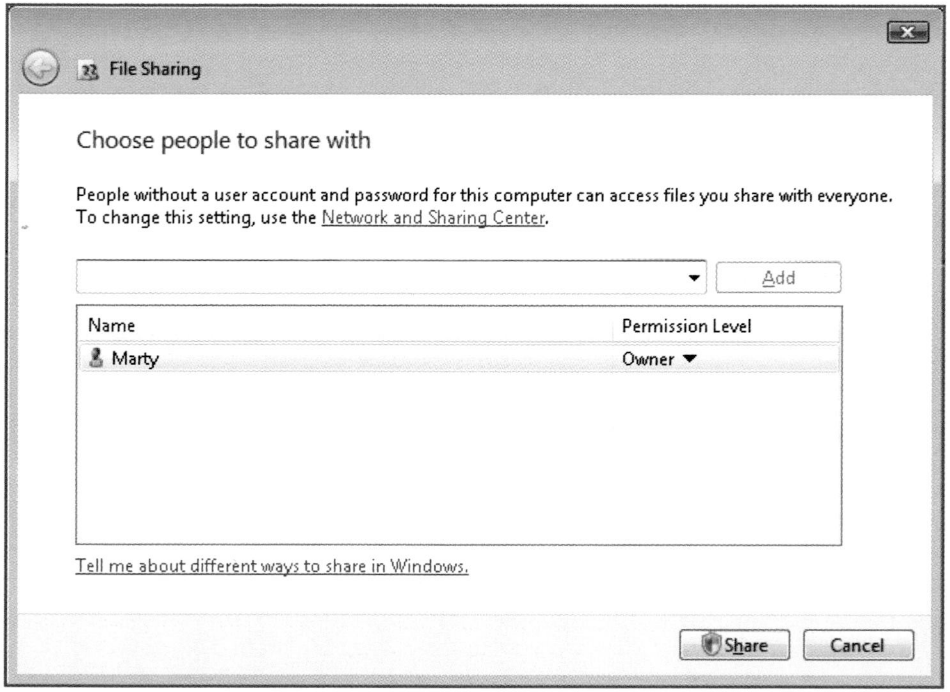

Figure 8-9: *The sharing of normal folders takes you directly to a permissions dialog box.*

4. If you want to close one of the Sharing And Discovery options without changing it, click the up arrow on the right.

5. When you have finished with the Network And Sharing Center, click **Close**.

SHARE NORMAL FOLDERS

The final layer of sharing settings is with the objects you want to share. Normal drives and folders are shared differently than the primary system drives and folders, such as the C: drive and Users folder. To share normal folders:

1. Click **Start** and click **Computer**. Drag **Folders** to the top of the navigation pane. In Folders, open the disk and folders necessary to see in the right pane the folder you want to share.

2. Right-click the folder and click **Share**. The File Sharing dialog box will appear, as shown in Figure 8-9.

3. Click the down arrow on the right of the top text box to open a list of users and groups known to your computer. Click the user or group, possibly the Everyone group, you want to give permission to use this disk or folder, and click **Add**. The user or group is added to the list in the lower part of the dialog box with the minimal permission level of Reader.

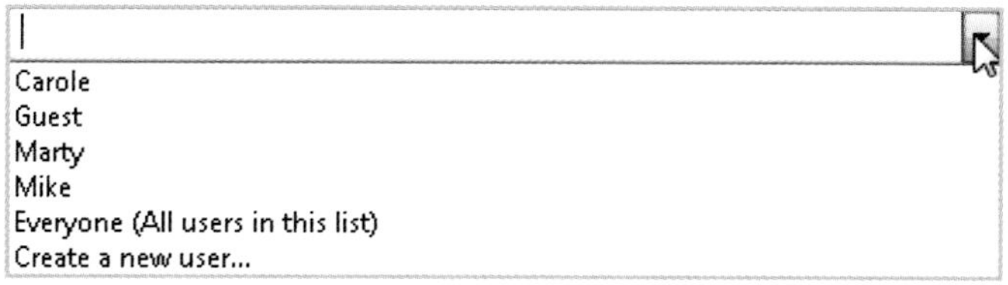

4. Click the **Permission Level** down arrow for your new user or group to open the alternative permission levels. Click the level you want for the addition:

- **Reader** allows the user to view the files in the shared folder.

- **Contributor** allows the user to view existing files and to add files, which the new user can change and delete.

NOTE

When you share a folder, all folders and files within it are given the same sharing status due to inheritance. If that is not what you want for a particular folder, you must individually change the sharing status of the folders within it.

- **Co-Owner** allows the user to view, add, change, and delete any of the files in the shared folder.

Name	Permission Level
Everyone	Reader
Marty	Owner

Reader ✓
Contributor
Co-owner

Remove

5. Click **Share** and click **Continue**; or type a password, and click **OK**. Click **Done** to complete the sharing process.

SHARE DRIVES AND SPECIAL FOLDERS

Drives and special folders—like primary user folders immediately under the User folder—have a more detailed sharing process.

1. Click **Start** and click **Computer**. Navigate to the drive or folder you want to share.

2. Right-click the drive or folder you want to share, and click **Share**. The Properties dialog box will appear with the Sharing tab displayed, as shown in Figure 8-10.

3. Click **Advanced Sharing** and click **Continue**; or type a password, and click **OK**.

4. Click **Share This Folder**, change the share name if desired, and click **Permissions**.

5. Select a listed user or group; or, if the one you want is not listed, click **Add**, click **Advanced**, click **Find Now**, double-click a user or group, and click **OK**.

6. With the user or group selected, click the permission level you want for that entity. The levels of permission are:

- **Read** allows the user or group to read but not change or delete a file or folder.
- **Change** allows the user or group to read and change but not delete a file or folder.
- **Full Control** allows the user or group to read, change, or delete a file or folder.

7. Click **OK** twice and close the Properties dialog box.

Local Disk (F:) Properties

Security	Previous Versions	Customize
General	Tools	Hardware	Sharing

Network File and Folder Sharing

F:\
Not Shared

Network Path:
Not Shared

Share...

Advanced Sharing

Set custom permissions, create multiple shares, and set other advanced sharing options.

Advanced Sharing...

Password Protection

People without a user account and password for this computer can access folders shared with everyone.

To change this setting, use the Network and Sharing Center.

OK   Cancel   Apply

Figure 8-10: *Drives and special folders use a different sharing procedure.*

NOTE

Windows Vista Home Basic edition doesn't support the addition or changing of groups.

NOTE

"Standard Users" are called just "Users" in the list of groups.

Use and Add Groups

Groups, or *group accounts*, are collections of user accounts that can have permissions, such as file sharing, granted to them. Most permissions are granted to groups, not individuals, and then individuals are made members of the groups. You need a set of groups that handles both the mix of people and the mix of permissions that you want to establish. A number of standard groups with preassigned permissions are built into Windows Vista, but you can create your own groups, and you can assign users to any of these.

OPEN EXISTING GROUPS

To open the groups in Windows Vista and see what permissions they contain:

1. Click **Start** and click **Control Panel**. In Control Panel Home, click **System And Maintenance**, and then click (or double-click in Classic view) **Administrative Tools**.

2. In the right pane, double-click **Computer Management** and click **Continue**; or type a password, and click **OK**.

3. In the left pane, click the triangle opposite **System Tools** to open it, click the triangle opposite **Local Users And Groups** to open that, and click **Groups**. The list of built-in groups is displayed, as shown in Figure 8-11.

4. Double-click a few groups to open the Properties dialog box for each and see the members of that group.

Computer Management

File   Action   View   Help

Computer Management (Local)	Name	Description	Actions
System Tools	Administrators	Administrators have complete and unrestr...	Groups
Task Scheduler	Backup Operators	Backup Operators can override security re...	More Actions
Event Viewer	Cryptographic Operat...	Members are authorized to perform crypt...	
Shared Folders	Distributed COM Users	Members are allowed to launch, activate a...	
Local Users and Groups	Event Log Readers	Members of this group can read event log...	
Users	Guests	Guests have the same access as members ...	
Groups	IIS_IUSRS	Built-in group used by Internet Informatio...	
Reliability and Performan	Network Configuratio...	Members in this group can have some ad...	
Device Manager	Performance Log Users	Members of this group may schedule log...	
Storage	Performance Monitor ...	Members of this group can access perfor...	
Disk Management	Power Users	Power Users are included for backwards c...	
Services and Applications	Remote Desktop Users	Members in this group are granted the rig...	
	Replicator	Supports file replication in a domain	
	Users	Users are prevented from making acciden...	

*Figure 8-11: **There are a number of built-in groups to which users can be assigned.***

UNDERSTANDING PERMISSIONS

Permissions authorize a user or a group to perform some function on an object, such as files, folders, disks, and printers. Objects have sets of permissions associated with them that can be assigned to users and groups. The specific permissions depend on the object, but all objects have at least two permissions: Read and either Modify or Change. Permissions are initially set in one of three ways:

- The application or process that creates an object can set its permissions upon creation.

- If the object allows the inheritance of permissions and they were not set upon creation, a parent object can propagate permissions to the object. For example, a parent folder can propagate its permissions to a subfolder it contains.

- If neither the creator nor the parent sets the permissions for an object, then the Windows Vista system default settings will do it.

Once an object is created, its permissions can be changed by its owner, by an administrator, and by anyone else who has been given authority to change permissions.

ADD USERS TO GROUPS

1. Right-click a group to which you want to add a user, and click **Add To Group**. Click **Add**. The Select Users dialog box will appear.

2. Either type a name in the text box and click **Check Names**, or click **Advanced** and then click **Find Now**. A list of users on that computer will be displayed. Select the user that you want to add (hold down CTRL to select several), and click **OK**.

3. When you are done, click **OK** twice.

ADD A GROUP

1. In the Computer Management window, in the list of groups in the middle or Subject pane, right-click in a white area so that no group is selected, and then click **New Group**. The New Group dialog box appears.

2. Enter a group name of up to 60 characters (Windows Vista lets you enter more, but if you ever want to use the group in Windows 2000 or NT systems, it will not work). It cannot contain just numbers, periods, or spaces; it can't contain " / \ [ ] : ; | = ,+ * ? < >; and leading spaces or periods are dropped.

3. Enter the description of what the group can uniquely do, and click **Add**. Then follow the instructions in "Add Users to Groups" except for clicking OK the final time in step 3.

4. When your group is the way you want it (see Figure 8-12), click **Create** and then click **Close**. The new group will appear in the list on the right of the Computer Management window. Close the Computer Management window.

Figure 8-12: **Creating your own group lets you give it your own set of permissions.**

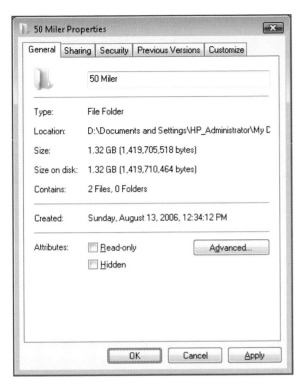

50 Miler Properties					

General | Sharing | Security | Previous Versions | Customize

50 Miler

Type:	File Folder
Location:	D:\Documents and Settings\HP_Administrator\My D
Size:	1.32 GB (1,419,705,518 bytes)
Size on disk:	1.32 GB (1,419,710,464 bytes)
Contains:	2 Files, 0 Folders
Created:	Sunday, August 13, 2006, 12:34:12 PM
Attributes:	☐ Read-only Advanced...
	☐ Hidden

OK   Cancel   Apply

Figure 8-13: Protecting files and folders is accomplished from the files and folders Properties dialog box.

Protect Stored Data

Protecting stored data is another layer of protection. It works to make unusable whatever is found on the computer by someone who managed to break through the other layers of protection.

Protect Files and Folders

You can protect files and folders in two ways: hide them and encrypt them. Start by opening the Properties dialog box for the file or folder.

1. Click **Start**, click **Computer**, and drag **Folders** to the top of the pane. In the Folders pane, open the disks and folders necessary to locate in the right pane the file or folder you want to protect.

2. Right-click the file or folder you want to protect, and click **Properties**. The Properties dialog box will appear, as shown for a folder in Figure 8-13 (there are slight differences between file and folder Properties dialog boxes).

HIDE FILES AND FOLDERS

Hiding files and folders means to prevent them from being displayed by Windows Explorer. This assumes the person from whom you want to hide them does not know how to display hidden files or how to turn off the hidden attribute. To hide a file or folder, you must both turn on its hidden attribute and turn off the Display Hidden Files feature.

1. In the file or folder Properties dialog box, click **Hidden**, click **OK**, and click **OK** again to confirm the attribute change. Click **Continue**; or type a password, and click **OK** (the object's icon becomes dimmed).

2. In the Windows Explorer window click the **Organize** menu, click **Folder And Search Options**, click the **View** tab, and make sure **Do Not Show Hidden Files And Folders** is selected. Click **OK** to close the Folder Options dialog box. Close and reopen the parent folder, and the file or folder you hid will disappear.

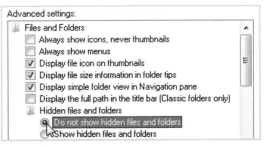

Advanced settings:
- Files and Folders
  - ☐ Always show icons, never thumbnails
  - ☐ Always show menus
  - ☑ Display file icon on thumbnails
  - ☑ Display file size information in folder tips
  - ☑ Display simple folder view in Navigation pane
  - ☐ Display the full path in the title bar (Classic folders only)
  - Hidden files and folders
    - ● Do not show hidden files and folders
    - ○ Show hidden files and folders

3. To restore the file or folder to view, click the **Organize** menu, click **Folder And Search Options**, click the **View** tab, click **Show Hidden Files And Folders**, and click **OK**. Then, when you can see the file or folder, open its Properties dialog box, and deselect the **Hidden** attribute.

ENCRYPT FILES AND FOLDERS

File and folder encryption, called the *Encrypting File System (EFS)*, is built into Windows Vista using NTFS (but it is not available in either Home Basic or Home Premium editions). Once EFS is turned on for a file or a folder, only the person who encrypted the file or folder will be able to read it. However, you can backup the encryption key and use that to access the file or folder. For the person who encrypted the file, accessing it requires no additional steps, and the file is re-encrypted every time it is saved.

To encrypt a file or folder from Windows Explorer:

1. From the General tab in the file or folder Properties dialog box, click **Advanced**. The Advanced Attributes dialog box appears.

2. Click **Encrypt Contents To Secure Data**.

3. Click **OK** twice. If you are encrypting a file, you will see an encryption warning that the file is not in an encrypted folder, which means that when you edit the file, temporary or backup files might be created that are not encrypted. Choose whether to encrypt only the file or to encrypt both the file and its parent folder, and then click **OK**.

4. If you are encrypting a folder, the Confirm Attribute Changes dialog box appears, asking if you want to apply the encryption to this folder only or to both the folder and its contents. If you click **This Folder Only**, *existing* files and folders in the folder will *not* be encrypted, while files and folders later created in or copied to the encrypted folder will be. If you click **This Folder, Subfolders, and Files**, all files and folders will be encrypted. Choose the setting that is correct for you, and click **OK**. Click **Continue**; or type a password, and click **OK**.

5. Log off as the current user, and log on as another user. Click **Start**, click **Computer**, and open the drive and folders necessary to display in the right pane the file or folder you encrypted. You can see that the file exists, but when you try to open it, edit it, print it, or move it, you will get a message that access is denied.

6. To decrypt a file or folder, log on as yourself (given you're the person that encrypted it), reopen the file or folder Properties dialog box, click **Advanced**, and deselect **Encrypt Contents To Secure Data**.

Advanced Attributes

Choose the settings you want for this folder.
When you click OK or Apply on the Properties dialog, you will be asked if you want the changes to affect all subfolders and files as well.

Archive and Index attributes

☐ Folder is ready for *a*rchiving

☑ *I*ndex this folder for faster searching

Compress or Encrypt attributes

☐ *C*ompress contents to save disk space

☑ *E*ncrypt contents to secure data   [Details]

[OK]   [Cancel]

TIP

Because many applications save temporary and secondary files during normal execution, it is recommended that folders rather than files be the encrypting container. If an application is then told to store all files in that folder, where all files are automatically encrypted upon saving, security is improved.

CAUTION

If you encrypt a shared folder and select **This Folder, Subfolders, and Files**, any files or subfolders belonging to others will be encrypted with your key, and the owners will not be able to use what they created.

LOCKING A COMPUTER

By default, when your screen saver comes on and you return to use your system, you must go through the logon screen. If you have added a password to your account, you have to enter it to get back into the system, which is a means of preventing unauthorized access when you are away from your running computer. If you don't want to wait for your screen saver to come on, you can click **Start** and click the **Lock** button in the lower-right corner of the Start menu, or you can press 🪟 (the Windows logo key)**+L** to immediately bring up the logon screen, from which your screen saver will open at the appropriate time.

Depending on your environment, having to go through the logon screen every time you come out of the screen saver may or may not be beneficial. To turn off or turn back on the screen saver protection:

1. Right-click the desktop and click **Personalize**. Click **Screen Saver**.
2. Select or deselect **On Resume, Display Logon Screen**, depending on whether or not you want to display the logon screen on returning to your system. (See Figure 8-14.)
3. Click **OK** to close the Display Properties dialog box.

TIP

To use a backed up encryption key, insert the removable media with the key, open the drive in the Windows Explorer, and browse to and double-click the file with the key. In the Certificate Wizard that opens click **Next**, confirm that you have the right file, and click **Next**. Type the password used to backup the key, select how you want to use the key, and click **Next**. Select the certificate store you want, click **Next**, and click **Finish**.

BACKUP YOUR ENCRYPTION KEY

If you use file encryption it is important to backup your file encryption key so that you do not lose the information you have. It is also important, of course, to keep the media that you backup the key on safe so that it can't be used. The key is part of a digital certificate, so the terminology here is to back up the certificate.

1. Click **Start** and click **Control Panel**. In Control Panel Home, click **User Accounts And Family Safety**, and then click (or double-click in Classic view) **User Accounts**. Your User Account window opens.
2. Click **Manage Your File Encryption Certificates**, and click **Continue**; or type a password, and click **OK** to open the Encrypting File System dialog box.
3. Read about what you can do with this wizard and click **Next**. Click **Select Certificate**; select the most recent certificate whose purpose is "Encrypting File System;" and click **OK**. That certificate should appear in the Certificate Details. Click **Next**.

Issued to	Issued by	Intended Purposes	Friendly name	Expiratio...
Marty	Marty	Encrypting File Syst...	None	8/29/2106

Encrypting File System

Select the certificate you want to use.

OK Cancel View Certificate

4. Click **Browse** and navigate to the removable disk and folder you want to hold the certificate. Type a file name and click **Save**.
5. Type a password and confirm it, then click **Next**. Select the folders with encrypted files that you want the new certificate and key applied to, and click **Next**. Your files will be updated with the new key.
6. When you are told the files have been updated and where the key is stored, click **Close**, anc close the User Accounts window.
7. Store the removable disc or USB flash drive in a safe place.

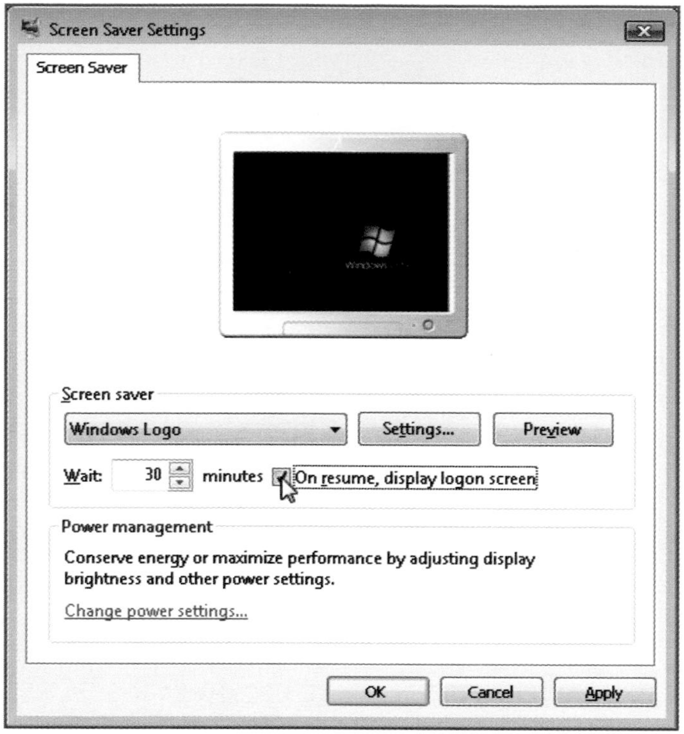

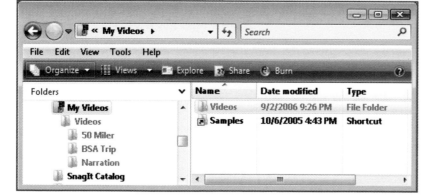

Figure 8-14: *You can password-protect your system when you leave it unattended by having the logon screen appear when you return after using the screen saver.*

Use Encrypted Files and Folders

If you are the person who encrypted a file or folder and you log on as yourself, you can use the file or folder exactly as you would if it hadn't been encrypted. The only way you know the files or folders are encrypted is that Windows Explorer shows them in green, as shown in Figure 8-15. If you log on as someone else, or someone else logs on as anyone other than you, they will not be able to use the files or folders. Copying and moving encrypted files and folders, however, has a special set of rules:

- If you copy or move a file or folder to an encrypted folder, the item copied or moved will be encrypted.

- If you copy or move a file or folder to an unencrypted folder, the item moved remains as it was prior to being moved. If it was unencrypted, it remains so. If it was encrypted, it is still encrypted after being moved.

- Someone other than the owner who tries to copy or move encrypted files or folders to a different computer sees an error message that access is denied.

- If the owner copies or moves an encrypted file or folder to another file system, such as Windows NT 4 NTFS or Windows 98 FAT32, the encryption is removed, but a warning message is generated before the copy or move is complete.

- Backing up encrypted files or folders with Windows Vista Backup leaves the items encrypted.

Figure 8-15: *Windows Explorer shows the information for encrypted files and folders in green.*

How to...

- Select a Type of Network
- Selecting Wired Ethernet Hardware
- Select a Network Standard
- Selecting Wireless Hardware
- Set Up Network Interface Cards
- Enable Vista's Networking Functions
- Configure a Networking Protocol
- Getting a Block of IP Addresses
- Test a Network Setup and Connection
- Review Network Security

Chapter 9
Setting Up Networking

Networking is the ability to connect two or more computers and allow them to share information and resources, whether at home, in an organization, or around the world. The Internet, as was discussed in Chapter 4, is a form of networking. This chapter discusses a *local area network,* or a *LAN*, which is generally confined to a single residence or building or perhaps just a section of a building. (The Internet is a *wide area network*, or a *WAN.*) You'll see what comprises a LAN, how to set it up, and how to use it.

Plan a Network

Windows Vista is a *network operating system.* This allows the interconnection of multiple computers for many purposes:

- **Exchanging information**, such as sending a file from one computer to another
- **Communicating**, for example, sending e-mail among network users
- **Sharing information** by having common files accessed by network users
- **Sharing network resources**, such as printers and Internet connections

Networking is a system that includes the connection between computers that facilitates the transfer of information, as well as the scheme for controlling that transfer. The scheme makes sure that the information is transferred correctly and accurately. This is the function of the networking hardware and software in your computer and the protocols, or standards, they use.

Select a Type of Network

Today, the majority of LANs use the *Ethernet* standard, which determines the type of network hardware and software needed by the network, and *TCP/IP* (Transmission Control Protocol/Internet Protocol), which determines how information is exchanged over the network. With this foundation, you can then choose between using a peer-to-peer LAN or a client-server LAN.

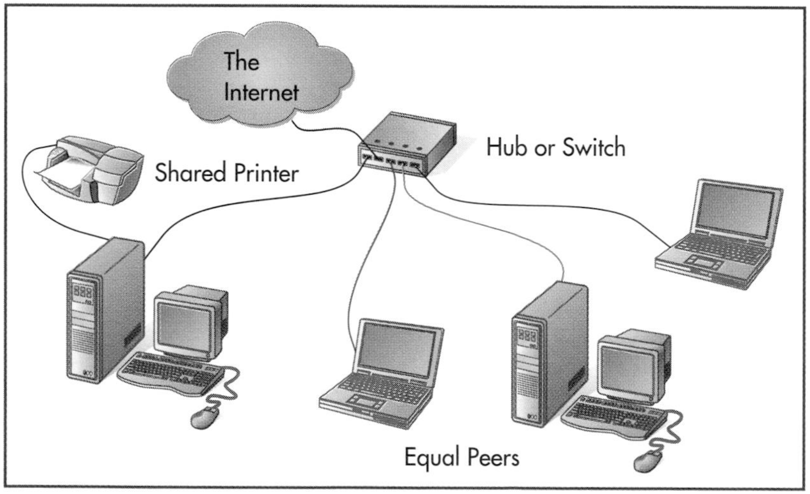

PEER-TO-PEER LANS

All computers in a *peer-to-peer LAN* are both servers and clients and, therefore, share in both providing and using resources. Any computer in the network may store information and provide resources, such as a printer, for the use of any other computer in the network. Peer-to-peer networking is an easy first step to networking, accomplished simply by joining computers together, as shown in Figure 9-1. It does not require the purchase of new computers or significant changes to the way an organization is using computers, yet resources can be shared

Figure 9-1: *In a peer-to-peer LAN, all computers are both servers and clients.*

QUICKSTEPS

SELECTING WIRED ETHERNET HARDWARE

Selecting networking hardware for wired Ethernet means selecting a NIC, a hub or switch, and cabling. For all hardware, I recommend a brand-name product, giving you a company that stands behind the product you are buying. Respected brands of networking gear are 3Com and its subsidiary U.S. Robotics, D-Link, Intel, Linksys (a division of Cisco Systems), and Netgear.

SELECT A NETWORK INTERFACE CARD (NIC)

Many new computers come with a built-in 10/100 Ethernet NIC, so you may not need to add this. You already have a NIC if your computer has two telephone-style jacks, one slightly larger than the other. The larger one is the connection to the NIC. The other jack is for the modem.

If you don't have a NIC, you can generally add one to your computer. For a desktop computer, you will need to open the computer case and plug in the card. If you are uncomfortable doing that, most computer stores will do it for little more than the cost of the card ($25 to $50). You need to carry in only the computer itself, not the monitor, keyboard, or mouse. You want a 10/100 NIC for

Continued . . .

(as is the printer in Figure 9-1), files and communications can be transferred, and common information can be accessed by all.

Peer-to-peer LANs tend to be used in smaller organizations that do not need to share a large central resource, such as a database, or to have a high degree of security or central control. Each computer in a peer-to-peer LAN is autonomous and often networked with other computers simply to transfer files and share expensive equipment. Putting together a peer-to-peer LAN with existing computers is fairly easy, and can be inexpensive (less than $50 per station).

CLIENT/SERVER LANS

The computers in a *client/server LAN* perform one of two functions: they are either servers or clients. *Servers* manage the network, centrally store information to be shared on the network, and provide the shared resources to the network. *Clients,* or *workstations*, are the users of the network and are standard desktop or laptop computers. To create a network, the clients and server(s) are connected together, with the possible addition of standalone network resources, such as printers, as shown in Figure 9-2.

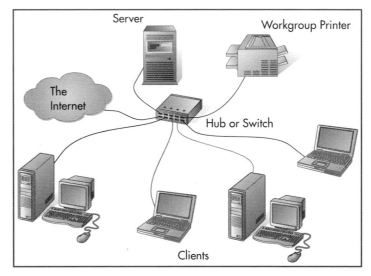

Figure 9-2: In a client/server LAN, one or more computers are servers and the rest are clients.

QUICKSTEPS

SELECTING WIRED ETHERNET HARDWARE *(Continued)*

the PCI (Peripheral Component Interconnect) bus in your computer.

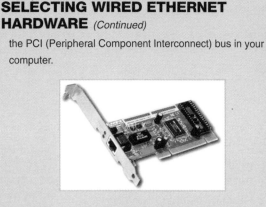

For a laptop computer, the NIC plugs in from the outside, so it is very easy to add. It uses a PCMCIA (Personal Computer Memory Card International Association), or *PC Card* for short, slot on the side of the computer. You want a 10/100 PC Card NIC.

SELECT CONNECTING DEVICES

There are two common connecting devices: hubs, which are like a party-line telephone system where everybody hears all the traffic; and switches, which are like a private-line telephone system. Switches once cost a lot more, so hubs were used. Today, switches and hubs are virtually the same price. A simple switch runs from under $50, for a four- or five-port one,

Continued . . .

The management functions provided by the server include network security, managing the permissions needed to implement security, communications among network users, and management of shared files on the network. Servers generally are more capable than clients in terms of having more memory, faster (and possibly more) processors, larger (and maybe more) disks, and more special peripherals, such as large, high-speed tape drives. Servers, generally, are dedicated to their function and are infrequently used for normal computer tasks, such as word processing.

Clients generally are less capable than servers and, infrequently, may not even have a disk. Clients usually are standard desktop and laptop computers that perform the normal functions of those types of machines in addition to being part of a network. Clients can also be "mini-servers" by sharing some or all of their disk drives or other resources. So the principal difference between peer-to-peer networks and client/server networks is the presence of a dedicated server.

Windows Vista and either Windows Server 2007 or Windows Server 2003 work together to form a client/server network operating environment, with Windows Server performing its function and Windows Vista being the client. Several Windows Vista computers can operate in a peer-to-peer network.

There are simple client/server networks, and there are client/server networks where one or more servers are set up as *domain controllers* and the entire network is considered a *domain*. In a large organization, a domain provides many benefits—most importantly, a central registry for all users so that one registration provides access to all the computers and resources in the domain. Domains, however, are complex and require significant expertise to set up and manage. This book, therefore, focuses on setting up and using a peer-to-peer network and on connecting to a client/server network.

Select a Network Standard

Windows Vista supports the two predominant networking standards: wired Ethernet and wireless. These, in turn, determine the type of hardware you need.

QUICKSTEPS

SELECTING WIRED ETHERNET HARDWARE *(Continued)*

to under $150 for a 24-port switch. You need a port for each user on the system, plus one for your broadband (DSL) Internet connection, but you can stack switches by plugging them into one another. You want an Ethernet 10/100 switch with the number of ports to meet your needs.

SELECT CABLING

For 10/100 Ethernet networking, you need either Category 5 or Category 5e (for enhanced) cabling (these are called "Cat 5" or "Cat 5e," respectively) with RJ-45 male connectors on each end. Such cables come in various colors and lengths, up to 100 feet with the ends molded on, or in lengths up to 1,000 feet without the ends, where you need a crimping tool to add the ends. Cat 5e cable, which provides better transmission capability, is almost the same price as Cat 5, so we recommend it.

NOTE

In the name for the Ethernet standard, 10/100BaseT, the "10/100" indicates the alternative operating speeds in Mbps; the "Base" is for baseband, a type of transmission; and the "T" stands for the type of cabling (twisted-pair).

USE WIRED ETHERNET

The wired Ethernet standard comes in several forms based on speed and cable type. The most common, called 10/100BaseT, provides a network that operates at either the regular Ethernet speed of 10 Mbps (megabit, or a million bits, per second) or at the newer Fast Ethernet speed of 100 Mbps.

A wired Ethernet 10/100BaseT system, shown in Figure 9-3, has three major components:

- The **network interface card (NIC)** plugs into your computer, or is built into it, and connects it to the network.
- A **hub**, **switch**, or **router** joins several computers together to form the network:
  - A **hub**, the simplest and cheapest device, is where all computers are on the equivalent of a telephone party line (everybody can hear everybody else).
  - A **switch** is more expensive than a hub, but all computers are on the equivalent of a private telephone line.
  - A **router** joins two different networks, for example, the Internet to a local area network. Often, a router is combined with a hub or a switch, either in one device or in two devices, to join the Internet to several computers.

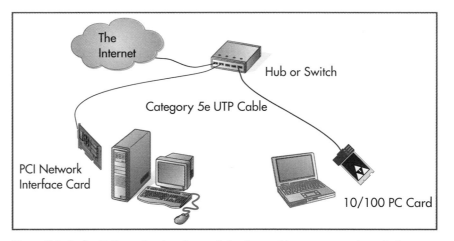

Figure 9-3: **A wired Ethernet network consists of a card in your computer, a hub or switch into which other computers are connected, and a cable connecting the two.**

- An **unshielded twisted-pair (UTP)** telephone-like cable with a simple RJ-45 telephone-like connector joins the NIC to the hub, switch, or router. This cable is called Category 5 or enhanced Category 5 ("Cat 5" or "Cat 5e," respectively).

Ethernet networks are easy to set up (see "Set Up a Network" later in this chapter), have become pervasive throughout organizations, and have an average cost for all components of less than $50 per computer on the network.

USE A WIRELESS LAN

Wireless LANs (WLANs) replace the cable used in a wired network with small radio transceivers (transmitter and receiver) at the computer and at the hub or switch. There are several wireless standards, but the two most common are 802.11b and 802.11g. 802.11b is older, is WiFi-compliant (WiFi is a trademark for a set of wireless fidelity standards), and provides data transfer of up to 11 Mbps using a secure transmission scheme. The newer standard, 802.11g, is now the dominate standard because it is five times faster than 802.11b (54 Mbps), is WiFi-compliant and compatible with 802.11b, and is not that much more expensive.

A WLAN has two components (see Figure 9-4):

- An **access point** is connected to the wired Ethernet network by being plugged into a hub, a switch, or a router. It uses a transceiver to communicate wirelessly with cards that are added to computers using the WLAN.

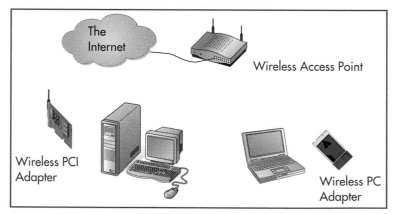

*Figure 9-4: **A wireless network consists of an adapter that plugs into or is built in your computer and an access point that is connected to a wired network, the Internet, or both.***

NOTE

In addition to the WLAN standard, the WiFi (wireless fidelity) standard makes sure that the hardware from different manufacturers is compatible. Thus, you can walk into any office, airport, or coffee shop with a WiFi standard wireless system and be able to connect to the WLAN at that location if you have the appropriate permissions. In many airports, hotels, and coffee shops, you see signs for "WiFi hotspots," meaning that you can use a wireless connection to access the Internet at that location.

NOTE

Lessened security is also a potential downside with wireless if it isn't set up properly. For example, if you don't turn on encryption and the use of passwords, your neighbor (or hacker cruising your neighborhood) might be able to get on your network or look at your network traffic.

UICKSTEPS

SELECTING WIRELESS HARDWARE

Selecting networking hardware for a wireless network means selecting a wireless adapter and a wireless access point. We recommend the same manufacturers as were listed for wired Ethernet hardware.

SELECT A WIRELESS SPEED

If you are installing a new wireless network, the 54-Mbps 802.11g standard is really your only choice. The 11-Mbps 802.11b standard is not any cheaper and is becoming harder to find. Also, if you should go into an 802.11b reception area with an 802.11g computer, it will work fine, just slower.

SELECT A WIRELESS ADAPTER

Many new laptops come with a built-in wireless adapter, so you may not need to buy one. For a desktop computer, you will need a PCI wireless adapter for the speed you have chosen, and you will need to open up the computer to plug it in or have a store do it. For a laptop computer without the built-in capability, you need a PC Card wireless adapter of the appropriate speed, which you can easily plug in.

SELECT A WIRELESS ACCESS POINT

Wireless access points come in simple versions that plug into a wired Ethernet network, as well as more sophisticated versions,

Continued . . .

- An **adapter** plugs into or is built into your computer, and has a transceiver built in to communicate wirelessly to an access point within its range. There are PC adapters for use in notebook computers and PCI adapters for use in desktop computers.

If the access point is plugged into a hub or switch on a wired network, the wireless computers within the range of the access point operate on the network in exactly the same way, except for being a little slower, as they would with a cable connection. A WLAN has some significant benefits over a normal wired LAN:

- You do not have the expense of cabling and the even higher expense of installing and maintaining cabling.
- Adding and removing users from the network is extremely easy.
- Users can move easily from office to office.
- Users can roam within an area, say, carrying their laptops to a meeting.
- Visitors can easily get on the network.

The downsides, of course, are cost, speed, and (potentially) security, but all of these are manageable. The cost per computer of a wired network, as was said previously, is less than $50 per computer. The cost per computer of a wireless network is generally above $50, but the two prices are getting closer. The speed difference is more significant, not just because of the difference between an 11- or 54-Mbps access point and a 100-Mbps network, but because of the net rate of dividing the 11- or 54-Mbps access point by the number of people trying to use it. Despite these drawbacks, there is a large movement to WLANs, and a number of systems are being sold for both offices and homes.

Set Up a Network

When you installed Windows Vista, a basic set of networking services was installed and configured using system defaults. This setup may, but doesn't always, provide an operable networking system. Look at these three areas to

SELECTING WIRELESS HARDWARE

(Continued)

called "wireless broadband routers," that terminate a DSL or cable Internet connection. You have that choice and a choice of speeds when you choose a wireless access point.

TIP

If you want to network only two computers, you can do so without a hub or a switch, but you need a special *crossover* cable where the connections are reversed on each end. Most computer stores carry such a cable.

NOTE

If you need more than four levels of hubs (hubs plugged into hubs) in a 10BaseT network or more than two levels in a 100BaseT network (or a mixed 10/100BaseT network), you need to use a switch to add more levels.

set up *basic networking*, which means that your computer can communicate with other computers in the network:

- Be sure the network interface card (NIC) is properly set up.
- Install the networking functions that you want to perform.
- Review your network security settings.

Set Up Network Interface Cards

If the computer you are setting up has a NIC that is both certified for Windows Vista and fully Plug and Play–compatible, then your NIC was installed by Windows Setup without incident, and you don't need to read this section. Otherwise, this section examines how the NIC was installed and what you need to do to make it operational.

Assuming that a NIC *is* properly plugged into the computer, any of these things could be causing it to not operate:

- The NIC driver is not recognized by Vista; it is either missing or not properly installed.
- The NIC is not functioning properly.

Look at each of these possibilities in turn.

CHECK THE NIC AND ITS DRIVER

Check the status of your NIC and whether you have a driver installed. If you don't, you can install one.

1. Click **Start** and click **Control Panel**. In Control Panel Home, click **Network And Internet**, and then click (or double-click in Classic view) **Network And Sharing Center**. The Network And Sharing Center window opens.

2. Click **Manage Network Connections** in the left pane. The Network Connections window opens. If you have an icon in the window labeled "Local Area Connection," as shown on the right, you have the NIC driver properly installed and you can go on to the section "Enable Vista's Networking Functions."

TIP

You can change the name, "Local Area Connection," that appears in the Network Connections window. For example, if you install two NIC cards, you can give each of them a descriptive name by right-clicking the icon and clicking **Rename**.

TIP

I went through the process of downloading a driver and found it painless. The hard part is figuring out what type of card you have, because often it is not written on the card. You may be able to see it in step 6 of "Check the NIC and Its Driver." If not, you need to locate purchase records or documentation—if you know which records go with the card.

3. If you do not have a Local Area Connection icon, you cannot create one by clicking Connect To A Network or Set Up A Connection Or Network. You must first install a Windows Vista driver for the NIC. Since it was not automatically installed by Vista, you will need to get one before proceeding. If a driver did not come with the NIC (most likely on a CD), you need to use another computer attached to the Internet.

4. On the other computer, bring up the manufacturer's Web site, locate and download the Windows Vista driver (you need to know the make and model of the NIC), copy it onto a disk, and then go back to the original computer.

5. Click **Start** and click **Control Panel**. In Control Panel Home, click **Hardware And Sound**, and then click (or double-click in Classic view) **Device Manager**. The Device Manager window opens.

6. Double-click **Network Adapters** to display the network adapter in your computer. If you see your NIC and it doesn't have a problem icon (an exclamation point), then Windows thinks that the NIC is installed and running properly. If you double-click the device, you should see the device status, "This device is working properly." If so, then you may need to only install a new driver. Skip to step 13.

```
Monitors
Network adapters
    Realtek RTL8139/810x Family Fast Ethernet NIC
Portable Devices
```

Device status

This device is working properly.

7. If you see your NIC with a problem icon, double-click the NIC. You will most likely see a device status message telling you that a driver was not installed. Skip to step 13.

8. If you don't see your NIC in the Device Manager window, click the **Action** menu, and click **Add Legacy Hardware**. The Add Hardware Wizard will open. Click **Next**. Click **Install The Hardware That I Manually Select From A List**—you don't want Windows to search for new hardware; if it was going to find it, it would have—and click **Next**.

9. Double-click **Network Adapters** in the Common Hardware Types list. A list of network adapters appears. If your NIC had been on the list, Windows Setup would have found it, so you need to insert and use the disk that you made prior to step 3 or the disk that came with the NIC.

10. Click **Have Disk**. Click **Browse**, locate the appropriate drive, and click **OK**. When it is displayed, select the driver for your adapter, and click **Next**. When told that the device will be installed, click **Next** again.

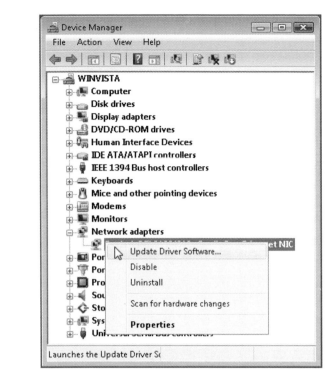

Figure 9-5: *It is common to have to install device driver software for older hardware.*

11. You may see a message stating that the driver you are about to install does not have a Microsoft digital signature. Click **Yes** to go ahead and install it anyway. The driver and its necessary supporting software will be installed.

12. Click **Finish**. The Network Connections window should now show the Local Area Connection icon. If you see this icon, go to the section "Enable Vista's Networking Functions."

13. If you saw your NIC in the Device Manager window, with or without a problem icon, you can install or reinstall a driver from there. Place the disk with the driver software in the drive. Right-click your NIC and click **Update Driver Software**, as shown in Figure 9-5.

14. Click **Browse My Computer For Driver Software**, click **Browse**, locate the drive and folder with the driver, and click **Next**. You will be told when the driver is installed. Click **Close** to close the Update Driver Software dialog box.

If you still do not have a Local Area Connection icon, or if some other problem occurred in the preceding process that does not point to an obvious solution, continue through the next section to see if a solution is presented.

DETERMINE IF A NIC IS FUNCTIONING

If installing a NIC driver did not cause the Local Area Connection icon to appear, it is likely that the NIC itself is not functioning properly. The easiest way to test that is to replace the NIC with a known good one, ideally one that is both Windows Vista–certified and Plug and Play–compatible. It is wise to have a spare NIC; they are not expensive ($25 and under), and switching out a suspected bad one can quickly solve many problems.

Enable Vista's Networking Functions

Vista's networking functions provide the software for a computer to access other computers and, separately, for other computers to access the computer you are working on. In other words, the two primary functions allow the computer to be a client (it accesses other computers) and to be a server (other computers access it). Make sure that these two services are enabled by following these steps.

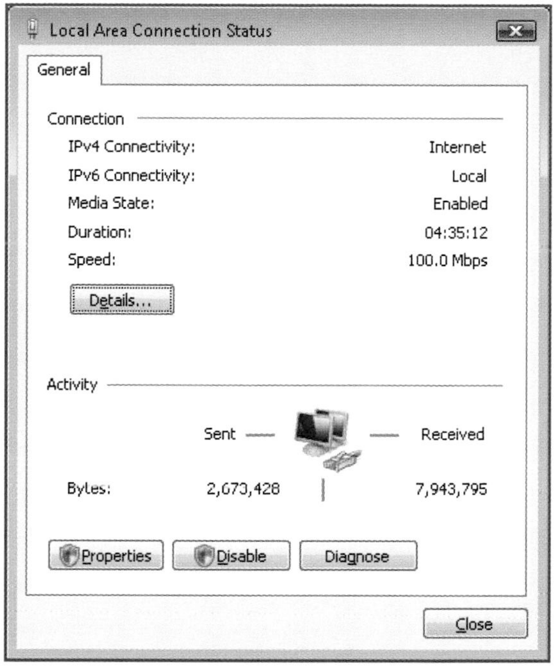

Figure 9-6: *If your NIC is working correctly, you should see a lot of information being sent and received.*

1. Click **Start** and click **Control Panel**. In Control Panel Home, click **Network And Internet**, and then click (or double-click in Classic view) **Network And Sharing Center**. The Network And Sharing Center window opens. Click **Manage Network Connections** in the left column. The Network Connections window opens and displays an icon labeled "Local Area Connection."

2. Right-click the **Local Area Connection** icon, and click **Status**. The Local Area Connection Status dialog box appears, as shown in Figure 9-6. In the particular case shown here, the computer indicates it is connected to the network and that it is sending and receiving information indicating it is correctly set up.

3. Click **Properties**. The Local Area Connection Properties dialog box, shown in Figure 9-7, appears and displays the services and protocols that have automatically been installed.

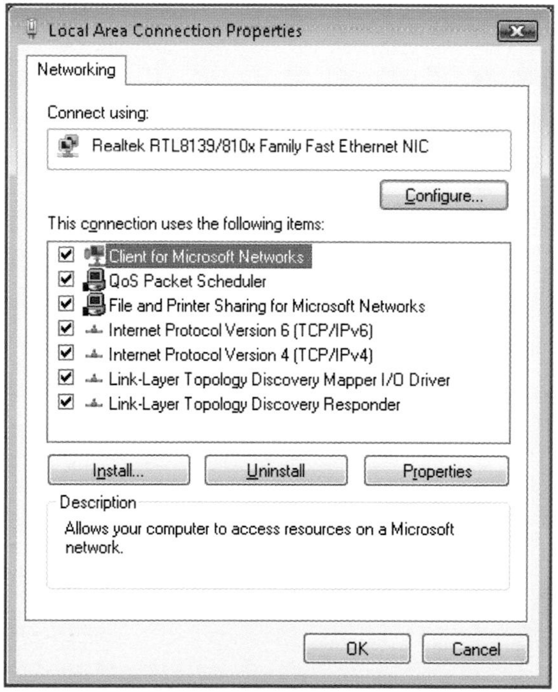

Figure 9-7: *By default, Vista installs the networking services and protocols shown here.*

The minimum services needed for networking are Client For Microsoft Networks and File And Printer Sharing For Microsoft Networks, plus one protocol, Internet Protocol Version 4 (TCP/IPv4). Vista, by default, installs an additional service and three additional protocols.

Click **Install**. The Select Network Feature Type dialog box appears, in which you can add clients, services, and protocols.

INSTALL A CLIENT

1. Double-click **Client**. If you already have Client For Microsoft Networks installed, you will not have any services to install.

2. If Client For Microsoft Networks is not installed, select it and click **OK**.

INSTALL A SERVICE

Windows Vista provides two services, both of which are automatically installed:

- **File And Printer Sharing For Microsoft Networks** handles the sharing of resources on your computer.

- **QoS (Quality of Service) Packet Scheduler** helps balance a network and alleviate bottlenecks when one part of the network is fast and another part is slow.

1. In the Select Network Feature Type dialog box, double-click **Service**. If you already have File And Printer Sharing For Microsoft Networks and QoS Packet Scheduler installed, you will not have any services to install.

2. If File And Printer Sharing For Microsoft Networks and QoS Packet Scheduler are not installed, select them and click **OK**.

Configure a Networking Protocol

Networking protocols are a set of standards used to package and transmit information over a network. The protocol determines how the information is divided into packets, how it is addressed, and what is done to assure it is reliably transferred. The protocol is, therefore, very important to the success of networking, and its choice is a major one. Windows Vista offers three Internet protocols and two network-mapping protocols:

- **Internet Protocol Version 4 (TCP/IPv4)**, for use with the Internet and most LANs

- **Internet Protocol Version 6 (TCP/IPv6)**, the newest system for use with the widest variety of networks

NOTE

Vista's default installation of Internet Protocol Version 6 (TCP/IPv6) is done in preparation for a rapidly approaching future when TCP/IPv6 becomes the Internet and LAN standard. TCP/IPv6 provides for a greatly expanded address space, increased speed, and increased security.

NOTE

In the Local Area Connection Properties dialog box, you should see at least one protocol installed, as shown previously in Figure 9-7. In most cases, both TCP/IPv4 and TCP/IPv6 should already be installed.

- **Reliable Multicast Protocol**, which is a special one-to-many protocol used in conferencing
- **Link-Layer Topology Discovery Mapper I/O Driver** that goes out and finds devices on the network
- **Link-Layer Topology Discovery Responder** that responds when it is queried by a Discovery Mapper

All of these protocols, except Reliable Multicast Protocol, are installed by default. If the computer you are working on is or will be connected to the Internet, it will require TCP/IPv4. TCP/IP is a robust protocol, suitable for a demanding environment (like the Internet), and accepted worldwide. Because of this, Microsoft recommends that TCP/IP be installed as your protocol of choice for both your LAN and the Internet.

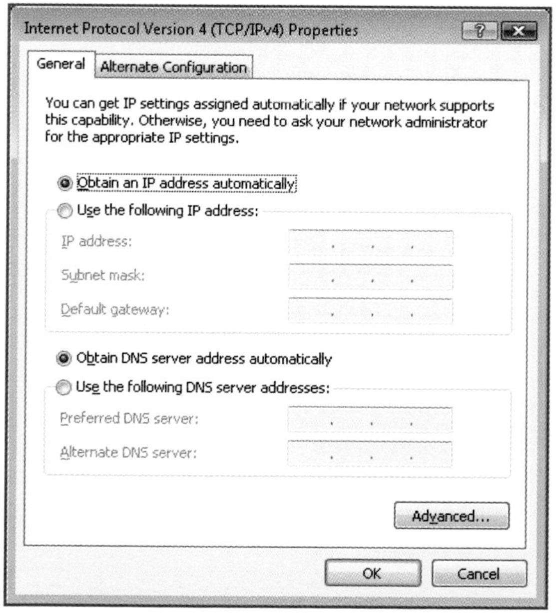

CHECK AND CHANGE PROTOCOLS

Check (and change if necessary) the protocols that have been installed and the settings that are being used.

1. Click **Start** and click **Control Panel**. In Control Panel Home, click **Network And Internet**, and then click (or double-click in Classic view) **Network And Sharing Center**. The Network And Sharing Center window opens. Click **Manage Network Connections** in the left column. The Network Connections window opens and displays an icon labeled "Local Area Connection."

2. Right-click the **Local Area Connection** icon, and click **Status**. The Local Area Connection Status dialog box appears.

3. Click **Properties**, click **Install**, and double-click **Protocol**. The Select Network Protocol dialog box appears listing the available protocols.

4. If you see any protocol you want installed, double-click it. If you want to install another protocol, repeat steps 3 and 4. Otherwise, click **Cancel** twice to close the Select Network Protocol and Select Network Feature Type dialog boxes.

5. Select the **Internet Protocol Version 4 (TCP/IPv4)** protocol in the Local Area Connection Properties dialog box, and click **Properties**. The Internet Protocol (TCP/IP) Properties dialog box appears, shown in Figure 9-8. Here you can choose either to use a dynamic IP (Internet Protocol) address automatically assigned by a server or DSL router or to enter a static IP address in this dialog box.

Figure 9-8: If you use dynamic IP addresses that are automatically assigned, you don't have to worry about having two devices or computers with the same IP address.

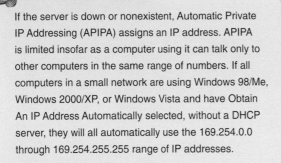

TIP

If the server is down or nonexistent, Automatic Private IP Addressing (APIPA) assigns an IP address. APIPA is limited insofar as a computer using it can talk only to other computers in the same range of numbers. If all computers in a small network are using Windows 98/Me, Windows 2000/XP, or Windows Vista and have Obtain An IP Address Automatically selected, without a DHCP server, they will all automatically use the 169.254.0.0 through 169.254.255.255 range of IP addresses.

TIP

If your organization doesn't plan to directly access an outside network like the Internet or you have a router between your network and the Internet, then the static IP address can be from the block of APIPA numbers or from several other blocks of private IP addresses. (See the "Getting a Block of IP Addresses" QuickSteps.)

QUICKSTEPS

GETTING A BLOCK OF IP ADDRESSES

The block of IP addresses you use with the Internet Protocol depends on whether the computers to be assigned the addresses will be private or public.

GET PRIVATE IP ADDRESSES

If the computers will be operating only on an internal network, where they are separated from the public network by a router, bridge, or hardware firewall, they are *private* and need only organizational uniqueness.

Continued . . .

If you have a server or a DSL router that automatically assigns IP addresses, then you need to leave the Obtain An IP Address Automatically option selected (it is selected by default).

ENTER YOUR OWN IP ADDRESS

1. If you are working on a computer that you know must have a static IP address, click **Use The Following IP Address** and enter an IP address. The IP address that you use should be from the block of IP addresses that an Internet service provider (ISP) or other authority has assigned to your organization.

2. If you entered a static IP address, you must also enter a subnet mask. This mask tells the IP which part of an IP address to consider a network address and which part to consider a computer, or *host*, address. If your organization was assigned a block of IP addresses, it was also given a subnet mask. If you used the APIPA range of addresses, then use 255.255.0.0 as the subnet mask.

OBTAIN AN IP ADDRESS AUTOMATICALLY

1. If you don't have a specific reason to use a static IP address, click **Obtain An IP Address Automatically**, and use the addresses from either a server or DSL router on the network or APIPA.

2. Click **OK** to close the Internet Protocol Version 4 (TCP/IPv4) Properties dialog box, click **Close** to close the Local Area Connection Properties dialog box, click **Close** to close the Local Area Connection Status dialog box, and click the **Close** button on both the Network Connections window and Control Panel.

3. Click **Start**, click the **Shut Down** arrow, and click **Restart**. This is required to utilize your network settings.

VERIFY YOUR CONNECTION

1. When the computer restarts, reopen the Network Connections window (click **Start** and click **Control Panel**; in Control Panel Home, click **Network And Internet** and then click **Network And Sharing Center**; click **Manage Network Connections** in the left column). Double-click **Local Area Connection** to open the Local Area Connection Status dialog box. You should see activity on both the Sent and Received sides, as was shown earlier in Figure 9-6.

2. If you do not see both sending and receiving activity, click **Start**, click in the **Start Search** text box, and enter a computer name in your same subnet in the form *computername*\. You should see the drives on the computer appear in the Start menu,

UICKSTEPS

GETTING A BLOCK OF IP ADDRESSES *(Continued)*

Four blocks of IP addresses have been set aside and can be used by any organization for its private, internal needs without any coordination with any other organization, but these blocks should not be used for directly connecting to the Internet. These private-use blocks of IP addresses are:

- 10.0.0.0 through 10.255.255.255
- 169.254.0.0 through 169.254.255.255 (the APIPA range)
- 172.16.0.0 through 172.31.255.255
- 192.168.0.0 through 192.168.255.255

GET PUBLIC IP ADDRESSES

If your computer(s) will be interfacing directly with the Internet, they are *public* and thus need a globally unique IP number. If you want a block of public IP addresses, you must request it from one of several organizations, depending on the size of the block that you want. At the local level, for a moderate-sized block of IP addresses, your local ISP can assign it to you. For a larger block, a regional ISP may be able to handle the request. If not, you have to go to one of three regional Internet registries:

- American Registry for Internet Numbers (ARIN), at http://www.arin.net/, which covers North and South America, the Caribbean, and sub-Saharan Africa
- Réseaux IP Européens (RIPE), at http://www.ripe .net/, which covers Europe, the Middle East, and northern Africa
- Asia Pacific Network Information Centre (APNIC), at http://www.apnic.net/, which covers Asia and the Pacific

as shown in Figure 9-9. If you see this, then the computer is networking. If this doesn't work, then you need to double-check all the possible settings previously described:

- If you are using APIPA, make sure that the computer you are trying to contact is also using that range of numbers, either as a static assigned address or with automatic assignment.
- If all the settings are correct, check the cabling by making a simple connection of just several computers.
- If you do a direct connection between two computers, remember that you need a special *crossover* cable with the transmitting and receiving wires reversed.

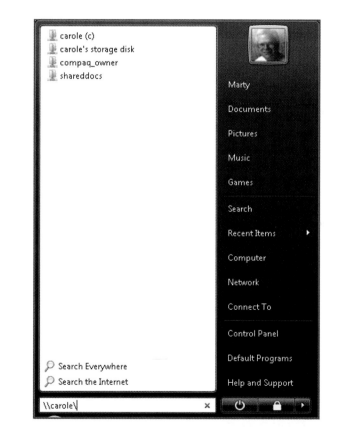

*Figure 9-9: **When networking is working properly, you'll be able to see shared resources on other computers in your network.***

CAUTION

Remember that private ranges work only with other computers in their own subnets and with IP addresses from the same range. You can tell what the subnet is from the subnet mask. For example, with a subnet mask of 255.255.255.0, all computers in the network must have IP addresses with the same first three groups of numbers and vary only in the last group. For example, computers with the numbers 192.168.104.001 and 192.168.104.002 are in the same subnet.

NOTE

The 127.0.0.1 IP address is a special address set aside to refer to the computer on which it is entered.

- If all else fails, replace the NIC.
- It could also be that network security is getting in your way of seeing the drives and resources on the other computer. See "Review Network Security" later in this chapter.

With a good NIC, good cabling, the correct settings, and network security properly handled, you'll be able to network.

Test a Network Setup and Connection

You can use several command-line utilities to test a TCP/IP installation. The more useful of these commands are the following:

- **Ipconfig** is used to determine if a network configuration has been initialized and if an IP address is assigned. If an IP address and valid subnet mask are returned, then the configuration is initialized and there are no duplicates for the IP address. If a subnet mask of 0.0.0.0 is returned, then the IP address is a duplicate.

- **Hostname** is used to determine the computer name of the local computer.

- **Ping** is used to query either the local computer or another computer on the network to see whether it responds. If the local computer responds, you know that TCP/IP is bound to the local NIC and that both are operating correctly. If the other computer responds, you know that TCP/IP and the NICs in both computers are operating correctly and that the connection between the computers is operable. Figure 9-10 shows the testing results on my system.

1. Click **Start**, click **All Programs**, click **Accessories**, and click **Command Prompt**. The Command Prompt window opens.

2. Type ipconfig and press **ENTER**. The IP address and subnet mask of the current computer should be returned. If this did not happen, there is a problem with the current configuration.

3. Type hostname and press **ENTER**. The computer name of the local computer should be returned.

4. Type ping, type the name of another computer on your network, and press **ENTER**. You should get four replies from the other computer.

5. If Ping did not work with a remote computer, try it on the current computer by typing ping 127.0.0.1 and pressing **ENTER**. Again, you should get four replies, this time from the current computer. If you didn't get a reply here, then you have a problem with either the

```
Command Prompt                                                    _ □ ✕

C:\>ipconfig

Windows IP Configuration

Ethernet adapter Local Area Connection:

   Connection-specific DNS Suffix  . :
   Link-local IPv6 Address . . . . . : fe80::c8f4:def7:53f3:b1cc%7
   IPv4 Address. . . . . . . . . . . : 192.168.1.35
   Subnet Mask . . . . . . . . . . . : 255.255.255.0
   Default Gateway . . . . . . . . . : 192.168.1.1

Tunnel adapter Local Area Connection* 4:

   Connection-specific DNS Suffix  . :
   IPv6 Address. . . . . . . . . . . : 2001:0:4136:e378:2c3d:198d:3f57:fedc
   Link-local IPv6 Address . . . . . : fe80::2c3d:198d:3f57:fedc%9
   Default Gateway . . . . . . . . . : ::

Tunnel adapter Local Area Connection* 3:

   Connection-specific DNS Suffix  . :
   Link-local IPv6 Address . . . . . : fe80::5efe:192.168.1.35%8
   Default Gateway . . . . . . . . . :

C:\>hostname
Winvista

C:\>ping marty-pc

Pinging Marty-PC [fe80::11aa:5d54:582d:b3c4%7] from fe80::c8f4:def7:53f3:b1cc%7
with 32 bytes of data:

Reply from fe80::11aa:5d54:582d:b3c4%7: time<1ms
Reply from fe80::11aa:5d54:582d:b3c4%7: time<1ms
Reply from fe80::11aa:5d54:582d:b3c4%7: time<1ms
Reply from fe80::11aa:5d54:582d:b3c4%7: time<1ms

Ping statistics for fe80::11aa:5d54:582d:b3c4%7:
    Packets: Sent = 4, Received = 4, Lost = 0 (0% loss),
Approximate round trip times in milli-seconds:
    Minimum = 0ms, Maximum = 0ms, Average = 0ms
```

Figure 9-10: You can test a network with TCP/IP utilities such as Ipconfig, Hostname, and Ping.

network setup or the NIC. If you did get a reply here, but not in Step 4, then there is a problem either in the other computer or in the cable and devices connecting them.

6. Type <u>exit</u> and press **ENTER** to close the Command Prompt window.

If you do find the problem here, go on to the next section on network security, and then review earlier sections on setting up network hardware, functions, and protocols to isolate and fix the problem.

Review Network Security

Chapter 8 discusses network security in depth. This section provides a brief synopsis of the specific steps you need to take to share your computer across

TIP

There are really only two types of networks: public and private. When you select the location of a network, the first two options, Home and Work, create a private network that is reasonably protected from the outside world and networking can be freely carried out. Selecting Public Location creates a public network and limits networking.

a LAN so that other computers similarly set up can see your computer and access the drives, folders, and printers. You will be able to see and access other computers that do the same thing. The steps to take in the appropriate order are described next. The specific steps to open the required windows and dialog boxes, as well as the specific settings to use, are provided in Chapter 8.

1. When you complete the installation of Vista, or the first time you turn on a new computer with Vista already installed, you are asked if the network you want to be a part of will be at home, at work, or in some public location, as shown in Figure 9-11. Both Home and Work are considered private locations where you want your computer to be seen and shared. You can change this later on (see step 2).

Figure 9-11: *Decide if the network you use is private or public.*

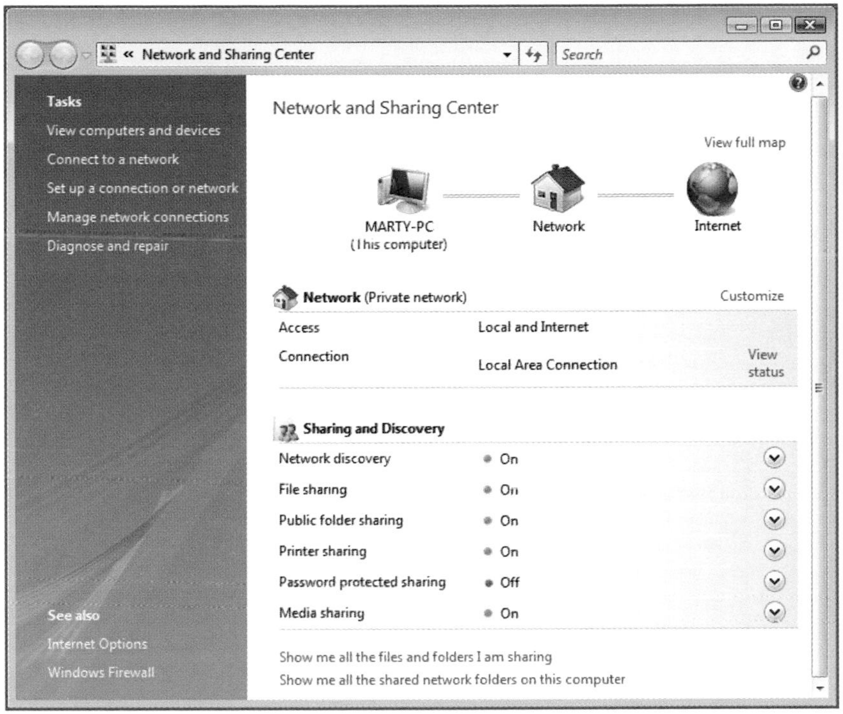

*Figure 9-12: **Turn on the sharing of your computer.***

2. If you want to share your computer's resources, such as files, folders, disk drives, and printers, you need to turn on that capability (it is turned off by default). This is done in the Network And Sharing Center, shown in Figure 9-12. This is also where you can change the private versus public aspect of the network interface for this computer by clicking **Customize**.

3. To share individual drives, folders, and printers, you must turn on that capability for the most senior drive or folder you want to share (also known as the parent). Subsidiary folders and the files within those folders will inherit the sharing aspect of the parent, although you cannot share the full C: drive. Sharing a drive, folder, or printer is done through the object's Properties dialog box, shown in Figure 9-13.

*Figure 9-13: **Share the specific objects you want others to be able to use.***

4. Finally, you must set up the Windows Firewall to allow the network and its sharing aspects to come through even though you have Windows Firewall turned on (which is highly recommended). Setting up the firewall exceptions to allow networking is done in the Windows Firewall Settings dialog box, shown in Figure 9-14.

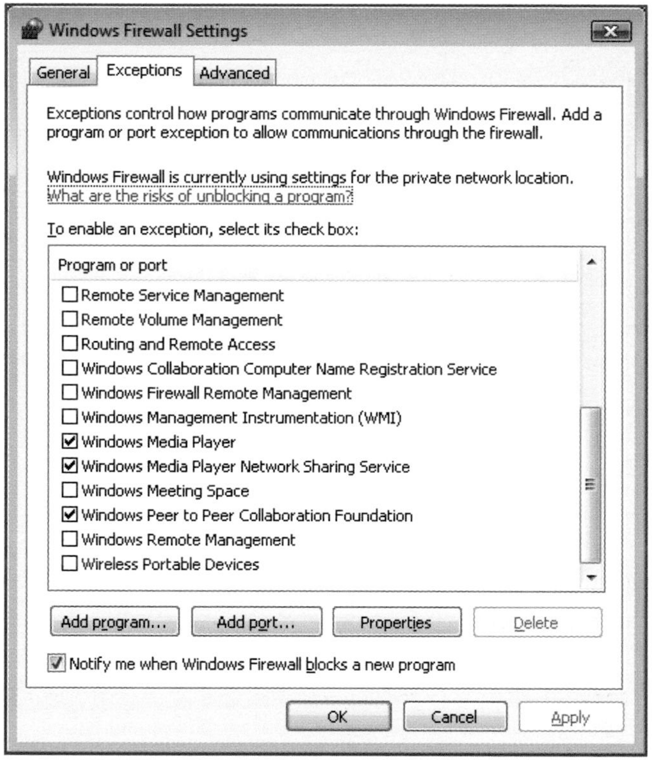

TIP

Correctly setting up the Windows Firewall is a secrete to successful networking while at the same time protecting yourself from unwanted intrusion. Review the tasks you perform on the network and then select only those options in the Firewall Exceptions that support those tasks.

Windows Firewall Settings

General | **Exceptions** | Advanced

Exceptions control how programs communicate through Windows Firewall. Add a program or port exception to allow communications through the firewall.

Windows Firewall is currently using settings for the private network location.
What are the risks of unblocking a program?

To enable an exception, select its check box:

Program or port

☐ Remote Service Management
☐ Remote Volume Management
☐ Routing and Remote Access
☐ Windows Collaboration Computer Name Registration Service
☐ Windows Firewall Remote Management
☐ Windows Management Instrumentation (WMI)
☑ Windows Media Player
☑ Windows Media Player Network Sharing Service
☐ Windows Meeting Space
☑ Windows Peer to Peer Collaboration Foundation
☐ Windows Remote Management
☐ Wireless Portable Devices

[Add program...] [Add port...] [Properties] [Delete]

☑ Notify me when Windows Firewall blocks a new program

[OK] [Cancel] [Apply]

Figure 9-14: **Make sure Windows Firewall allows networking.**

How to...

- *Explore a Network*
- *Permanently Connect to a Network Resource*
- *Connect Outside Your Workgroup or Domain*
- *Using Network Addresses*
- *Copy Network Files and Information*
- *Finding or Adding a Network Printer*
- *Print on Network Printers*
- *Access a Network Internet Connection*
- *Share Your Files*
- *Share Folders*
- *Set Up a Remote Desktop Connection*
- *Connect to a Remote Desktop over a LAN*
- *Use a Remote Desktop Connection*
- *Set Up a Wireless Connection*
- *Manage Wireless Network Sharing*
- *Implementing Windows Defender*
- *Use a Wireless Network*

Chapter 10
Using Networking

Networking brings a vastly enlarged world of computing to you, giving you access to all the computers, printers, and other devices to which you are connected and have permission to access. Using a network and its resources is no more difficult than accessing the hard disk or printer that is directly connected to your computer. Your network connection can be either wired or wireless, and you'll notice no difference, except for the hardware and the possibility that wireless is slower.

In this chapter you'll see how to access other computers and printers over a local area network (LAN), how to let others access your computer and resources, and how to access your computer remotely—across a LAN, through a telephone connection, or over the Internet.

NOTE

This chapter assumes that you have networking operating on your computer, as discussed in Chapter 9, and that you and others on your network have set up sharing and security parameters such that networking can take place, as described in Chapters 8 and 9.

NOTE

In many of the steps in this chapter, you will be interrupted and asked by User Account Control (UAC) for permission to continue. So long as it is something you started, then you want to click **Continue** or enter an administrator's password. To keep the steps as simple as possible, I have left out the UAC instructions. Chapter 8 discusses UAC in more detail.

Access Network Resources

Begin by looking at the network available to you through your computer. Then access a disk and retrieve files and folders from another computer, use a network printer, and access the Internet over the network.

Explore a Network

Whether you have just installed a small home network or have just plugged into a large company network, the first thing you'll probably want to do is explore it—see what you can see. You can do that from Windows Explorer Network or Computer view.

USE WINDOWS EXPLORER NETWORK VIEW

1. Click **Start** and click **Network**. The Network window opens, as shown in Figure 10-1. This shows the computers on your network that have been shared and are available to you.

Figure 10-1: Opening your network displays the computers that are shared, as well as media being shared (the top two and fourth icons are used to share media).

2. Double-click one of the shared computers on your network. It will open and display
   the drives, printers, and other resources (such as tape drives and removable disks)
   on that computer.

3. Double-click one of the drives to open it, and then double-click one or more of the
   folders to see the files available to you (see Figure 10-2).

4. Click **Back** one or more times, and then open other computers, drives,
   and folders to more fully explore your network.

5. Click **Close** to close Windows Explorer.

USE WINDOWS EXPLORER COMPUTER VIEW

Network is just one particular view of Windows Explorer. You can also navigate
to a network resource through the Windows Explorer Computer view.

1. Click **Start**, click **Computer**, and drag **Folders** to the top of the navigation pane.

2. In the Folders list, click **Network** to open it. The network resources will be displayed,
   as you saw in Figure 10-1.

3. Close Computer view.

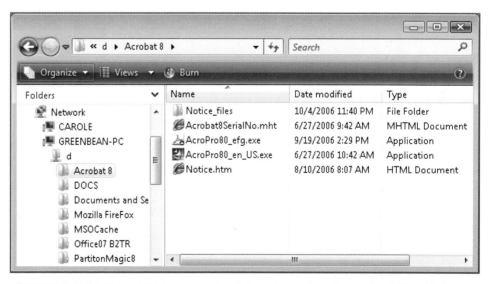

*Figure 10-2: If the computers on your network have been shared, you should be able to see
the folders, files, and other resources that are available to you.*

Permanently Connect to a Network Resource

If you use a specific network drive or folder a lot, you may want to connect to it permanently so that you can use it as if it were a drive on your computer. This permanent connection is called a "mapped network drive." Note that it is only "permanent" until you decide to disconnect from the drive. See "Disconnect a Mapped Drive" later in this chapter.

CONNECT TO A MAPPED NETWORK DRIVE

To set up a mapped network drive:

1. Click **Start**, click **Computer**, and, if needed, drag **Folders** to the top of the navigation pane. In Folders, click the triangle opposite **Network**, and click the computer that contains the drive you want to connect to permanently. You should see the drive in the subject pane.

2. Right-click the drive in the Subject pane, and click **Map Network Drive** (see Figure 10-3). The Map Network Drive dialog box will appear.

3. Select the drive letter you want to use for the mapped drive or the specific folder, if that is applicable, and choose whether you want to reconnect to the drive every time you log on to your computer.

4. Click **Finish**. The drive will open in a separate window. Close that window.

5. In the Folders list of the original Windows Explorer window, click the triangle to the left of **Network** to close it. Then, if it isn't already displayed, click **Computer** to open that view. Both in the Folders list and in the Subject pane, you should see the new network drive, as shown in Figure 10-4.

6. Close Computer view.

DISCONNECT A MAPPED DRIVE

1. Click **Start**, click **Computer**, and, if needed, drag **Folders** to the top of the navigation pane.

2. In the Folders list, right-click the mapped network drive, and click **Disconnect**. The drive will disappear from the Folders list and in the Subject pane.

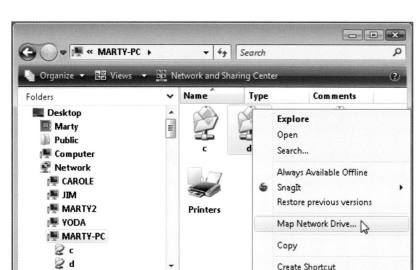

Figure 10-3: Mapping a network drive gives you a permanent connection to that device.

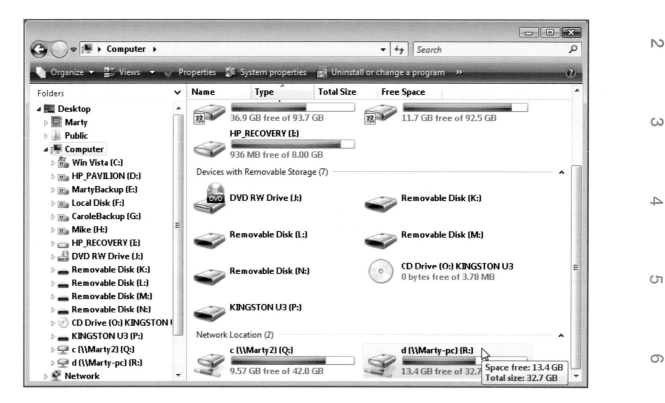

Figure 10-4: A mapped network drive across a network gives you the same access as any drive on your computer.

Connect Outside Your Workgroup or Domain

If you want to connect to another computer or network resource outside of your workgroup or domain, you will not see that computer or resource when you open Network view. You must use a different procedure to connect to it.

1. Click **Start** and click **Network**. The Network window opens, as you saw in Figure 10-1.

2. Click **Network And Sharing Center** on the toolbar. The Network And Sharing Center window will open.

3. Click **Connect To A Network**. A list of the networks you can connect to is displayed. Click the network you want, and click **Connect**.

4. If requested, enter a user name and a password, and click **OK**. Given the appropriate permissions, you'll see and be able to open the computers in the other network.

5. Close Windows Explorer.

QUICKSTEPS

USING NETWORK ADDRESSES

Network addressing uses the *Uniform Naming Convention*, or UNC, to identify files, folders, and other resources on any computer on the network.

IDENTIFYING A NETWORK RESOURCE

A network resource, which is a folder or disk on a computer on the network, is identified by:

\\computername\drivename:\pathname\folder name

For example, on a computer named "Marty-PC" a folder named "2007 Budgets" in the Budgeting folder would have the full network address of:

\\Marty-PC\D:\Budgeting\2007 Budgets

IDENTIFYING A NETWORK PRINTER

Identifying a network printer is similar to identifying any other network resource. It takes the form of:

\\computername\printername

For example, a printer named HP4500 on Server 1 would have the UNC of:

\\Server1\HP4500.

Copy Network Files and Information

Once you have opened a network resource, it is easy to copy information from the resource to your local hard disk.

1. Click **Start**, click **Computer**, and, if needed, drag **Folders** to the top of the navigation pane.
2. In the Folders list, click the triangle opposite **Network** to open it. Then open the computer, drive, and folder(s) in order to see the files that you want to copy in the Subject pane.
3. In the Folders list, click the triangle opposite the drive and folder to display the folder you want to hold the information from the network.
4. Click the first file or folder you want to copy, and then hold down CTRL, clicking the remaining files and/or folders you want. When all are selected, drag them to the folder on the left in which you want them, as you can see in Figure 10-5.
5. Close Windows Explorer.

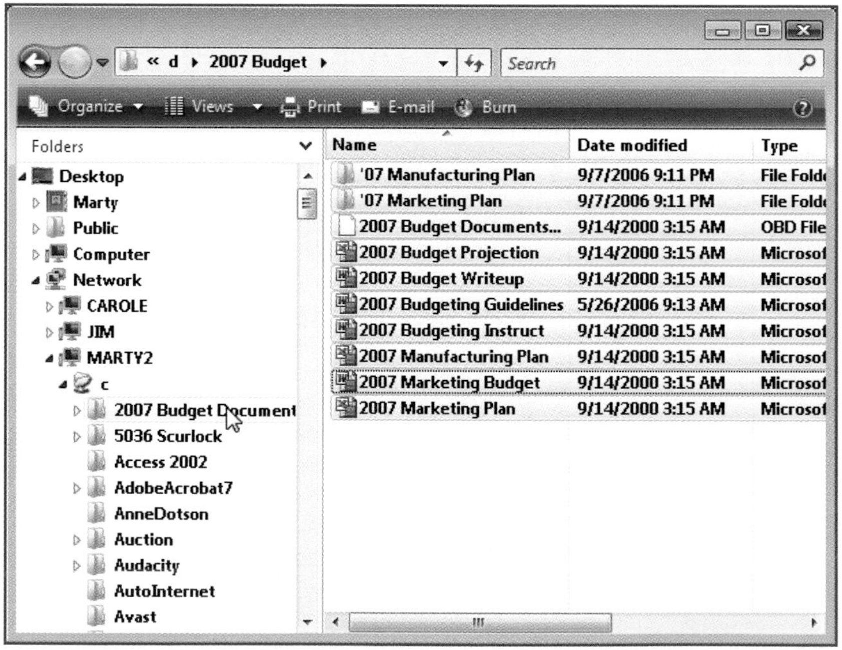

Figure 10-5: You can locate and copy files and folders across the network.

There are two ways to find a network printer: by using Find Printer in the Print dialog boxes of some programs and by using Add A Printer in the Printers And Faxes dialog box.

USE FIND PRINTER

Recent versions of Microsoft Office products and other applications have included a Find Printer button to search for and locate network printers. This is the same as the printer search capability, which uses the Windows domain's Active Directory service. To use this, you must be in a domain and not in a workgroup.

1. In an Office 2007 application, click the **Office Button**, click **Print**, and click **Find Printer**. If your network is not part of an Active Directory domain, you will get a message to that effect. Otherwise, the Find Printers dialog box will appear and begin a search for a printer.

2. A list of printers will be displayed. When you have located the printer you want, right-click that printer and click **Connect**.

3. Close the Search Results window.

USE ADD A PRINTER

Add A Printer is the most common way to locate a network printer, and is available to both workgroup and domain users.

1. Click **Start**, click **Control Panel**, and, in Control Panel Home, click **Printer** under Hardware And Sound; or, in Classic view, double-click **Printers**. The Printers window opens.

Continued . . .

Print on Network Printers

Like using other network resources, using a network printer is not much different from using a local printer. To locate a network printer, see the "Finding or Adding a Network Printer" QuickSteps.

To use a network printer that has been previously found, either automatically or manually—from Microsoft Word 2007, for example:

1. Click the **Office Button**, and click **Print** to open the Print dialog box.
2. Under Printer, click the **Name** down arrow, and choose the network printer you want to use.

3. Make any needed adjustments to the printer settings, and click **OK** to complete the printing.

Access a Network Internet Connection

If the network you are on has an Internet connection, you are automatically connected to it and can use it directly, unless it requires a user name and password. In most instances, you simply have to open your browser (click **Internet** on the Start menu) or your e-mail program (click **E-Mail** on the Start menu and enter your e-mail and ISP information), and you are on and using the Internet. See Chapter 4 for more information.

Let Others Access Your Resources

The other side of the networking equation is sharing the resources on your computer to allow others to use them. This includes sharing your files, folders, and disks, as well as sharing your printers. The mechanics of setting up your

FINDING OR ADDING A NETWORK PRINTER *(Continued)*

2. Click **Add A Printer**. Click **Add A Network, Wireless, Or Bluetooth Printer**. If you are on an Active Directory domain, a list of printers will be presented to you (see Figure 10-6). Select one and click **Next**.

3. If you don't see a list of printers, click **The Printer That I Want Isn't Listed**. Click **Browse**, double-click the computer that has the printer you want, and then double-click the printer. You should see the printer you want in the Add Printer dialog box, as shown in Figure 10-7.

4. Click **Next**. A permanent connection will be made to the printer. Click **Install Driver** if you are asked to do so. Type a name for the printer if you don't want to use the default name, determine if you want this printer to be your default, click the **Set As The Default Printer** check box as needed, and click **Next**.

5. Click **Print A Test Page**. When a test page prints, click **Close** and then click **Finish**. If a test page does not print, click **Troubleshoot Printer Problems**, and follow the suggestions.

6. Close Control Panel.

NOTE

Unlike earlier versions of Windows, Vista, by default, does not share its resources and further protects them with a strong firewall. To share resources, you must set up file, folder, and printer sharing and enable the appropriate exceptions in the Windows Firewall, as described in Chapters 8 and 9.

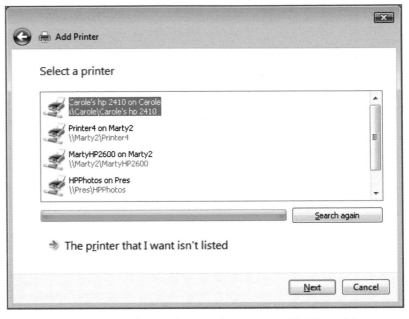

Figure 10-6: The automatic search for a printer may not find the printer you are looking for if you are not on an Active Directory domain.

computer to share its resources is discussed in depth in Chapters 8 and 9 (in particular, see "Set File and Folder Sharing" in Chapter 8). Here we'll look at how that is used once it is turned on.

Share Your Files

You can share your files by putting them into a shared folder. By default, your computer has a series of folders called Public that can be shared; however, the folders aren't shared by default. You can also create more shared folders (see Chapters 8 and 9).

1. Click **Start**, click **Computer**, and open the disk and folder(s) needed to locate and display the files you want to share in the subject pane.

2. In the navigation pane, click the triangle opposite **Public** to display the public folders.

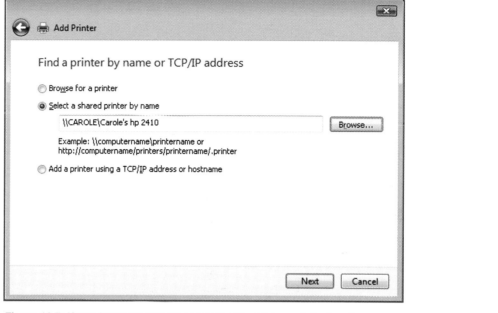

Figure 10-7: *If you know a network computer to which a printer has been attached and it has been shared, you can connect to it easily.*

NOTE

You cannot share the primary disk drive, normally labeled "C:," on a computer running Windows Vista, and while you can share the Users folder, that sharing does not carry over to any of the user folders.

3. Drag the files you want to share from the subject pane to one of the Public folders in the navigation pane, as shown in Figure 10-8.

4. Close the Computer window.

Share Folders

Any folder can be shared, as described in Chapters 8 and 9, but you can also do it by moving the folder into the Public folder.

1. Click **Start**, click **Computer**, and, if needed, drag **Folders** to the top of the navigation pane. Open the disk and folder(s) needed to locate and display the folder you want to share in the subject pane.

2. In the navigation pane, click the triangle opposite **Public** to open and display the public folders.

10

Figure 10-8: You can share a file by putting it into one of the Public folders.

3. Drag the folder you want to share from the subject pane to where you want it within the public folders.

4. Close the Computer window.

Work Remotely

Windows Vista allows you to work remotely from another computer, for example, from a remote computer to one in your office, using Vista's Remote Desktop Connection. The objective is to transfer information and utilize resources from a distance using a local area network (LAN) connection. To use Remote Desktop Connection requires both a Remote Desktop host and a Remote Desktop client.

Set Up a Remote Desktop Connection

Remote Desktop Connection enables you to literally take control of another computer and do everything on it as if you were sitting in front of that computer. Remote Desktop Connection is run over a LAN, where the computer you are sitting at is the *client* and the computer you are accessing is the *host*. To set up the host, you must first establish user accounts and then enable a LAN-based host.

SET UP REMOTE DESKTOP ACCOUNTS

To use Remote Desktop Connection, the host must have user accounts established for that purpose, and the user accounts must have a password. Therefore, the first step in setting up the account is to set up one or more such accounts on the host.

1. Click **Start** and click **Control Panel**. In Control Panel Home, click **User Accounts And Family Safety**, and then click (or double-click in Classic view) **User Accounts**.

2. Click **Manage Another Account**, click **Create A New Account**, enter the name for the account (this example uses "Remote"), select the type of account you want, and click **Create Account**.

3. Click the new account, click **Create A Password**, enter the password, press **TAB**, type the password again, press **TAB** twice, enter a hint if you wish (anyone can see the hint), and click **Create Password**. Close the Change An Account window.

4. Click **Start** and click **Control Panel**. In Control Panel Home, click **System And Maintenance** and then click (or double-click in Classic view) **Administrative Tools**.

5. In the subject pane, double-click **Computer Management**. In the Computer Management window that opens, in the left column, click the triangle opposite **System Tools** to open it, click the triangle opposite **Local Users And Groups** to open it, and click **Users**. In the list of users in the subject pane, shown in Figure 10-9, double-click the new user you just created.

6. In the Properties dialog box that appears, click the **Member Of** tab, and click **Add**. In the Select Groups dialog box, click **Advanced** and then click **Find Now** to search for groups. Click **Remote Desktop Users**, click **OK** three times, and close both the Computer Management and Administrative Tools windows.

Name (RDN)	In Folder
Performance Monitor Users	WINVISTA
Power Users	WINVISTA
Remote Desktop Users	WINVISTA
Replicator_ploc	WINVISTA
Special	WINVISTA
Users	WINVISTA

Search results:

OK   Cancel

10

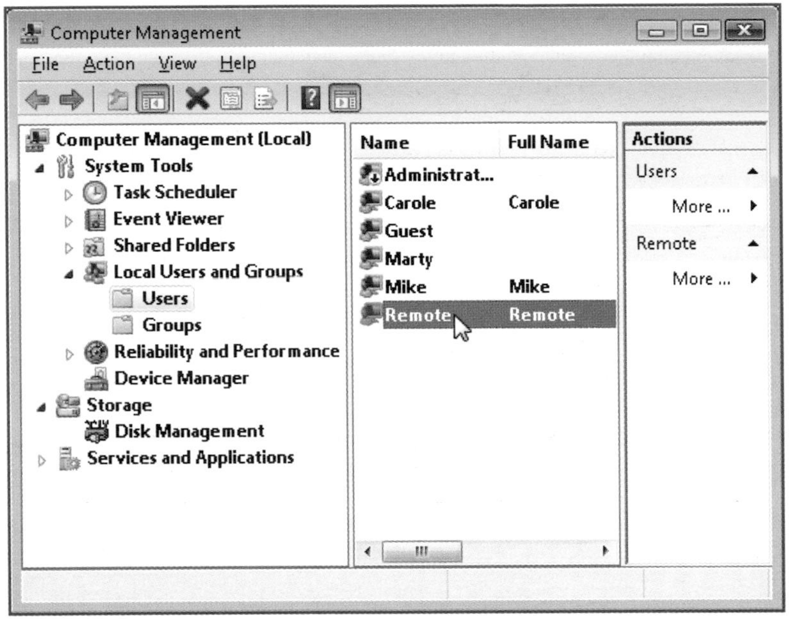

Figure 10-9: User accounts must be members of the *Remote Desktop Users group in order to use Remote Desktop Connection.*

SET UP A LAN–BASED HOST

Set up the host for using Remote Desktop Connection within a LAN.

1. Click **Start** and click **Control Panel**. In Control Panel Home, click **System And Maintenance**, and then click (or double-click in Classic view) **System**. Click **Remote Settings**. The System Properties dialog box will appear.

2. Click the **Remote** tab. In the bottom Remote Desktop panel, click **Allow Connections From Computers Running Any Version Of Remote Desktop**, as shown in Figure 10-10.

3. Click **Select Users**. Users that you added to the Remote Desktop Users group are displayed.

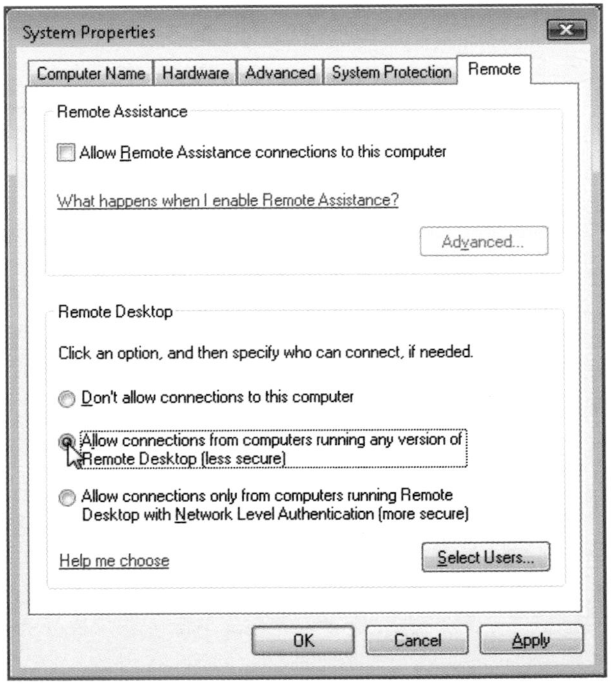

Figure 10-10: *Remote Desktop Connection is not turned on by default.*

The process in "Set Up a LAN–Based Host" adds users from the host computer to the Remote Desktop Users group. If you are part of a domain and want to add users from other computers, you need to enter them in the Enter The Object Names To Select field in the form *computername\username*.

4. If you want to add more users, click **Add**, click **Advanced**, and click **Find Now**. Select the users you want to include by holding down **CTRL** while clicking them, and then click **OK** four times to close all open dialog boxes. Close Control Panel.

SET UP A REMOTE DESKTOP CLIENT

The Remote Desktop Connection client is probably already installed on the computer you will be using for the client, since it is part of the default Windows Vista installation. Verify this, and, if it is not installed, do so.

Click **Start**, click **All Programs**, click **Accessories**, and click **Remote Desktop Connection**.

If you see the Remote Desktop Connection dialog box, you need to do nothing further here. If you do not see Remote Desktop Connection, you'll possibly need to reinstall Windows Vista.

Connect to a Remote Desktop over a LAN

When you are sitting at the client computer connected to a LAN, to which the host is also connected, you can connect to the Remote Desktop host.

1. Click **Start**, click **All Programs**, click **Accessories**, and click **Remote Desktop Connection**. The Remote Desktop Connection dialog box appears.

2. Enter the name or IP address of the computer to which you want to connect. If you are not sure of the computer name, click **Browse For More** in the Computer drop-down list box, which will display a list of the computers in your immediate domain or workgroup.

3. After you have entered the computer name, click **Connect**. The Windows Security dialog box appears. Enter the user name and password for the Remote Desktop host computer (this was the "Remote" user you created earlier), and click **OK**. If you see a message that someone is currently logged on to the remote host, decide if you can disconnect them, and click the appropriate choice. (See "Use a Remote Desktop Connection.")

The Remote Desktop toolbar appears in the top center of the screen with the name of the computer that is hosting you.

Figure 10-11: When the remote desktop is reduced from full screen, the Remote Desktop toolbar, the Connection bar, disappears.

Use a Remote Desktop Connection

Once you are connected to the host computer, you can perform almost any action that you could if you were sitting in front of that computer—you can run programs, access data, and more. In addition, the Remote Desktop toolbar, called the Connection Bar, allows you to close the Remote Desktop window without logging out so that your programs will keep running, to minimize the window so that you can see the computer you are sitting at (see Figure 10-11), and to maximize the window. In addition, there is a pushpin icon that determines whether the Connection Bar is always on the desktop or if it is only there when you move the mouse to the upper-center portion of the screen. Remote Desktop Connection also gives you the ability to transfer information between the host computer and the client computer you are using. This means that you can:

- Print to a local printer connected to the client (this is enabled by default)

- Work with files on both the remote host and the client computers in the same window (this is not enabled by default)
- Cut and paste between both computers and documents on either one (this is enabled by default)

The local client resources that are available in a Remote Desktop session are controlled by the Remote Desktop Connection dialog box options.

1. From the Remote Desktop, click **Start**, click **All Programs**, click **Accessories**, and click **Remote Desktop Connection**. The Remote Desktop Connection dialog box appears. Click **Options**, and the box expands to give you a number of controls for Remote Desktop.

2. Click the **Display** tab. The default for a LAN is to use Full Screen mode and up to the maximum color level your computer can use, as well as to display the Connection Bar.

3. Click the **Local Resources** tab. As you can see in Figure 10-12, you can determine if you want sound brought to the client and if you want the ability to use shortcut keys. Also:
   - If you want to print on the printer attached to the local client, keep the default Printers selection.
   - If you want to transfer information using the Cut and Paste commands between the two computers, the Clipboard should be selected.
   - If you want to transfer information by dragging between disk drives, click **More** and click **Drives** to select them all; or click the plus sign (+) next to **Drives**, and select individual drives.
   - If you intend to use a modem or another serial device on the local client, choose **Serial Ports**.

4. If you want to start a program when you open the Remote Desktop Connection, click the **Programs** tab, click the relevant check box, and enter the path and file name of the program and the starting folder to use.

5. Click the **Experience** tab, and select the connection speed you are using. This will determine which of the items below the drop-down list box are selected. You can change the individual items if you want.

6. Click the **Advanced** tab. Look at the choices for authentication, and select the one that is correct for you. If you have to go through a Terminal Services Gateway (generally in larger organizations), click **Settings**, select the option that is correct for you, type any needed information, and click **OK**.

TIP

If your LAN has particularly heavy traffic and is slow, you might want to lower the screen size and colors.

Remote Desktop Connection

Remote Desktop
Connection

General | Display | Local Resources | Programs | Experience | Advanced

Remote computer sound

Bring to this computer ▼

Keyboard

Apply Windows key combinations (for example ALT+TAB)

In full screen mode only ▼

Local devices and resources

Select the devices and resources you want to use in your remote session:

☑ Printers   ☑ Clipboard

More...

Connect | Cancel | Help | Options <<

Figure 10-12: You can control what client devices are available with Remote Desktop.

1 2 3 4 5 6 7 8 9

10

Click the **General** tab. If you will use several settings, save the ones you just made by clicking **Save As**, entering a name, and clicking **Save**.

8. If you are not already connected, enter your password and click **Connect**. Otherwise, close the Remote Desktop Connection dialog box.

9. When you are done using Remote Desktop, you may leave it in any of three ways:

- Click **Close** on the Connection Bar. This leaves you logged on, and any programs you have will remain running. If you restart Remote Desktop Connection with the host computer and no one else has logged on locally, you will return to the same session you left.

- Click **Start**, click the shut down arrow, and click **Log Off**. This terminates your Remote Desktop session and all programs are stopped. If you restart Remote Desktop Connection with the host computer and no one else has logged on locally, you will begin a new session.

- Click **Start** and click **Disconnect**. This is the same as clicking the Close button on the Connection Bar.

Set Up and Use a Wireless Network

Wireless networks have become a popular way to create small networks in homes and small business for the simple reason that you don't have to run cables everywhere. With a wireless access point connected to the Internet, any wireless-enabled computer within approximately 100 feet of the access point can connect to the Internet and communicate with any other wireless-enabled computer. If the access point is also connected to a wired network, all the members of the wired network are also available to the wireless computers. Chapter 9 talked about the hardware requirements needed to do this. Here we will talk about what is needed to set up and use a wireless network in Windows Vista and make it secure.

Currently connected to:

linksys
Access: Local and Internet

Connect or disconnect...
Network and Sharing Center

6:26 PM

Set Up a Wireless Connection

The first task is to make a connection with a wireless access point and then set it up so its use is secure. If you have a recent computer with wireless capability that is turned on (there may be a small switch on your computer to do that) and are near a wireless access point, your computer may automatically connect and, if you click on the network connection in the notification area, you will get a message you are connected. In any case continue on here to set up and secure the connection.

1. Click **Start** and click **Control Panel**. In Control Panel Home, click **Network And Internet** and then click (or double-click in Classic view) **Network And Sharing Center**. If you are already connected you will see your connection both graphically and textually. Skip to step 6.

linksys (Private network)		Customize
Access	Local and Internet	
Connection	Wireless Network Connection (linksys)	View status
	Signal strength: Good	Disconnect

2. If you don't see a wireless connection already established, click **Set Up A Connection Or Network**. Click **Set Up A Wireless Router Or Access Point**, and click **Next**. Read what the Network Wizard will help you do, and click **Next**. Your system will search for a wireless adapter in your computer and then for a wireless access point.

3. When a wireless network is found, you are asked to name your network. Type a name and click **Next**. Type a "passphrase" or password of at least eight characters, and click **Next**.

4. Choose the file and printer sharing option you want, or keep you current settings, and click **Next**.

5. Insert a USB flash drive on which you can save your settings, and click **Next**. This drive can be used to transfer these settings to other computers and wireless devices. Click **Close**.

6. In the Network And Sharing Center window look at the type of wireless network you have, Private, or Public and determine the type you situation requires. If you need to change the type, click **Customize**, click the type you want, change the icon if desired, click **Next**, and click **Close**.

7. Review the Sharing And Discovery options and change those as desired by clicking the Off or On, clicking the choice you want, and clicking **Apply**. When you have finished making the changes you want, click **Close**.

Manage Wireless Network Sharing

When you use a wireless connection, you most likely do not want other network users to access your computer. That is the default setting, but check and make sure that it is way your connection is set up.

1. From the Network And Sharing Center, click **Manage Network Connections** in the Tasks list. The Network Connections window opens, displaying the connections available on the computer.

2. Double-click **Wireless Network Connection** to open the Wireless Network Connection Status dialog box, shown in Figure 10-13.

3. Click **Properties**, click the **Sharing** tab, and look at your connection-sharing settings. In most circumstances where you are using a public WiFi hotspot, you want these check boxes *not* selected. The primary instance in which you would want this enabled would be in a secure organizational setting.

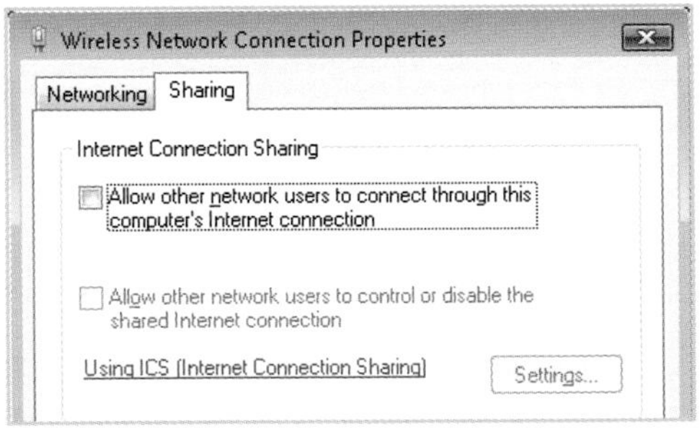

4. When you have assured yourself that the settings are the way you want them, click **OK**, click **Close** in the Status dialog box, and close both the Network Connections and Control Panel windows.

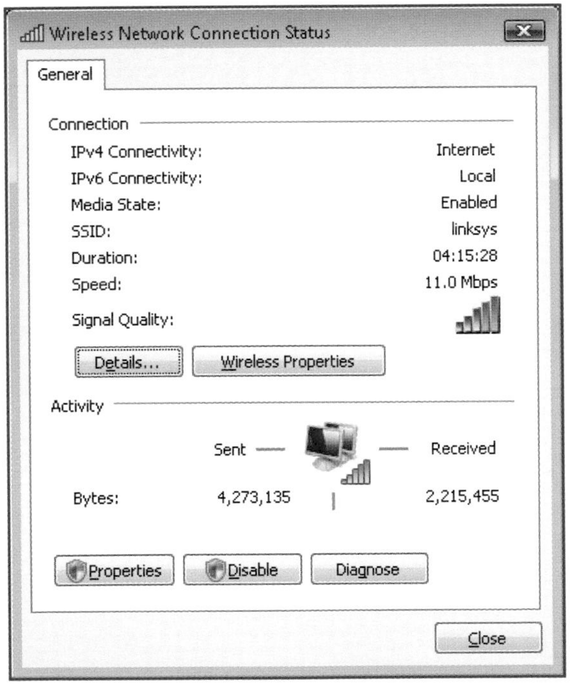

Figure 10-13: A wireless network is particularly susceptible to intrusion and needs to be protected.

![QuickSteps clock logo] **QUICKSTEPS**

IMPLEMENTING WINDOWS DEFENDER

Windows Defender guards your computer against spyware and other unwanted programs. It watches what is happening on your computer and looks for programs that are trying to install themselves or change important Windows settings, both without your approval. Windows Defender does this on a real-time basis, as well letting you manually start a scan of your computer. It uses a Microsoft database called the SpyNet Community that tracks, with the user's approval, what programs people think might be dangerous.

REVIEW WINDOWS DEFENDER SETTINGS

By default Windows Defender is running on your computer and you must take some action to turn it off (not recommended), if that is what you want. To open, review, and possibly change the Windows Defender setting:

1. Click **Start**, click **All Programs**, and click **Windows Defender**. Windows Defender appears.

2. Click **Tools** on the toolbar and click **Options** to display the many settings to can make to have Defender run the way you want, as shown in Figure 10-15.

3. Scroll down the options and make any changes that meet your needs.

4. When you have finished, click **Save** to return to the Tools And Settings window and check out the other options there.

Continued . . .

Use a Wireless Network

Once you have a wireless network up and running the way you want, you can use it in the same way you use a wired network.

1. Click **Start** and click **Internet** to open Internet Explorer, and explore the Internet in the same way you would with a wired network, as shown in Figure 10-14.

Figure 10-14: You can use a wireless network connection in the same way you used a wired one.

UICKSTEPS

IMPLEMENTING WINDOWS DEFENDER *(Continued)*

DO A MANUAL SCAN

If you suspect that software you don't want had gotten on you computer, you can run a manual scan to see what Windows Defender finds.

1. While in Windows Defender, click **Scan** on the toolbar. The scanning will immediately start. When it completes, you will be told what was found and given the scan statistics.

2. When you have finished, click **Close**.

Figure 10-15: Windows Defender provides some protection against spyware and unwanted programs.

2. Close Internet Explorer, click **Start**, and click **E-Mail** to open your default e-mail program, which you can use in the same way as with a wired network connection.

3. Close your mail program, and try any other networking program you use.

Index

Numbers

10/100BaseT Ethernet standard
explanation of, 217
using, 217–218
10BaseT networks, hub and switch
requirement for, 220
802.11b and 802.11g wireless standards
explanations of, 218
speeds for, 219
127.0.0.1 IP address, significance of, 228

Symbols

" (quotation marks), using with Internet
searches, 77
; (semicolon), using with addressees in
Windows Mail, 89

A

A: drive, meaning of, 52
access points
role in WLANs, 218–219
selecting, 220
accessory programs, running, 110–111
account types, changing, 191
accounts
changing, 192
setting up for Remote Desktop
Connection, 243
adapters, using with WLANs, 219
Add A Printer feature, using, 239–240
Add Fonts dialog box, selecting fonts
in, 151
Add To Contacts option, using with
Windows Mail, 92
address bar in Windows Explorer
window
description of, 10
function of, 47
identifying, 9
navigating with, 54
address box, identifying, 76
addressees
adding to Contacts list, 92

entering in Windows Mail, 89
selecting in Windows Mail, 92
using network addresses, 238
administrator
logging on as, 190–191
use of standard user account by, 190
Administrator accounts
setting up, 192
use of, 190
advanced system information,
viewing, 117–118
All Media Results page, components
of, 164
All Programs menu, 8
ALT key. See keyboard shortcuts
American Registry for Internet
Numbers (ARIN), Web address
for, 227
analog signals, recording with Movie
Maker, 171
APIPA (Automatic Private IP
Addressing), assignment of
IP addresses by, 226, 227
APNIC (Asia Pacific Network
Information Centre), Web address
for, 227
Appearance Settings dialog box,
displaying, 21
ARIN (American Registry for Internet
Numbers), Web address for, 227
Asia Pacific Network Information
Centre (APNIC), Web address
for, 227
Ask area of Help, using, 15
audio clips, placing in
movies, 183–184
audio files
availability to Movie Maker, 180–181
playing on Internet, 87
Audio Levels dialog box,
displaying, 185
automatic updates
applying, 112
turning on, 111–112
AutoPlay dialog box, opening, 135
AVI format, using, 173

B

Back button
in Internet Explorer, 76
in Windows Explorer, 47
backed up encryption keys, using, 209
backups
running immediate file backups, 65
scheduling, 63–64
biometric devices, replacing passwords
with, 196
BitLocker, using, 62
broadband connections, setting up, 73
browser navigation, using, 76
browsers, starting, 75
Burn files To Disk option, choosing, 66
burning music CDs, 167–169
buttons, grouping, 32

C

C: drive
meaning of, 52
restriction on sharing of, 241
cabling, selecting for wired
Ethernet, 215, 217
Calculator, using, 110
camcorder video, making movies
from, 174–176
camcorders, importing video
from, 172
camera images, importing, 134–135
cameras, installing, 131–132
Categories of cabling, using with
wireless LANs, 217
CD drive, labeling of, 52
CDs
advisory about installing printers
from, 140
burning music CDs, 167–169
copying to computers, 165–167
installing software from, 119
playing, 160–162
ripping to computers, 165–167
writing files and folders to, 65–66

certificates, backing up digital
certificates, 211
Character Map, using, 110–111
characters, restrictions for using with
groups, 208
check box in dialog box
function of, 13
identifying, 12
Classic menus
appearance of, 28
turning on, 11
Classic view
configuring Internet connections in, 74
configuring modems in, 71
displaying, 41
setting up dial-up connections in,
72–73
ClearType, using, 22
client devices, controlling with Remote
Desktop, 247
clients
enabling computers as, 223–224
setting up for Remote Desktop
Connection, 245
client/server LANs, function of,
215–216
clip, definition of, 176
clips. See video clips
clock icon, identifying, 32
Close button
description of, 10
identifying, 9, 12
stopping programs with, 106
collection of clips, explanation
of, 176
colors
changing with Personalization
window, 20–21
selecting for e-mail, 93
command buttons in dialog box
function of, 13
identifying, 12
Command Prompt window, reversing
text colors in, 106
communications, setting up, 70–74

Compress Contents To Save Disk Space
     attribute, description of, 63
computer information, viewing, 117
computer resources, sharing, 224, 231
Computer view, using, 235
computers
   enabling as clients and
        servers, 223–224
   locking, 211
   monitoring with UAC (User Account
        Control), 191–192
   networking two computers, 220
   protecting unattended computers, 212
connecting devices, selecting for wired
     Ethernet, 215–217
connections. *See also* Internet
     connections; network connections;
     Remote Desktop Connection
   to network resources, 236
   outside workgroups or domains, 237
   setting up broadband connections, 73
   setting up dial-up
        connections, 72–73
   setting up wireless
        connections, 248–249
   types of, 70
   verifying network
        connections, 226–227
Contacts list
   adding addresses to, 92
   using, 91–92
content. *See* Web content
context menus, opening for objects, 4
control menu icon in dialog box,
     identifying, 12
Control Panel
   Classic View of, 41
   icon for, 7
   using, 39
cookies, handling, 85
copying network files and
     information, 238
copyright issues, considering with
     recorded CDs, 171
copyrighted material, copying with
     Media Player, 166

cover pages
   coded fields in, 156
   creating for faxes, 156–158
   saving, 158
   selecting for fax messages, 154
   using drawing tools with, 156–158
CTRL key. *See* keyboard shortcuts

D

D: drive, meaning of, 52
date
   displaying and setting, 5
   setting and using, 36–37
day and date, displaying, 5
Default Programs icon, function of, 8
Defragment Now option, choosing, 68
deleted files and folders, recovering, 56
desktop
   adding icons to, 26
   changing background of, 22
   items on, 2
   starting programs from, 8
   switching programs on, 104
   using, 5
desktop icons. *See also* icons;
     program icons
   aligning, 27
   arranging, 27–28
   renaming, 28
   resizing, 27
   using, 5
Details pane in Windows Explorer
   function of, 47
   turning off, 47
device drivers. *See* drivers
devices, sharing, 200–201
dialog boxes
   components of, 12
   controls in, 12
   using, 11–13
   versus windows, 12
dial-up connections
   comparing to DSL, 70
   setting up, 72–73
digital certificates, backing up, 211

digital music devices, synching
     with, 169–171
Disk Cleanup feature, using, 67
Disk Defragmenter, using, 68
disk drives, selecting and
     opening, 52–53
disks
   bringing in documents from, 131
   defragmenting, 68
   navigating through, 53–54
disks recently displayed, listing, 54
Display Settings dialog box,
     opening, 21
document priorities, changing in print
     queue, 150
documents
   bringing in from disks, 131
   creating with programs, 130
   downloading across
        networks, 131–132
   downloading from Internet, 132
   printing, 142
   scanning and faxing, 155
domains
   connecting outside of, 237
   role in client/server networks, 216
DOS commands, typing at command
     prompt, 106
double-click, explanation of, 4
downloaded files, saving, 120
drawing tools, using with fax cover
     pages, 156–158
drivers
   explanation of, 121–122
   locating, 122, 123
   reinstalling for modems, 72
drivers and NICs, checking, 220
drives
   connecting to mapped network
        drives, 236
   sharing, 200–201, 206
drop-down list box in dialog box,
     identifying, 12
DSL connections, comparing to
     dial-up, 70
DVD drive, labeling of, 52

DVD Options dialog box, displaying
     for publishing movies, 187
DVDs
   burning for movies, 187
   playing, 171
   writing files and folders to, 65–66

E

E: drive, meaning of, 52
Ease of Access settings
   changing, 37–39
   function of, 37
   turning on, 37
effects, adding to movies, 183
Effects dialog box, opening, 22
EFS (Encrypting File System), function
     of, 210
e-mail accounts, establishing with
     Windows Mail, 88–89
e-mail messages. *See also* fax messages;
     Windows Mail
   applying formatting to, 92–95
   attaching files to, 95
   attaching signatures to, 94–95
   creating and sending with Windows
        Mail, 89–90
   displaying with Task Scheduler, 103
   including background images in, 92
   receiving in Windows Mail, 90–91
   responding to, 91
   selecting fonts and colors for, 93
   sending with Task Scheduler, 103
encrypted containers, folders as, 210
encrypted files and folders, copying
     and moving, 212
encrypting files and folders, 61–62
encryption keys
   backing up, 211
   using backed up keys, 209
Error Checking feature,
     using, 67–68
Ethernet hardware, selecting wired
     hardware, 215
Ethernet standards, 10/100BaseT, 217

even pages, printing, 143
Exit command, stopping programs
  with, 106

F

Fast User Switching, using with
  users, 197
FAT file system, relationship to Parental
  Controls feature, 198
Favorite Sites, saving and opening, 78
Favorites, putting in folders, 81–82
Favorites list, rearranging, 81
Fax And Scan feature
  availability of, 133
  receiving faxes with, 155–156
Fax Cover Page Editor, using, 156–158
fax cover pages
  coded fields in, 156
  creating for faxes, 156–158
  saving, 158
  selecting for fax messages, 154
  using drawing tools with, 156–158
fax messages, sending, 153–154. *See also*
  e-mail messages
faxes
  creating cover pages for, 156–158
  forwarding, 156–157
  printing, 155
  receiving, 155–156
  sending by printing, 154–155
faxing
  documents, 155
  setting up, 153
Figures
  Add Printer window, 241
  advanced system information, 118
  All Programs on Start menu, 8
  Appearance Settings dialog box, 21
  audio and video files played on Web
    pages, 87
  Automatic Updates, 112
  background picture selection, 23
  Browse for Printer window, 141
  burning playlists, 168
  CD and DVD formats, 66

Classic View of Control Panel, 41
client/server LANs, 215
command prompt, 106
computer information, 117
Contacts list, 91
Control Panel Home, 40
cookie management, 85
date and time settings, 37
defragmenting disks, 68
device driver installation for older
  hardware, 222
dialog boxes, 12
dial-up connections, 73
digital music devices mirroring Media
  Player Library, 170
Disk Cleanup feature, 67
disk drive and folder hierarchies, 52
document properties in print
  queue, 151
document-creation programs, 130
drive and folder sharing, 206
driver software, 122
drivers, 123
drives and folders open in subject
  pane, 53
DV camcorder, 173
dynamic IP addresses, 225
Ease of Access settings, 38
editing video clips in Timeline
  view, 177
effects in movies, 184
e-mail messages in Windows Mail, 90
encrypted file information, 212
fax cover page, 157
file and folder protection, 209
File Download dialog box, 120
file sharing in Public folders, 242
firewall settings, 202
firewall tests, 203
Folder Details view in Windows
  Explorer, 49
folder sharing, 205
folders, 46
fonts, 152
Google search, 77
group creation, 208

group types, 207
Import Video window, 174
Inbox in Windows Mail, 90
Internet connection setup, 75
Internet connection verification, 74
Internet Explorer search box, 76
invitation for Remote Assistance, 127
logon screen, 3
mapped network drives, 236, 237
Media Player's Library, 167
Media Player's Radio Tuner, 163
minimized program, 102
mouse pointer, 25
Mouse Properties window, 42
moviemaking, 175
music on Internet, 165
navigating video clips, 178
Network And Sharing Center, 204
network computers, 234, 235
network files and folders, 238
networking services and
  protocols, 218, 223
New Fax message window, 154
newsgroups, 96, 97
NIC testing, 223
notification area icons turned off, 33
notification area with programs and
  system icons, 34
object selection, 56
Paint program, 110
paper type and size settings, 147
Parental Controls, 199
Parental Controls feature, 86
password creation, 194
password protection from Screen
  Saver tab, 212
password-protection, 212
peer-to-peer LAN, 214
Performance tab in Task Manager, 105
Personalization window, 20
Photo Gallery, 137
Photos screen saver, 23
Plug and Play printer, 139
power plans, 119
Print dialog box, 142
printer installed manually, 140

printer selection, 240
printer sharing, 201
printer window, 149
private versus public network
  selection, 231
programs started from Startup
  folder, 101
Publish Movie window, 186
Quick Tabs button, 79
Recycle Bin, 57
Regional and Language Options, 44
Remote Assistance, 124, 125
Remote Desktop Connection
  accounts, 244
remote screen for remote
  assistance, 128
removing programs, 121
resolution, 21
Review Fax Status dialog box, 155, 156
scanned images, 134
Scanners and Cameras window, 132
scanning software, 133
Scientific view of Calculator, 110
search criteria for files and folders, 59
shared network resources, 214, 215
sharing computers, 231
signature in Windows Mail, 94
sounds associated with events, 24
Start menu, 6
Start menu customization, 29
System Configuration utility dialog
  box, 108
System Restore, 113
system restore at restore points, 115
tab capabilities, 79
Task Manager, 104
Task Scheduler, 102, 103
taskbar movement, 32
TCP/IP utilities, 229
Themes tab, 25
titles added in Movie Maker, 182
User Accounts, 193
user setup, 191
Web History feature, 83
Web mail accounts, 95
Web site organization, 82

Figures *(cont.)*
  Web-site categorization, 84
  Windows Defender, 252
  Windows Explorer, 47
  Windows Explorer folder and file
    information, 51
  Windows Explorer folder options, 50
  Windows Explorer window, 9
  Windows Explorer's toolbar, 48
  Windows Firewall set to allow
    networking, 232
  Windows Help and Support
    window, 16
  Windows indexing, 109
  Windows Mail, 89
  Windows Media Center, 188
  Windows Media Center setup, 187
  Windows Media Player, 161
  Windows Photo Gallery, 136
  wired Ethernet network, 217
  wireless connection, 249
  wireless network, 251
  wireless network components, 218
  wireless network susceptible to
    intrusion, 250
File And Printer Sharing service,
  enabling, 224
file attributes, changing, 62–63
file backups, running immediate
  backups, 65
file formats, availability to Movie
  Maker, 180–181
File Or Folder Is Ready For Archiving
  attribute, description of, 63
file sharing. *See also* Network And
  Sharing Center; sharing computer
  resources
  advisory about, 198
  implementing, 240–241
  limiting, 198
  testing Internet firewalls for, 202
File System (UDF) option, using with
  CDs and DVDs, 66
files
  attaching to e-mail, 95
  copying and moving, 59–60
  copying between folders, 60

copying network files, 238
creating, 60
encrypting, 61–62, 210
extracting zipped files, 64
hiding, 209–211
importing with Movie Maker, 180–181
printing to, 143–145
protecting, 209–211
recovering after deletion, 56
renaming and deleting, 55–56
saving downloaded files, 120
searching for, 58–60
selecting from subject pane, 55
sending to zipped folders, 63–64
sharing, 240–241
using encrypted files, 212
writing to CDs and DVDs, 65–66
zipping, 63–64
Filter Keys tool for Ease of Access,
  description of, 39
Find Printer feature, using, 239
firewalls
  setting up Windows Firewall, 201–203
  setting up Windows Firewall for
    networking, 232
  testing Internet firewalls, 202–203
floppy drive, labeling of, 52
folder attributes, changing, 62–63
folders
  copying and moving, 59–60
  copying files between, 60
  copying pictures from Internet
    to, 85–86
  as encrypted containers, 210
  encrypting, 61–62, 210
  extracting zipped folders, 64
  hiding, 209–211
  moving to Public folder, 241–242
  navigating through, 53–54
  navigating with, 54
  opening system-related folders, 7
  opening user-related folders, 7
  protecting, 209–211
  putting Favorites in, 81–82
  recovering after deletion, 56
  renaming and deleting, 55–56
  searching for, 58–60

selecting and opening, 52–53
selecting from subject pane, 55
sending to zipped folders, 63–64
sharing, 200–201, 205–206, 241–242
types of, 6
using encrypted folders, 212
writing to CDs and DVDs, 65–66
zipping, 63–64
folders recently displayed, listing, 54
fonts
  adding, 152
  deleting, 152–153
  selecting for e-mail, 93
  selecting in Add Fonts dialog box, 151
  using, 153
  using ClearType with, 22
Forward button
  function of, 47
  navigating browsers with, 76
Forward option in Windows Mail,
  using, 91
frames
  relationship to clips, 176
  removing from middle of clips, 178
  trimming, 179
FreeCell, playing, 16–18

G

Games folder, running programs in, 106
Google search, performing, 77
Google's Gmail, Web address for, 94
groups
  adding, 208
  adding users to, 208
  opening, 207

H

hard drive, labeling of, 52
hardware
  adding, 121–122
  requirements for making movies, 172
Hearts, playing, 16
Help, getting, 15–16
Help and Support icon, function of, 8

Hibernate
  explanation of, 14
  restarting from, 15
Hidden attribute, description of, 63
High Contrast tool for Ease of Access,
  description of, 39
history, deleting and setting, 83–85
History pane, opening, 82
home page
  changing, 81
  opening in own tab, 81
hostname command-line utility, testing
  TCP/IP installations with, 228–229
Hotmail, accessing, 94
HTML option, using with e-mail, 93
hubs
  description of, 216
  using switches with, 220

I

icons. *See also* desktop icons;
    program icons
  adding from menus, 27
  adding to desktop, 26
  hiding inactive icons, 34
  using, 5
IE7 (Internet Explorer 7), tab
  functionality in, 78–81
Import Pictures option, using, 135
Import Video option, using, 172
imported camcorder video, making
  movies from, 174–176
Inbox contents in Windows Mail,
  sorting, 90
Index This Folder For Faster Searching
  attribute, description of, 63
indexing, controlling, 109–110
inheritance attribute, relationship to file
  sharing, 198
Internet
  browsing, 75–76
  changing Start menu programs used
    for, 30
  copying pictures from, 85–86
  copying text from, 86–87

copying Web pages from, 87
downloading documents from, 132
entering search criteria for, 77
installing software from, 120
locating music on with Windows
    Media Player, 164
playing audio and video files on, 87
searching, 75–77
Internet connections. *See also*
    connections; network connections
accessing on networks, 239
configuring, 74–75
requirements for, 73
speeds, costs, and reliability of, 70
verifying, 74
Internet Explorer
searching Internet from, 76
starting, 77
viewing menus in, 80
Internet Explorer (IE7), tab
    functionality in, 78–81
Internet firewalls, testing, 202–203
Internet Options dialog box
closing, 84
opening, 83
Internet Protocol Version 4
description of, 224
selecting, 225
Internet Protocol Version 6, description
    of, 224
Internet protocols, enabling, 224–228
Internet registries, accessing for blocks
    of IP addresses, 227
Internet security, controlling, 84–86
Internet sites, searching from, 77
Internet-related programs, starting, 7
invitations, sending for Remote
    Assistance, 125–126
IP addresses
entering, 226
getting block of, 226–227
obtaining automatically, 226–227
ipconfig command-line utility, testing
    TCP/IP installations with, 228–229
ISO option, using with CDs and
    DVDs, 66

K

keyboard, stopping programs from, 106
keyboard shortcuts
for closing tabs, 80–81
for closing Web pages, 80
for copying and moving files and
    folders, 60
for getting hits in FreeCell, 18
for new tabs, 79
for opening History pane, 82
for opening home pages in tabs, 81
for opening Start menu, 6
for placing windows on top, 35
for Quick Tabs, 79
for starting Task Manager, 105
for stopping programs, 106
for switching among tabs, 80
for switching to tabs, 80
for undoing moves in FreeCell, 18
for viewing menus in Internet
    Explorer, 80
keyboards
copying and moving files and folders
    with, 60
customizing, 41–42
personalizing with Ease of Access
    settings, 37–39

L

LAN-based host, setting up for Remote
    Desktop Connection, 244–245
LANs (local area networks)
client/server LANs, 215–216
connecting to Remote Desktops
    from, 245–246
peer-to-peer LANs, 214–215
versus WLANs (wireless LANs), 219
Layout options in Windows Explorer,
    opening, 47
link, definition of, 75–76
Link-Layer Topology Discovery
    Mapper I/O Driver protocol,
    description of, 225

Link-Layer Topology Discovery
    Responder protocol, description
    of, 225
Links folder, contents of, 53
list box, function of, 12
List pane, closing in Windows Media
    Player, 161
"Local Area Connection," changing in
    Network Connections window, 220
local Plug and Play printers,
    installing, 138–139
Lock button, identifying, 211
Lock option, explanation of, 14
Log Off option, explanation of, 14
logging on to Windows, 3
logon screen, displaying while away
    from computers, 212

M

magnifier, using with clips, 178
Magnifier tool for Ease of Access,
    description of, 39
Mail. *See* Windows Mail
mapped network drives
connecting to, 236
disconnecting from, 236
Mastered (ISO) option, using with CDs
    and DVDs, 66
Maximize button in Windows Explorer
    window
description of, 10
identifying, 9
media, displaying shared media in
    Windows Media Player, 235
Media Player. *See* Windows
    Media Player
menus
adding icons from, 27
relationship to browsing Internet, 76
turning on classic menus, 11
using, 11
using in Windows Explorer, 50–51
viewing in Internet Explorer, 80
messages. *See* e-mail messages

Microsoft Word documents, copying
    text from Web pages to, 86–87
Minesweeper, playing, 16–17
Minimize button in Windows
    Explorer window
description of, 10
identifying, 9
modems, installing, 70
month, changing, 36
mouse
copying files and folders with, 59
customizing, 39–41
personalizing with Ease of Access
    settings, 37–39
using, 4
mouse pointers
changing, 24
identifying, 2
sing, 6
Movie Maker
importing files with, 180–181
opening Tasks view in, 180
recording analog signals with, 171
Movie Maker projects
naming and saving movies as, 176
opening, 187
placing still images in, 181
Movie Maker window, components
    of, 176
movies
adding effects to, 183
adding sounds to, 183–184
adding titles to, 181–183
making, 173–176
opening, 187
preparing for making of, 172–173
publishing, 186–188
using transitions in, 184
MSConfig program, using, 107
MSN's Hotmail, Web address for, 94
music
copyright issues related to, 171
locating on Internet with Windows
    Media Player, 164
organizing with Media Player
    Library, 167

music CDs, burning, 167–169
music players, copying to, 169–171
My Stations, listening to stations saved in, 164

N

narration, recording, 185
Narrator tool for Ease of Access, description of, 39
navigation pane in Windows Explorer window
  description of, 11, 47
  identifying, 9
  using, 53
network addresses, using, 238
Network And Sharing Center, using, 204–205. *See also* file sharing
Network Connection icon, identifying, 5
network connections. *See also* connections; Internet connections
  testing, 228–229
  verifying, 226–227
Network Connections window, changing "Local Area Connection" in, 220
network drives, connecting to mapped drives, 236
network files and information, copying, 238
network Internet connections, accessing, 239
network operating system, Windows Vista as, 214
network printers
  finding and adding, 239–240
  identifying, 238
  installing, 140–141
  printing on, 239
network protocols
  checking and changing, 225
  configuring, 224–228
network resources
  connecting to, 236
  identifying, 238

network security, reviewing, 229–232
network setup, testing, 228–229
network standards
  wired Ethernet, 215–216
  wireless LANs, 218–219
network types
  client/server LANs, 215–216
  peer-to-peer LANs, 214–215
Network view, using, 234–235
networking functions, enabling, 222–223
networking gear, brands of, 215
networking standards, types of, 216
networks
  downloading documents across, 131–132
  managing wireless network sharing, 250
  using wireless networks, 251–252
newsgroup accounts, setting up, 96
newsgroup messages, responding to, 98
newsgroups
  reading and posting messages in, 97–98
  subscribing to, 97
NIC type, determining, 221
NICs (network interface cards)
  selecting, 216–217
  testing, 222
  troubleshooting, 220
  using, 217
NICs and drivers, checking, 220–222
Notepad, using, 111
notification area
  changing, 33–34
  customizing, 34
  icon for, 32
  identifying, 2
  starting programs from, 8
  using, 5
NTFS (NT File System)
  function of, 197
  security descriptors related to, 198

O

objects
  altering appearance of, 21–22
  manipulating with mouse, 4
  sharing, 231
odd pages, printing, 143
On Screen Keyboard tool for Ease of Access, description of, 39
option buttons in dialog box
  function of, 13
  identifying, 12

P

pages. *See also* Web pages
  determining for printing, 142
  printing odd and even pages, 143
  using separator pages, 147–148
Paint program, using, 111
panes, turning on and off, 11
paper trays, assigning, 146–147
Parental Controls
  requirement for, 198
  setting, 198–200
  using, 86
Password Protected Sharing, turning off, 204
password protection, using, 212
passwords
  adding for Parental Controls, 199
  changing, 192, 194
  removing, 194–195
  replacing, 195–196
  resetting, 193–195
  setting up, 193–194
  using smart cards with, 195–196
  using strong passwords, 192
Pcl.sep file, explanation of, 148
peer-to-peer LANs, function of, 214
Permission Level options, using with folder sharing, 205
permissions
  appropriate setting of, 198
  setting, 208

Personalization window
  altering appearance of objects with, 21–22
  changing desktop background with, 22
  changing mouse pointers with, 24
  changing resolution and color with, 20–21
  creating themes with, 25–26
  opening, 20
  picking screen savers with, 22–24
  selecting sounds with, 24
  selecting themes with, 24–25
Photo Gallery, using, 136–137
pictures. *See also* Windows Photo Gallery
  copying from Internet, 85–86
  creating, 130
  printing, 143
  scanning, 133–134
  viewing outside Photo Gallery, 138
ping command-line utility, testing TCP/IP installations with, 228–229
PINs, using with smart cards for passwords, 195–196
playlists
  burning, 168
  shuffling, 167
Plug and Play hardware
  explanation of, 121
  printer installation, 138–139
port vulnerability, testing Internet firewalls for, 202
power options, setting, 118
preview area in dialog box
  function of, 13
  identifying, 12
Preview pane in Windows Explorer window
  description of, 11, 47
  identifying, 9
  turning on, 48
print jobs, redirecting, 150
print order, changing, 149

print queue
  changing document properties
    in, 150–151
  formation of, 148
print time, setting, 151
print to file, selecting, 144–145
printer pooling, enabling, 146
printer priority, setting, 146
printer window, opening, 148
printers
  choosing, 142
  configuring, 145–148
  creating text file printers, 144
  finding and adding network
    printers, 239–240
  identifying default printers, 142
  identifying on networks, 238
  installing local Plug and Play
    printers, 138–139
  installing network printers, 140–141
  preparing for installation of, 138
  settings for, 145
  sharing, 143, 200–201
printing
  canceling, 150
  faxes, 155
  to files, 143–145
  on network printers, 239
  notification of completion of, 151
  odd and even pages, 143
  pausing, resuming, and restarting, 149
  pictures, 143
  using Quick Print option for, 143
  Web pages, 145
priority, changing when printing
  documents, 150
private IP addresses, getting, 226
program files, moving with mouse, 59
program icons. *See also* icons
  adding to desktop, 26
  identifying, 32
  program installation,
    troubleshooting, 120
Program menu, adding icons from, 27
programs
  adding to Quick Launch Toolbar, 35

adding to Start menu, 301
controlling automatic programs, 107
creating documents with, 130
opening, 5
removing from Quick Launch
  Toolbar, 35
removing from Start menu, 30
running accessory programs, 110–111
running in background, 101
running manual scans for unwanted
  programs, 252
scheduling, 102–104
starting, 8
starting automatically, 100–101
starting from Remote Desktop
  Connection, 247
starting in Run, 106
starting minimized, 101
starting older programs, 106
starting with Task Scheduler, 103
stopping, 105–106
switching, 104–105
projects in Movie Maker
  naming and saving movies as, 176
  opening, 187
  placing still images in, 181
Protected Mode, turning on and off, 83
protocols. *See* network protocols
Pscript.sep file, explanation of, 148
Public folder
  limiting sharing of files and folders
    to, 198
  moving folders to, 241–242
public IP addresses, getting, 227–228
Publish Movie dialog box,
  displaying, 186
Pulse Dialing, configuring, 71

Q

QoS (Quality of Service), enabling, 224
queue. *See* print queue
Quick Launch toolbar
  adding programs to, 35
  identifying, 2, 5

removing programs from, 35
turning on, 34
Quick Print option, using, 143
Quick Tabs feature, using, 79
QuickFacts
  Understanding Permissions, 208
  Understanding User Account
    Control, 190
QuickSteps
  Acquiring a Document, 130–132
  Adding Other Program Icons to the
    Desktop, 27
  Browsing the Internet, 75–76
  Changing Taskbar Properties, 31–33
  Changing the Notification Area, 33–34
  Changing the Visualizations in
    Windows Media Player, 169
  Changing Window Layout, 11
  Changing Windows Explorer
    Layout, 48
  Controlling Internet Security, 84–86
  Copying and Moving Files and
    Folders, 59–60
  Drag Favorites in the List, 81–82
  Employing Effects and
    Transitions, 183–184
  Exploring Windows Media Center, 188
  Finding or Adding a Network
    Printers, 239–240
  Getting a Block of
    IP Addresses, 226–227
  Handling Fonts, 152–153
  Having Fun with Windows, 16–17
  Implementing Windows
    Defender, 251–252
  Locking a Computer, 211
  Preparing to Make a Movie, 172–173
  Printing, 142
  Rearranging the Quick Launch
    Toolbar, 35
  Renaming and Deleting Files and
    Folders, 55–56
  Running Accessory Programs, 110–111
  Selecting Wired Ethernet
    Hardware, 216–218
  Selecting Wireless Hardware, 219–220

Setting Passwords, 193–195
Starting a Program, 8
Stopping Programs, 106
Switching Programs, 104–105
Testing an Internet Firewall, 202–203
Using Network Addresses, 238
Using the Contacts List, 91–92
Using the Control Panel, 39
Using the Mouse, 4
Using the Notification Area, 5
Using Web Mail, 94
Viewing Other Pictures, 138
Zipping Files and Folders, 63–64
quotation marks ("), using with Internet
  searches, 77

R

radio stations, listening to in Windows
  Media Player, 163–164
Radio Tuner in Media Player,
  displaying, 163–164
Reading pane in Windows
  Explorer window
  description of, 10–11
  identifying, 9
Read-Only attribute, description of, 63
Recent Pages button, navigating
  browsers with, 76
Recycle Bin
  deleting files and folders to, 55
  identifying, 2
  using, 56–57
Refresh area in Windows Explorer,
  function of, 47
Refresh button, identifying, 76
regional settings, changing, 43
Reliable Multicast Protocol, description
  of, 225
Remote Assistance
  function of, 122
  protection from misuse of, 127
  providing, 127
  requesting, 124–126
  setting up, 123–124

Remote Desktop Connection. *See also* connections
  controlling client devices with, 247
  description of, 243
  exiting, 247–248
  setting up accounts for, 243
  setting up client for, 245
  setting up LAN-based host for, 244–245
  using, 246–248
Remote Desktop host, using, 242
Remote Desktops, connecting over LANs, 245–246
repeat, turning on and off in Windows Media Player, 162
Reply All option in Windows Mail, using, 91
Reply option in Windows Mail, using, 91
Réseaux IP Européens (RIPE), Web address for, 227
reset disk, creating for passwords, 193–194
resolution, changing with Personalization window, 20–21
Restart option, explanation of, 14
Restore All Items option, explanation of, 57
restore points, creating, 114
Rich Text (HTML) option, using with e-mail, 93
Rip Status column, checking, 166
RIPE (Réseaux IP Européens), Web address for, 227
router, description of, 217
Run, starting programs in, 8, 106

S

Safe Mode, running System Restore from, 116
Safely Remove Hardware icon, identifying, 5
scanned images, locating, 134
scanners, installing, 131–132

scanning documents, 155
scans, running manual scans for unwanted programs, 252
scheduled tasks, creating, 102–104
screen, parts of, 4–5
screen saver protection, turning on and off, 211
screen savers, picking, 22–24
screen tips, displaying, 9
scroll arrow in Windows Explorer window
  description of, 10
  identifying, 9
scroll bar in Windows Explorer window
  description of, 10
  identifying, 9
scroll button in Windows Explorer window
  description of, 10
  identifying, 9
Search box in Windows Explorer, function of, 47
search criteria, entering for Internet, 77
Search pane in Windows Explorer window
  description of, 10
  identifying, 9
searching files and folders, 58–60
security
  considerations for wireless LANs, 218
  testing network security, 230–232
Security tab, opening, 83
semicolon (;), using with addressees in Windows Mail, 89
SEP separation files, availability of, 148
separator pages, using, 147–148
servers
  versus clients, 216
  enabling computers as, 223–224
  role in client/server LANs, 215
services, installing, 224
shared media, displaying, 235
shared resources, displaying in Network view, 235
sharing computer resources, 224, 231.
  See also file sharing

shortcuts
  creating, 58
  definition of, 26
  identifying, 58
shuffle, turning on and off in Windows Media Player, 162
Shuffle Music option, synching Media Player Library with, 171
shuffling playlists, 167
Shut Down option, explanation of, 14
Sidebar
  identifying, 2
  location of, 4
  managing, 43–44
signatures, attaching to e-mail, 94–95
site navigation, using, 75–76
sites
  entering directly, 75
  saving and opening Favorite Sites, 78
sizing handle in Windows Explorer window
  description of, 10
  identifying, 9
Sleep
  explanation of, 14
  resuming from, 14–15
slider in dialog box
  function of, 13
  identifying, 12
smart cards, replacing passwords with, 195–196
software
  installing from CDs, 119
  installing from Internet, 120
  removing, 120–121
Solitaire, playing, 17
sound tracks, mixing, 185
sounds
  adding to movies, 183–184
  changing, 42
  selecting, 24
special characters
  restrictions for using with groups, 208
  using, 110–111

spinner in dialog box
  function of, 13
  identifying, 12
Split button, using with video clips, 178
spyware, guarding computers against, 251–252
Standard User accounts, setting up, 192.
  See also users
Start button
  identifying, 2
  location of, 4
  using, 5
Start menu
  adding icons from, 27
  adding programs to, 30–31
  changing items displayed on, 29–30
  changing look of, 28
  opening, 6
  using, 6–8
Start menu programs used for Internet, changing, 30
stationery, adding to e-mail, 92
stations. *See* radio stations
Sticky Keys tool for Ease of Access, description of, 39
still image files, availability to Movie Maker, 180–181
Stop button, identifying, 76
storage devices, identifying, 52
Storyboard view, example of, 175
strong password, definition of, 192
subject pane in Windows Explorer window
  description of, 11, 47
  identifying, 9
  selecting files and folders from, 55
subnets, identifying, 228
switch, description of, 216
Switch User option, explanation of, 13
switches, using with hubs, 220
Sysprint.sep file, explanation of, 148
Sysprtj.sep file, explanation of, 148
System Configuration utility dialog box, opening, 107
system icons, showing, 34
system information, getting, 116–118

system management programs,
  opening, 7–8
System Restore
  function of, 112–113
  hard-drive requirement for, 113
  restoring from, 115
  running from Safe Mode, 116
  running from Windows, 114–115
  setting up, 113–114
system-related folders, opening, 7

T

tab in dialog box, identifying, 12
Tab List feature, using, 80
Tablet PC Input Panel, opening, 31
tabs
  closing, 80
  opening home pages in, 81
  opening Web pages in, 79
  switching among, 79–80
  switching to, 80
tape segments, recording, 173
task list
  identifying, 32
  switching programs on, 105
Task Manager, using, 104–106
Task Scheduler, using, 102–104
taskbar
  closing programs from, 106
  hiding, 32
  identifying, 2
  keeping on top, 32
  moving and sizing, 32–33
  switching programs on, 104–105
  ungrouping tasks on, 104
  unlocking, 31–32, 35
  using, 5
taskbar properties
  closing, 33, 34
  opening, 31
tasks, ungrouping on taskbar, 104
Tasks view, opening in Movie
  Maker, 180
TCP/IP installation, testing, 228–229

TCP/IPv4 protocol
  description of, 224
  selecting, 225
TCP/IPv6 protocol
  default installation of, 225
  description of, 224
text, copying from Internet, 86–87
text box in dialog box
  function of, 13
  identifying, 12
text file printer, creating, 144
themes
  creating, 25–26
  selecting, 24–25
threads, creating in newsgroups, 97
time, setting and using, 36–37
Timeline view
  editing video clips in, 177
  zoom features in, 180
title bar in Windows Explorer window
  description of, 10
  identifying, 9, 12
titles
  adding to movies, 181–183
  editing for movies, 183
toolbar in Windows Explorer window
  description of, 10, 47
  identifying, 9
toolbars, selecting for display, 32
transitions in video clips
  adjusting, 179–180
  using in movies, 184
trimming handles, using with video
  clips, 179
troubleshooting NICs (network
  interface cards), 221

U

UAC (User Account Control), function
  of, 20, 191–192
UDF option, using with CDs and
  DVDs, 66
Unpin From Start Menu option,
  accessing, 30

updates
  applying, 112
  turning on automatic updates, 111–112
user accounts
  customizing, 196–197
  setting up, 190–193
user-related folders, opening, 7
users. *See also* Standard User accounts
  adding to groups, 208
  Standard Users as, 207
  switching among, 197
UTP (unshielded twisted-pair) cabling,
  using with wired Ethernet, 218

V

video
  importing from camcorders, 172
  playing DVDs, 171
video capture cards, capabilities of, 173
video clips
  combining, 178
  editing, 177–180
  overlapping, 179–180
  removing transitions from, 184
  selecting, 176–177
  splitting, 178
  trimming, 179
video files
  availability to Movie Maker, 180–181
  playing on Internet, 87
video formats, examples of, 173
View submenu, opening, 26
Vista. *See* Windows Vista
visualizations, changing in Windows
  Media Player, 169
volume, controlling in Windows Media
  Player, 162–163

W

Web, definition of, 75
Web content, controlling, 85–86
Web History feature, using, 82

Web mail, using, 94
Web pages
  closing, 80
  copying from Internet, 87
  copying text from, 86–87
  opening in new tabs, 79
  playing audio and video files on, 87
  printing, 145
Web pages, keeping open multiple
  pages, 78–81
Web sites
  APNIC (Asia Pacific Network
    Information Centre), 227
  ARIN (American Registry for Internet
    Numbers), 227
  categorizing, 84
  entering directly, 75
  RIPE (Réseaux IP Européens), 227
Who to notify option, using with
  documents in print queue, 150–151
WiFi (wireless fidelity) standard,
  explanation of, 218
window layout, changing, 11
windows
  versus dialog boxes, 12
  placing on top, 35
  using, 9–11
Windows, controlling use of, 200
Windows Defender,
  implementing, 251–252
Windows Explorer
  components of, 47
  Computer view in, 235
  customizing, 48–50
  encrypting files from, 210
  Folder Details view in, 49
  Network view in, 234–235
  opening, 46–48
Windows Explorer menus,
  using, 50–51
Windows Fax And Scan
  availability of, 133
  receiving faxes with, 155–156
Windows Firewall
  setting up, 201–203
  setting up for networking, 232

Windows Firewall Exceptions list,
including programs in, 203
Windows indexing, controlling, 109–110
Windows Mail. *See also* e-mail messages
creating and sending e-mail
with, 89–90
establishing e-mail accounts
with, 88–89
reading and posting newsgroup
messages in, 97–98
receiving e-mail in, 90–91
responding to e-mail in, 91
running System Restore from, 114–115
selecting addresses in, 92
setting up newsgroup accounts in, 96
sorting Inbox contents in, 90
starting, 88
subscribing to newsgroups in, 97
Windows Media Center
setting up, 187
using, 188
Windows Media Player
changing visualizations in, 169

controlling volume in, 162–163
copying copyrighted material
with, 166
displaying shared media in, 235
features of, 160–162
listening to radio stations in, 163–164
locating music on Internet with, 164
making movies with, 173–176
opening, 160
playback controls in, 162
playing DVDs with, 171
ripping CDs to computers
with, 165–167
shuffling playlists in, 167
Windows Media Player Library
organizing music with, 167
synching, 171
Windows Movie Maker. *See* Movie
Maker
Windows Photo Gallery, using, 136–137.
See also pictures
Windows Security Alerts icon,
identifying, 5

Windows sessions, ending, 13–15
Windows Vista
as network operating system, 214
restoring, 112–116
updating, 111–112
wired Ethernet
selecting cabling for, 217
selecting connecting devices
for, 216–217
selecting hardware for, 216–217
using, 216–217
wireless connections, setting
up, 248–249
wireless hardware, selecting, 219–220
wireless network sharing,
managing, 250
wireless networks, using, 251–252
wireless speed, selecting, 219
WLANs (wireless LANs)
versus LANs (local area
networks), 219
using, 218–219

WMV format, using, 173
Word documents, copying text from
Web pages to, 86–87
workgroups, connecting outside
of, 237
workstations, role in client/server
LANs, 215

Y

Yahoo Mail, Web address for, 94
year, changing, 36

Z

zipped files, extracting, 64
zipped folders
creating, 63
extracting, 64
sending files and folders to, 63–64
Zoom button, function of, 78